CONTRIBUTORS

JAMES AITKEN is a tax expert who works at Legal Knowledge Scotland.

ARTHUR AUGHEY is Professor of Politics at the School of Criminology, Politics and Social Policy, University of Ulster.

ANTHONY BARNETT was the first Director of Charter 88 and co-founder of Open Democracy.

CHRISTINE BELL is Professor of Constitutional at the Law School, Edinburgh University.

GRAEME BLACKETT is an economist and Managing Director of Biggar Economics.

STEPHEN BOYD is Assistant Secretary of the Scottish Trades Union Congress.

NOREEN BURROWS is Emeritus Professor of European Law at the Law School, Glasgow University.

DANNY DORLING is Halford Mackinder Professor of Geography, School of Geography and the Environment, University of Oxford

SARA DYBRIS MCQUAID is Assistant Professor at the Department of Aesthetics and Communication, University of Aarhus.

NIAMH HARDIMAN is Senior Lecturer at the School of Politics and International Relations, University College Dublin.

GERRY HASSAN is Research Fellow in Cultural Policy at the School of Creative and Cultural Industries, University of the West of Scotland and a *Scotsman* columnist.

MARC LAMBERT is Chief Executive of the Scottish Book Trust.

JOHN KAY is an economist and *Financial Times* columnist.

GEORGE KEREVAN is a journalist and a columnist for *The Scotsman*.

COLIN KIDD is Professor at the History Department, St Andrews University.

COLIN MAIR is former Head of the Scottish Local Authorities Management Centre and currently Chief Executive of the Improvement Service.

JAMES MITCHELL is Professor of Public Policy at the School of Social and Political Science, Edinburgh University.

JAMES MCCORMICK was Director of Scottish Council Foundation and is Scotland Adviser to the Joseph Rowntree Foundation.

NICOLA MCEWEN is Senior Lecturer in Politics at the School of Social and Political Science, Edinburgh University.

AILEEN MCHARG is Professor of Public Law at the Law School, University of Strathclyde.

AILSA MACKAY is Professor of Economics at Glasgow Caledonian University.

FIONA MACKAY is Professor of Politics at the School of Social and Political Science, Edinburgh University.

PHILIP SCHLESINGER is Professor in Cultural Policy at the School of Culture and Creative Arts, Glasgow University.

KATHERINE TREBECK is Policy and Advocacy Manager for Oxfam.

NEIL WALKER is Regius Professor of Public Law and the Law of Nature and Nations at the Law School, Edinburgh University.

WILLIAM WALKER is Professor at the Department of International Relations, St Andrews University.

Luath Press is an independently owned and managed book publishing company based in Scotland, and is not aligned to any political party or grouping. Viewpoints is an occasional series exploring issues of current and future relevance.

After Independence

Edited by
GERRY HASSAN and JAMES MITCHELL

Luath Press Limited
EDINBURGH
www.luath.co.uk

First published 2013

ISBN: 978-1-908373-95-3

The paper used in this book is recyclable. It is made from
low chlorine pulps produced in a low energy, low emissions manner
from renewable forests.

Printed and bound by
Bell & Bain Ltd., Glasgow

Typeset in 11 point Sabon

Contents

Introduction: Scotland's Big Debate
GERRY HASSAN AND JAMES MITCHELL   11

    Alternative Futures and the Role of the Unknown   12
    The British Questions   14
    The Role and Importance of Citizenships   15
    Cultural Scotland: The Nation of Imagination   17

Independence in and Independent World
NEIL WALKER   21

    A New Geopolitcal Landscape   21
    The Spectrum of Scottish Self-Government   24

The Defence of the Union: Ironies and Ambiguities
COLIN KIDD   35

Varieties of Independence
JAMES MITCHELL   45

    The SNP's Independence   46
    Independent Statehood   49
    Independent from Whom or What?   50
    Changing Nature of Debate   52
    When is Independence?   54

The Size of States – An Economic Analysis
JOHN KAY   55

Concepts and Challenges Relating to the Economic
of Self-Government   64
STEPHEN BOYD AND KATHERINE TREBECK

    Introduction   64
    Bringing Democracy Back to Economic: Reconceptualising
      'Self-Government'   65
    A Critique of Current Economic Model   66
    More of Same? The Continuation of the Dominant Economic
      Orthodoxy No Matter What the Constitutional Scenario   67
    What Might an Alternative Model Look Like for Social
      Justice and Environmental Sustainability   68
    Reality Check   73
    Conclusion   74

The Continuing Battle for Scottish Tax Powers

JAMES AITKEN   76

    Introduction   76
    A Brief History of Tax in Scotland in Recent Times   77
    The Wider Context   79
    Taxes Devolved or Being Devolved Under Scotland Act 2012   80
    Likelihood of Additional Powers Being Devolved if Scotland
       Votes 'No'   80
    No Second Question   82
    Arguments Put Forward Against a Scottish Tax System   82
    Memo to Treasury and HMRC: Scotland Has Its Own
       Legal System   83
    What about Northern Ireland?   84
    This Would Complicate the Tax System   84
    Tax Competition is Bad   85
    Always Stay in Control   85
    Westminister Always Knows Best   86
    What Could Have Been Done?   86
    It Will Cost Too Much   87
    Conclusion   87

Scotland and the UK: Public Finances and the Economy

GRAEME BLACKETT   88

    Introduction   88
    The Size and Performance of the UK ad Scottish Economies   88
    Regional and National Economies in the UK   89
    Contribution of the Oil and Gas Sector   91
    Public Sector Spending Across the UK   93
    UK and Scottish Tax Revenues and Public Spending   94
    Public Spending and Value for Money   95
    Public Sector Deficit and Debt   97
    Conclusions   98

Arguing for a Citizen's Basic Income in a New Scotland

AILSA MCKAY   101

    The Future of Social Security Policy: A Scottish Debate?   101
    What is a Citizen's Basic Income – A Reform Proposal or a
       Radical Idea?   103
    Crisis, Cuts and Care Work: Who is Paying the Price?   106
    Gender Equality in a new Scotland – A Question of Values?   109

Public Service Reform In Scotland
COLIN MAIR   114

  Introduction   114
  The Pattern of Public Service Reform: 1999–2000   114
  Efficiency and Best Value   115
  Integration and Partnership   116
  Reducing inequalities and Extension of Entitlements   117
  The Watershed 2010–2012   118
  The Independent Budget Review   119
  The Christie Commission   119
  2011–Present   120
  The Impact of Reform   121
  Going Forward   122
  Public Service Reform and the 'Constitutional Debate'   125

Social Justice: Arguments on Independence and Self-Government
JIM MCCORMICK   127

  Introduction   127
  What Is Social Justice?   127
  Wanted: Welfare Reform to Reduce Poverty   130
  Welfare Reform and Mitigation   132
  Universal Credit: the Devil in the Detail   133
  Prelude: First, More within Existing Powers   134
  Pockets: How the Money is Raised and Spent   135
  Targeting Beyond Means-Testing   136
  Prospects: The Case for Closing the Quality Gap in Childcare   137
  Pre-school Care: Looking to Denmark Not 'going Dutch'   137
  Conclusion   140

Energy Policy, Nationalism and Scottish Independence
NICOLA MCEWEN   143

  Energy Policy under current constitutional arrangements   144
  Energy Independence   146
  Independence and Interdependence   147
  Governing Interdependence   149

Scotland in the Wider World: Does Size and Sovereignty Matter?
GEORGE KEREVAN   151

  A New Model: Small State Globalisation   152

Scotland and Small State Globalisation   155
Small State Sovereignty and Geopolitics   156
Foreign Policy in an Independent Scotland   157
Culture and Small Nation Sovereignty   159
Conclusion   160

Trident's Insecure Anchorage
WILLIAM WALKER   162
An Unbending Scottish Stance on Trident?   162
An Unbending UK Stance on Trident?   166
Trident and the Referendum's Early Aftermath   168
Conclusion   171

Scotland and the United Kingdom
AILEEN MCHARG   173
Intergovernmental Relations: Risks and Opportunities   173
Developing Machinery or Intergovernmental Relations   176
Maximising Scottish Influence   177
Securing Effective Accountability   179
Keeping Integration in Check   182
Conclusion   183

Scotland and the EU
NOREEN BURROWS   185

Have Scottish Dreams Diverged from English Ideals?
DANNY DORLING   196
Education – Is Scotland Aiming Higher than England in
    Aspiration for all its Children?   196
Employment – Should every Job be a Good Job or the Workless
    be Grateful for any job?   200
Housing – Is Social Housing art of the Mix or a Safety Net for
    the Poorest of the Poor?   201
Health – Can the health of all be improved or is health an
    individual responsibility?   204
Inequality and Exclusion within Scotland   207
Conclusion   209

Beyond 'the Global Kingdom': England after Scottish Self-Government
ANTHONY BARNETT   211
England-Britain   213

The Upturning of the British Axiom   218
The European Dimension   222

Faraway, so close: Scotland from Northern Ireland
ARTHUR AUGHEY   224

    Unionism   225
    Nationalist and Republicans   229
    Differences in Common   232
    Conclusion   233

The Irish Experience
NIAMH HARDIMAN   235

    Managing Economic Policy for Good or Ill   236
    Institutional Design and Political Accountability   241
    Economic Governmental and Democratic Debate in an
      Interdependent Europe   243

Nordic Horizons for the Isles? Instituting Regional Cooperation
SARA DYBRIS MCQUAID   246
    Introducing the Idea of a Council Model   247
    Introducing the Institutional Cooperation   249
    Parliamentary Cooperation: The Nordic Council (NC)   249
    Parliamentary Cooperation: The British-Irish Inter-Parliamentary
      Body/The British-Irish Parliamentary Assembly (BIPA)   250
    Intergovernmental cooperation: Nordic Council of Ministers
      (NCM)   251
    Intergovernmental Cooperation: The British-Irish Council (BIC)   251
    Relations between the Inter-Parliamentary Level and the
      Inter-Governmental Level of Cooperation   252
    Secretariats   253
    The Dynamics of Nordic Cooperation: New Debates   254
    New Nordic Debates   255
    Nordic Horizons for the Isles?   257

Women and constitutional debates: engendering visions of a new
Scotland
CHRISTINE BELL AND FIONA MACKAY   259

    Introduction   259
    Women, Devolution and Constitutional Change   259
    Women and the Independence Referendum debates: Mutual
      Indifference?   261

*The Difficulty of Holding onto Devolution Gains – Gender Parity
is (still) Not the Norm*   262
*The Legalism of the Process Debate – and its Gendered
Implications*   264
The Gendered Nature of Deal-Making   266
The Gendered Nature of Statehood   267
Political Contingency and 'Standpoint'   268
Is It Worth It?   270
Conclusion: How Could the Process be Engendered?   270

Cultural Policy and the Constitutional Question
PHILIP SCHLESINGER   272

Introduction   272
The Scope of Cultural Policy in Scotland   273
Inventing the Creative Economy   275
Making Cultural Policy in Scotland   279
Conclusion   281

Grasping the Fizzle: Culture, Identity and Independence
MARC LAMBERT   283

Cultural Wars I   283
Cultural Wars II   284
A Little History   286
Cultural Wars III   289
Grasping the Fizzle: Culture and Identity   290

Who Speaks for Scotland? Entitlement, Exclusion, the Power of
Voice and Social Change
GERRY HASSAN   297

Introduction   297
The Limits of the 'New Politics' Thesis   298
The Nature of 'Civic Scotland'   299
The New Class of Devolved Scotland   301
The Missing Scotland   303
Social Democracy of a Narrow Bandwidth   304
*Values, Voice and Vessels: Self-Government and
Self-Determination*   306

Scotland's Big Debate

GERRY HASSAN AND JAMES MITCHELL

THIS IS A MAJOR moment in the life of Scotland – as a nation, society and people. For some, this is a culmination of all they have ever hoped for politically and constitutionally; for others, it is either a threat or a diversion from the challenges of modern life. For another group, inarguably and by far the biggest, this opportunity is viewed more pragmatically, as a prospective opening for exploring some of the big issues facing Scotland: economically, socially, and democratically.

Our understanding of this debate is that it is constitutional in the widest sense. It is not simply about the machinery of government and relations between Scotland and the wider world. It is more than a debate about whether Scotland should have a seat at the United Nations between Saudi Arabia and Senegal, or whether an independent Scotland would automatically become a member of the European Union. This is fundamentally a debate about the kind of Scotland we want to live in, and how any changes in the formal institutions of government might affect the daily lives of people living in Scotland. Constitutional change in this sense is seen less as an end in itself but as something that has the potential, but we stress only the potential, to offer new opportunities but will also present new challenges.

Constitutional change can only offer a new framework in which choices are to be made. It will be the choices themselves that will determine what kind of Scotland emerges in the future. These choices will not be made on 18 September 2014, Referendum Day. But the decision made that day will determine whether elections to the Scottish Parliament or elections to Westminster will be most important in determining what kind of Scotland future generations will live in. No-one can tell with certainty who will be returned at these future elections to these different Parliaments and what kind of policies will pursued, far less the changing background against which these elections will be held. We should have no illusions. Some of the most important decisions affecting and constraining choice in the future will be made far beyond Edinburgh and London however we vote in September 2014. The likelihood must be that neither Scotland nor the UK will have as much autonomy as many advocates of independence or union respectively claim. The theme of interdependence that runs through many contributions in this book is important. This is a debate about power and manoeuvrability, to borrow the title of a book of essays written a generation ago on the same theme (Carty and McCall Smith, 1978).

Just as we will be significantly constrained in what we might wish to do whether within a UK or Scottish state, these constraints will also protect us in the bad choices that will undoubtedly be made from time to time. The constraints on our choices come with protections too. Our interdependent world both constrains and protects. But an interdependent world is one in which collaboration and cooperation by states is vital unless we are to place ourselves at the mercy of other forces. Again, how a state chooses to act within such a world will be important. No state in the world today is capable of tackling some of the most urgent and powerful economic and environmental challenges on its own. Advocates of union maintain that the relative size of the UK compared with that of an independent Scotland would give it greater weight in international relations. Advocates of independence emphasise the choices that are made and question whether choices made by the larger entity would be either in Scotland's best interests or conform to a role in world politics that would be chosen by most Scots. But this is not simply a choice between being a powerless small state in a dangerous world or a larger state with a 'special relationship' with the world's most powerful country. Scotland is not small by international standards and size, whether measured by economic wealth, population or geography, and these can be less important than the resources available and the use to which they are put. It is easier to focus on an immediate balance sheet – though even this is far from straightforward and has been highly contentious – than to focus on the more important dynamics that would follow from remaining within the union or voting for independence.

Alternative Futures and the Role of the Unknown

The recent economic and fiscal crisis should by now have taught us to be more circumspect in accepting the predictive sciences' ability to foresee what is about to happen. The Queen's 2008 question at the London School of Economics remains amongst the sharpest observations about the economic crisis – why did the predictive sciences fail to see the coming crisis? The premise of the question has implications when considering the referendum and Scotland's future: how much faith should we have in the same predictive sciences' ability to foresee the likely consequences of any constitutional decision we make?

This is particularly relevant when what will be more important than whether the framework is a UK or Scottish one, are the policy choices made in successive elections and the policies pursued by future governments. But while choices will be constrained, the main constraint comes from within. This is a debate about alternative futures, each involves taking risks but neither is quite as perilous as its opponents would have us believe. The referendum is a choice between two relative unknowns. We may have a sense of where we are going within the UK or with an independent Scotland, but no one can forecast with certainty the kind of society we will have in a few decades time. At one level that is a frightening proposition though it is a prospect faced everywhere at any time, whether or not confronting a constitutional choice. The difference is that the referendum gives us the opportunity, perhaps forces us, to confront the future as never before. This referendum debate is an opportunity to debate more than a choice of states but also a choice of societies. Election cycles limit our perspectives to a very short period of time but a referendum is unique in giving us an opportunity to consider our future over the long-term.

These essays attempt to make sense of where Scotland stands today within the UK and thereby what an independent Scotland would inherit as well as consideration of a variety of possible scenarios. But nothing written here should be taken as absolute truth. The emphasis in these essays has been to consider choices. Some of the choices on offer are available now and have been available under the present constitutional order just as they will be if Scotland votes for independence. The question is whether these choices or some variation should be made and whether it is felt that certain choices would more likely be made under one or other constitutional scenario. This constitutional debate is an opportunity to raise questions about the future, to challenge those who have taken up a position on the constitution to spell out what kind of society and economy they envisage. It is also an opportunity to raise issues onto the narrower constitutional agenda by those who feel, for example, that women have had an unfair deal in Scottish society or that we must address Scotland's position as one of the most economically and socially unequal liberal democracies in the world. There is no reason why the constitutional referendum should not be about gender, inequality or any number of other matters affecting people living in Scotland.

The British Questions

What would an independent Scotland or an unreformed United Kingdom have to offer? Or indeed, what would a reformed United Kingdom, if that is seriously on the agenda, offer? To date there has been no reason to believe that a reformed UK is seriously an option. Given our experience, we would be foolish to accept vague talk about 'more powers', DevoMax, DevoPlus and the rest without guarantees and evidence that this talk is not simply a cover for garnering votes, even if advocates of the variety of alternatives to the status quo and independence may themselves be sincere. Devolution of whatever variety is not just a Scottish process of change, but one involving a British context and crucially, veto; and as compared to 1997, devolution requires not just Scottish will and pan-British agreement. It also entails changing the nature of the UK political centre (something it has shown little interest in so far), and radically reforming and reconfiguring the constitutional character of the United Kingdom. All proposals need to address this missing British dimension.

Too much of the constitutional debate to date has been expressed in a hopelessly limited time frame. A debate on Scotland's future conducted only in terms of where we are now or in the few years after the referendum and not where we might be in the long-term is limiting and dangerous. Constitutional moments of this sort come around rarely. We are told that the decision made in 2014 will settle the matter for a generation, though whether anyone has the authority to make such a claim is doubtful, so we must consider the implications over the next generation at least. Success in Scottish politics during the 20th Century was largely measured in terms of how much could be wrung out of the Treasury. Scotland's representatives were remarkably successful in this regard. It has been treated generously at least in terms of receiving additional financial support. Scotland has never been treated as an internal colony. Yet, Scotland remains a deeply unequal society and its underlying social and economic problems remain far from resolved. The extra financial support Scotland has received has operated as a side-payment for losing out when it has come to mainstream public policies designed to assist the greater number.

Scotland receives more because it loses out more. This may simply be the best of all possible worlds and reflect that some believe Scotland is 'unable to stand on its own feet' and is fortunate to be part of what they see as a generous union. We may not like this but have no alternative. On the other hand, this attitude might be seen as defeatist and limiting our ambitions. Either way, this may come down to attitudes towards risk. What would an independent Scotland be able, and choose, to do differently? There might be less interest in leaving the union if the union had been more successful and Scotland had less need for these side payments. Scotland's current state needs to be taken into account as this will be our inheritance, but the debate needs to look beyond where we are now and consider where we might be in the future. Scotland's current state, of what some choose to describe as 'dependency', may simply reflect realities no matter that alternative policies might allow for a greater focus on Scottish needs and the stages of growth and development Scotland has to go through to make mature choices.

The Role and Importance of Citizenship

The current debate is more than a formal constitutional one but is about citizenship. It is about who belongs and what this belonging means in terms of rights and obligations. If it was simply about which flag to fly over public buildings then turnout deserves to be low. But this is about visions of citizenship, and what kind of Scotland we wish to aspire to, create and inhabit. Scotland may be deeply unequal but that is not inevitable under current or any other constitutional arrangements. Many of the essays in this book outline alternative visions and the possibility of constitutional change as a catalyst to economic and social change. Whether the reader is attracted to any of these alternative Scotlands will make up part of the mixed motivations of how people approach and vote in the referendum and raises the question of which constitutional scenario is most likely to approximate to these agendas and visions.

Not only is it difficult to make sense of the claims and counter-claims in this debate and figure out what kind of Scotland will emerge under the different constitutional scenarios but there is an added dimension that adds to our difficulties. Regardless of Scotland's constitutional status, formidable challenges lie ahead. Scotland's population is ageing. It has been estimated that there will be a 50 per cent increase in people aged 60 and over, and an 84 per cent increase of those aged over 75 between 2008 and 2033. OECD estimates suggest that long-term demographic change will require a doubling of spending on health as a proportion of GDP without changes in policy. Income inequality widened in Scotland during the years of devolution as the top 30 per cent of the population grew richer, while lower socio-economic groups remained static. The average learning outcomes of the bottom 20 per cent has not changed since devolution. The gap in life expectancy between the poorest and wealthiest in Scottish society has grown. Yet, the first decade of devolution saw five per cent annual real terms growth in public expenditure, fuelled without solid foundations, now leading to unprecedented cuts in spending. An independent Scotland will inherit this mess and it may take a generation to return to levels of spending recently known and then only if that is the choice that is made and capabilities permit. We should not pretend that an independent Scotland will start with a blank canvas or at 'Year Zero'.

But perhaps the greatest challenge, whether Scotland remains within the union or as an independent state, will be how Scotland transforms its decision-making processes to allow it to focus on its underlying problems. Scotland's capacity to win additional resources and to address the immediate effects of social and economic weaknesses have simply not been matched by an ability to prevent problems arising. Treasury largesse has been welcome but allowed us to evade difficult choices. We have pretended that we are radical by making a noise complaining that we need more money but we avoid confronting underlying problems ourselves. One former Health Minister expressed it, 'We are great at picking up bodies that have fallen off the cliff and putting them back together but not so good at stopping them falling off the cliff in the first place'. These are amongst the biggest challenges ahead and while interest in the constitution is at its height we should not lose sight of these matters. Creating independent human beings and independent communities, in the sense of people being able to able to lead full and fulfilling lives, may prove the greatest challenge whether in an independent Scottish state or the UK. The question in the referendum is whether one side is more capable of convincing us that their preferred option offers greater capacity, incentives and intention to address these matters than the other.

Cultural Scotland: The Nation of Imagination

But the rationale of this book is not only about what might be called everyday socio-economic public policy. Scotland is a cultural nation, something agreed by almost everyone engaged in this debate. The extent to which constitutional frameworks affect culture and identity is disputed. The economic and political interdependencies of the modern world have their equivalent in the world of communications and culture. The challenges posed by 'globalisation' can act as stimulants and the absence of such challenges can result in stagnation, introversion and parochialism. But parochialism is not a function of size but of insularity and defensiveness. A more confident and outward looking culture is a living, changing culture. The challenges posed to Scottish culture are no less significant than those outlined above in society and economy, and are given due attention in our essays. These observations lead to no obvious constitutional conclusion but that does not mean that they have no constitutional implication. It will be for protagonists for independence and their antagonists to explain why and how their preferences will affect these cultural matters.

A number of essays consider experiences elsewhere, and others consider Scotland's relations with other places. There is much to be learned from experiences elsewhere whether to copy good practice or to avoid mistakes. Manichean thinking in much of this debate has even infected efforts to learn from elsewhere, whether identifying arcs of prosperity or arcs of despair. The reality is more complex and, in keeping with one of our themes, we believe we should view these matters over the long haul. What appeared to be an arc of prosperity became an arc of despair but is now turning into an arc of resilience less easily defined in Manichean terms. It becomes clear from observing the world of international interactions that there is a variety of potential ways in which Scotland might interact with its closest neighbours as well as others. It is also worth paying attention to the implications of Scottish independence for other parts of the UK. This debate is being watched with great care in many other places including our near neighbours. We consider this important, and thus include essays offering perspectives from outside Scotland and on how changes might affect other places.

These essays offer insights, give warnings, raise questions and in some cases propose ideas in the spirit of enlightening a debate which can be overly heated. Bruce Ackerman, one of the most distinguished constitutional lawyers in the United States, has distinguished between 'constitutional politics' and 'normal politics', with the former defined as 'intermittent and irregular politics of public virtue associated with moments of constitutional creation' and the latter as periods when 'factions try to manipulate the constitutional forms of political life to pursue their own narrow interests' (Ackerman 1984: 1022–1023). For Ackerman, constitutional politics are superior to normal politics. We take issue with this distinction. We would like to make such a claim for Scotland's constitutional moment as one marked by 'public virtue' but fear that few would recognise it as such, at least as the debate has been conveyed in the media, though fully acknowledging that our experience has been that serious, virtuous debate is possible. We are aware of exciting, important, enlightening debates taking place under the broad heading of the referendum and believe that these essays make such a contribution.

For us, Scotland's 'constitutional moment' is an opportunity to reflect on 'normal politics', to consider how we can improve the processes of decision-making, create a fairer and more equal society, address some of our underlying problems and face the future. Our contributors were asked to explore the key issues in this debate, behind which can be found the terrain of different futures, values and choices – of different possible Scotlands, and different possible Britains.

These futures are informed by the present and also contested understandings and collective memories of the past, both far removed and in more recent times. To some, 1707 and what they believe are the perceived injustices of the union in relation to Scotland matter and are the defining factors; to others there is the story of progressive Britain, and harking back to a Ken Loach style 'Spirit of '45'. Many people will not approach or think of the independence debate in these terms, but will come to it much more pragmatically, with an open mind and influenced by memories of more recent events: Thatcherism, New Labour, devolution and the SNP in office. There is a potent sense for some of what can be gained (or to some reclaimed) and for others what might be lost. There is an over-enthusiasm of some on each of the options which recalls the 'fans with typewriters' sobriquet which so accurately described football journalists. And to some there is complete incomprehension as to how we have arrived at this point and why we are having this debate. The political choice has also to extend beyond two variants of nationalism slogging it out, or in other scenarios, 'the fog of war' of the long Labour-SNP contest.

For all its limitations Scottish nationalism has contributed much to the making of modern Scotland and is 'out' as a nationalism, whereas British nationalism (which is what unionism is) is the historic majority nationalism of the UK but does not see and recognise itself as such thus ultimately posing problems for how it sees and acts in this debate.

Language matters in this debate: we would all do well to listen and learn from those with whom we may disagree. The importance of empathy for people of differing opinions cannot be understated, because unless those who find them on the losing side decide to stomp off, we will continue to share this common liberal democracy. It will be no less yours for being on the losing side, no more for being on the winning side. For all the Yes/No dimensions of the 2014 vote and the reality that some of the loudest voices in this debate will be the most simplistic, underneath this there is a very different Scotland, which is by far the majority and the critical constituency. It is one of movement, porous boundaries and fluid identities, resistant to labelling and point scoring, and which wants to be treated like adults and see a serious debate about Scotland's future, one which allows for ambiguity, uncertainty and a sense of hope. It is with this in mind and with this outlook that we have approached this book, conceived it and commissioned the enclosed essays.

We would even go as far as to argue that beyond the Yes/No certainties of each camp, that the most important divide in Scottish public life is actually between those with power, privilege and status, and those groups and individuals without these characteristics: in other words, between insider and outsider Scotland. As important is the related distinction between those who want to change this and those who do not; this debate is not a simple one of Yes/No, left versus right, Scottish nationalist versus unionist, but one which is complex, runs through all these terms, and which has always been with us (and always will).

The forthcoming debate cannot be seen in isolation or without backstory and context. This is informed by Scotland's constantly evolving status as a nation, political community, and imagined community; and whatever the decision in 2014 many key elements of this debate will continue into the foreseeable future – about how Scotland as a nation articulates its collective wishes, aligns and mobilises its public policy choices and institutions, chooses the stories we choose to tell ourselves and the world, and how we live on an island with the powerhouse of the 'world city' of London and the South East.

Part of this debate is about how we choose to invent and imagine ourselves as a people, with all its resultant myths and fictions, and about how we see this people as a community with all its diversities and contradictions (Morgan, 1989).

After Independence has at least two meanings explicit in the title. One is obvious: what tasks and serious work would Scotland need to mobilise itself towards in light of a Yes vote in 2014; the other is more ambiguous, about the challenges and priorities after the referendum irrespective of the result. We have approached the spirit of this book in viewing each of these outcomes as not mutually exclusive, but overlapping.

We have invited intellectually provocative contributors who are experts or authorities in their respective areas to explore the terrain of different possible Scotlands. We have discouraged, we hope successfully, dry academic styles and inaccessible jargon, but the reader can be the judge of how successful we have been in this endeavour.

In our task we have asked each contributor to rise above partisan and binary thinking. This book is not a prescriptive call to arms in any narrow sense, but a call to explore, think and reflect on the possibilities of a Scotland consciously and maturely debating, deciding and creating its own future, as much as any modern nation can in an age of interdependence. In this our primary motivation and hope is that this book can make a small contribution to the ongoing debate, adding some of the substance, seriousness and depth which it and Scotland's voters expect and deserve.

References

Ackerman, B. (1993), *We The People: Foundations*, London: The Belknap Press of Harvard University Press.

Carty, T. and McCall Smith, A. (eds) (1978), *Power and Manoeuvrability: The International Implications of an Independent Scotland*, Edinburgh: Q Books.

Morgan, E.S. (1989), *Inventing the People: The Rise of Popular Sovereignty in England and America*, London: W.W. Norton and Company.

Independence in an
Interdependent World

NEIL WALKER

SCOTLAND'S URGENT CONSTITUTIONAL question challenges many conventional assumptions about what is at stake in the struggle over sovereign authority and political identity, and about how that struggle might be treated or resolved. My essay investigates that challenge.

A New Geopolitical Landscape

In his fascinating study of the global impact of the American Declaration of Independence (Armitage, 2007), David Armitage alerts us to the distinctive political grammar of the modern world. He demonstrates how the famous 1776 Declaration was more than the collective self-assertion of one fledgling community – or community of communities – seeking to free itself from the colonial yoke. It was, in addition, the keystone of a new kind of global architecture. The Declaration was, of course, primarily addressed to the nascent American people, but it also sought and found a planetary audience. Its message reflected and reinforced the notion that national sovereignty – the governing idea of the emerging state system – possessed a double aspect. Sovereignty referred, in its internal orientation, to the idea that independent statehood should be consecrated in an act or process of popular self-authorisation. It involved an exercise of constituent power by which 'the people', typically through a constitutional scheme, mandated a comprehensive framework of self-rule. But sovereignty also referred, in its external orientation, to the necessity, if independent statehood was to mean what it said, that it be recognised by all other powers. These other powers would be required both to acknowledge the distinct title of the American people to participate in international relations as a newly independent state and to commit themselves to non-interference in the internal affairs of that new state.

Yet the Declaration acquired a broader global resonance. The Americans not only sought recognition for themselves. They also offered a model for general use. In proclaiming their 'separate and equal Station' as one of the

'Free and Independent States' among 'the Powers of the Earth', the Declaration's framers encouraged many other aspiring states over the following two centuries to adopt the same template. Popular self-determination was presented as a universally valid claim, and sovereign statehood treated as a 'Station' available to all nations. And crucially, the very quality of sovereignty as a title to authority that was both (internally) comprehensive and (externally) exclusive, meant that there need be no contradiction, at least in principle, between the full satisfaction of the particular claim and the notion that all were similarly entitled.

Of course, principle is far from everything in international politics. The idea of a global order of mutually exclusive and mutually respecting state sovereignties was only ever partially honoured. The modern world has seen many waves of imperialism, and much resistance to claims of self-determination by subaltern communities and other nationalist movements. Indeed, sovereignty has often been invoked to frustrate rather than promote equal standing between political communities. It has been used cynically by established states either to justify their non-recognition or suppression of other national movements or to resist interference by those who might protest against their internal or external abuses of power. Yet even as a heavily qualified good, and one disproportionately enjoyed by Western powers, the 1776 Declaration envisaged and inspired a system of global authority that was coherent in its own terms. It supplied a language and logic of justification that was not merely conservative of existing authority, but could also be used by many embryonic polities in pursuit of constitutional self-determination.

If the 'high modern' world ushered in by the 1776 Declaration emphasised universality of form, comprehensiveness of authority, and mutual exclusivity of claims, the 'late modern' world in which contemporary claims to independence are articulated in Scotland and elsewhere looks quite different. While the state remains the focus of political organisation, it is now merely first amongst equals. In place of a universal and uniform template of sovereign statehood we have a highly differentiated global mosaic of legal and political capacities. In place of internal sovereignty as comprehensive and monopolistic, authority is typically partial – distributed between various political sites and levels, states and otherwise. And in place of mutual exclusivity as the default condition of external sovereignty, we have overlap, interlock and mutual interference.

Why and how so? No single 'X' factor explains the ongoing movement from universality, comprehensiveness and mutual exclusivity to differentiation, partiality and overlap. Rather, there is a combination and accumulation of forces. Some tendencies challenge states and their borders as effective containers of power. The long post-war development of transnational markets, communication media and cultural forms, has gradually eroded the material capacity of the nation state as the axis of economic power and political authority, and, to a lesser extent, its symbolic locus as the core of political identity. Institutional responses to these changes have underscored the state-decentring trend. Globally inclusive entities such as the United Nations and exclusive groupings such as the G8, as well as regional institutions like the EU, have both tracked and reinforced the development of forms of collective action and public goods (and 'bads') beyond the state. Their remit ranges far and wide, from the provision of security to the protection of human rights, and from the making of transnational markets to market 'correction' in spheres as diverse as food safety, environmental protection, energy efficiency and criminal justice cooperation. Overlapping these umbrella institutions there is a dense network of powerful, functionally specialist transnational organisations, from state-controlled public bodies such as the World Trade Organisation and the International Atomic Energy Agency, through hybrid public/private entities such as the Internet Corporation for Assigned Names and Numbers, to purely non-state organs such as the International Olympic Committee.

Alongside these global and transnational tendencies, other disturbances to the authority of the state emanate from below. Ironically, the seeds of this challenge to the modern system were sown in the foundational American settlement. As well as the first modern state, the United States was also the first mature federation. It gave novel constitutional form to the idea of territorially distributed power *within* the polity. However, it did so in a way which – even if it required a Civil War to settle the matter definitively – understood the allocation of jurisdiction between federal government and provincial or 'state' institutions as an *expression* of the sovereign authority of the United States as an integrated whole rather than as an internal *challenge* to its integrity.

Federalism, US-style, was designed and rolled out in a particular way, involving a clear division between the two levels of authority and their respective policy spheres, a high degree of ethnic or cultural homogeneity between the different state units, and uniform and symmetrical legal and institutional treatment of these units. Contemporary federalism, or quasi-federalism, has gradually departed from that classical norm. Most newer federations, such as Germany, are 'cooperative' rather than 'dual' arrangements, involving a significant degree of policy overlap and institutional interlocking between central and local levels. Many, such as Canada, Spain or Belgium, are also multinational or multiethnic rather than merely territorial compacts, with some constituencies retaining aspirations towards stronger forms of constitutional recognition. And these multinational or multiethnic federations tend, in addition, towards uneven or asymmetrical treatment of their provinces; those with the clearest or most longstanding traditions of distinctiveness, or the strongest claim to national identity, are accorded more ample recognition of cultural goods such as language or religion, greater regional governmental autonomy, or disproportionate influence at the federal centre. All these factors combine to create a looser and more fluid political form, challenging the earlier conception of the federal state as a mere variation of the 'sovereigntist' ideal of a well ordered and permanently settled unity.

So when considering the overall challenge to the universality, comprehensiveness and mutual exclusivity of the modern state system we must look to both flanks – to pressures from the substate interior as well as from the transnational beyond. Furthermore, the two dynamics feed off one another. Claims to substate national recognition or protection are powerfully sponsored through global mechanisms for the promotion of individual or collective rights, while supranational institutions such as the EU provide a scale of policy and economic support which makes the ambition of greater regional autonomy within existing states more viable. By the same token, just because existing states have gradually ceded authority and capacity upwards to other territorial or functional institutions, they may become less attractive magnets for substate nations and less well equipped to maintain their sovereign integrity.

The Spectrum of Scottish Self-Government

How does this shifting geopolitical landscape illuminate the stakes and prospects in the Scottish independence debate? I begin with a series of outline propositions.

Under the 2012 Edinburgh Agreement, with its commitment to a single referendum question in 2014, the Scottish debate has now been firmly constitutionally coded in the familiar binary terms of high modernity – a straight choice between staying put in one sovereign state or going it alone in a new one. Yet, as the caution and delicacy with which both sides have sought to position themselves in the debate only serves to make clear – not least, ironically, on account of their shared tendency to deflect scrutiny of their own stance by exposing the fragilities and uncertainties of the other side – the underlying situation is more complex. Our islands are far from immune to the forces sketched above. In fact, the factors reshaping the geopolitical landscape towards a more varied range of polities exhibiting more restricted and more heavily overlapping forms of authority and capacity apply with particular force in our local context. The claims of comprehensiveness and autonomy associated with internal and external sovereignty are available neither to those who would argue for the retention of Scotland within the British state nor to advocates of Scottish independence. In the words of my title, any solution that retains Scotland as part of an 'interdependent' United Kingdom is still likely to be a relatively 'independent' solution – one permitting Scotland a significant degree of self-government and distinctive voice. Conversely, any solution that recognises Scotland's 'independent' statehood is nevertheless apt to retain a high level of 'interdependence' with the rest of the UK, the EU and the broader network of global institutions. Rather than categorical opposites, therefore, we are faced with a graduated range of possibilities clustered along a narrower spectrum.

This invites a number of conclusions. To begin with, it explains why, for all the early reluctance of the protagonists to commit themselves, the Scottish constitutional debate cannot avoid intricate questions of institutional architecture and policy content. What independence, or its absence, entails, and where its threshold lies, requires respecification, and detailed argument will be important in making the popular and political case for or against independence.

If the premium on institutional design and policy content is unsurprising and has been widely anticipated, two further implications of the spectral character of the constitutional debate are less well appreciated. In the first place, for all that the debate is geared towards constitutional settlement, the absence of bright-line solutions together with the broader unpredictability of constitutional politics in a multi-level, interlocking context means that we are likely to remain in a state of constitutional *unsettlement* for the foreseeable future. In the second place, as one special feature of unpredictability and uncertainty, the tendency towards less sovereign-

tist solutions is bound to alter the symbolic politics of constitutional identity in ways we cannot yet fully imagine. We are entering a phase where
the psychology of political belonging and self-identification must confront
a long-term shift in the availability, distribution and combination of the
practical means of individual and collective self-determination.

Let me now develop these points more fully.

(a) The Changing Environment of the Scottish Debate

Why is the Scottish constitutional debate particularly susceptible to the
various trends discussed above? Partly this has to do with the global
situation of the United Kingdom, partly with the European context, and
partly with the specific historical position of Scotland relative to the rest
of the UK.

In global terms, the post-imperial UK, though widely understood to be
in long-term decline, retains a relatively strong economic, cultural and
diplomatic presence. In a world of increasing variety and interconnected-
ness of political forms and of ever denser transnational regulation, however,
such strength does not manifest itself as independence from global networks. External sovereignty today involves more, not less, involvement
with other authority systems, and the restrictions as well as the opportunities associated with such involvement. Britain's permanent seat in the
UN Security Council, for example, or membership of the G8, or recognition as one of five 'nuclear weapon states' under the Nuclear Non-Proliferation Treaty, both reflect and underscore its international standing and
influence, as well as the constraints associated with collective engagement.

In regional terms, the European continent is one where classical understandings of sovereignty (internal and external) have become more generally transformed over the last half-century. Like all member states of the
supranational EU – originally six but rising to nine with British accession
in 1973 and now to 28 in 2013 – the UK has conceded to the demands of
the common European market all domestic control and external Treaty
authority over the circulation of the factors of production – persons, goods,
services and capital – and over much of the broader regulation of commerce. Increasingly, the EU institutions – Council, Commission, Parliament
and Court of Justice – have also acquired jurisdiction in other, more or
(increasingly) less market-related areas as wide-ranging as the environment, public health, energy and internal and external security. In a context
of gradual integration, reinforced by a common regime of human rights

protection in the wider framework of the Council of Europe, all members of the EU – even one as notoriously semi-detached as the UK – are experiencing the synergies and compromises, the accommodations and conflicts of multi-level governance more than any other region at any point in modern history.

As regards the internal UK context, our comparative reference point is the versatile model of federal authority. Yet so evolved rather than designed, so uneven rather than symmetrical, and so fluid rather than fixed has been the development of devolved power to Scotland and the other nations of the UK, that it would be a stretch too far to describe the resulting pattern in federal terms at all. Some prefer the older language of 1707 in characterising the UK as a 'Union state' (Rokkan and Urwin, 1982) comprising once distinct and still distinguishable nations, and required for its survival to continue nurturing some of these diverse institutional and cultural roots and the aspirations associated with them. The accommodation of diversity in the deep political culture is reinforced by the absence of the kind of settled constitutional blueprint we associate with the nominate federal tradition. Instead of a rigid frame in which both floor and ceiling of devolved authority are set in stone, we have a long, twisting, gradually accelerating and still open-ended narrative. This has embraced post-Union retention and selective cultivation of a distinctive Scots law and home-grown educational and religious institutions, a longstanding and gradually extended commitment to administrative devolution, the eventual establishment of a Scottish Parliament in 1999, and now, the introduction of a successor Scotland Act 2012 which foresees significantly extended fiscal powers to complement legislative and executive autonomy.

These factors combine to suggest that the choice between remaining in the UK and becoming an independent state cannot be well understood in classically binary sovereigntist terms. Even from a perspective of purely Scottish self-interest, the question of advantage becomes one of fine and shifting balance; between, on the one hand, remaining absorbed within the authority of a larger state, and all that implies in terms of a sacrifice of some decisional autonomy for sustained influence and capacity as part of the larger unit, and, on the other hand, full sovereign independence, and all that implies in terms of a sacrifice of some forms of influence and capacity for greater decisional autonomy in pursuit of national interests and aspirations.

The complexities of the new constitutional options, and the weighing and balancing involved, are profound indeed. As the global and European picture makes clear, in the presence of an increasingly powerful and intrusive transnational regulatory domain the purchase of influence and capacity at the price of autonomy is not just the lot of the substate nation. It is a price any traditionally sovereign state, the UK included, increasingly must pay in the late modern age – especially if it sits at or near the top table – just as it is a price any nascent state inevitably pays as it seeks to join the international community. And compounding the complexity, in our particularly fluid local environment, the underlying conceptual distinction between interdependence and independence appears ever fuzzier at the margins. Devolution in the Union state can be stretched to include significant autonomy from the central political system, just as independence, as we shall see, can be qualified to allow a wide range of continuing interdependencies with the rest of the UK and beyond.

(b) Redefining Independence

Ever since the publication by Scotland's first SNP government in 2007 of *Choosing Scotland's Future*, announcing a 'national conversation' on Scotland's constitutional outlook and setting the tone for the party's subsequent strategy, the nationalist movement has sought to define independence in a manner which takes considerable distance from the sovereigntist certainties of high political modernity. Externally, membership of the EU is fully embraced, and this automatically implies continued common UK regulation in many areas. Participation is also sought in key global organisations such as the Commonwealth, the World Health Organisation, the Organisation of Economic Co-operation and Development, the World Trade Organisation, and – in a recent change of policy – the North Atlantic Treaty Organisation. More tellingly, even within the ambit of the British Isles the nationalist approach emphasises continuity with certain lateral constitutional initiatives of recent years. Both the Joint Ministerial Committee framework, which provides for the various governments of the United Kingdom to work together, and the British-Irish Council, established in 1998 under the auspices of the Good Friday Agreement for co-operative amongst all the executives of the two states, are endorsed as vital confederal supports for a newly independent Scotland rather banished as relics of an outmoded settlement. Accordingly, while formal international sovereignty – the idea of a separate voice and seat in global affairs – is insisted upon as one non-negotiable fundamental of independence, much of that sovereignty is then to be re-pooled or re-mixed in the name of collective action or coordinated policy.

Even more striking is the willingness to countenance continuing UK influence over certain traditional areas of internal sovereignty. The 2007 prospectus launched the idea of a 'social Union', and subsequent debate has suggested this may extend to a common British platform of social welfare. Defence and the retention of a sterling currency Union, the latter revived in light of the diminishing attractiveness of the Euro, are two other high profile areas where the longstanding, complex intertwining of policy has provoked consideration of the continued pooling of resources and competences. In other areas, too, such as the media and immigration, the manifest and manifold cross-border and broader transnational policy 'externalities', recognised and reinforced by the tightening grip of common EU regulation, argue in favour of the retention of a common policy front.

From the Unionist side, conversely, we observe a willingness to push out the devolutionary boat – to 'define down' what is required by way of policy, institutional or fiscal commonality to retain the integrity of the United Kingdom. The Calman Commission, which reported to broad Unionist agreement in 2009, and which provided much of the impetus behind the 2012 Scotland Act, is one example. And while the different Unionist parties have been unwilling, either in their 'non-discussion' of a possible third referendum option or as a more general forward-looking initiative, to put their support behind a common conception of 'devo-max', each Party is committed to bring forward its own proposals for further constitutional reform.

And so the constitutional debate, deprived of sharp sovereigntist definition, moves towards a crowded middle. This opens up two key areas of contestation. One concerns the attractiveness and plausibility of the different alternatives. If the nationalists cannot simply point to the purity of the Promised Land, then, as already noted, they must make the case for a deliverable package that strikes an optimal balance between decisional autonomy and retention of capacity and influence. Likewise, if the Unionists concede that the *status quo* is not ideal, they must argue for a similarly optimal and deliverable solution from their end of the constitutional spectrum. A related controversy – one that will grow in significance as the referendum approaches and questions of definition come to the fore – concerns the authenticity of the self-positioning on the spectrum of the sponsors of each approach. Is the case for a heavily qualified form of independence still nevertheless a case for independence, or is it a case of false pretences? Equally, is the pitch for a heavily qualified form of Unionism still nevertheless a pitch for the UK, or is it simply a fig-leaf, a refusal to acknowledge a process of inexorable drift and dissolution? In a world of eroded and interlocking sovereignties there is no objective 'fact of the matter', no neutral test to determine whether or not this or that position is 'really' one of independence or 'truly' and stably Unionist. There are only the more or less persuasive arguments of either side that their position is both attractive and plausible in its own terms and can make genuine claim to the inheritance of the ideal of independence on the one hand or the legacy of the Union on the other.

(c) Towards Constitutional Unsettlement

It is true but trite to say that we live in unsettled constitutional times. The referendum debate will stretch over two years, and regardless of how the vote goes, there will be various consequential moves, either to further reform and consolidate the Union or to enter and conclude formal negotiations for the severance of the Union and develop an indigenous Scottish Constitution. These will throw up many additional matters of dispute and will take years to resolve. Beyond the obvious, however, there are other factors which suggest unsettlement is not simply a passing incident of a significant constitutional moment, but a deeper condition of our new geopolitical age.

In part, this is due to the disappearance of categorical constitutional answers in the changing climate. Faced no longer with a binary choice but with a continuum of constitutional options, it is less likely that the Scottish and British people will treat any particular resting point on that continuum as decisive. Politicians may talk as if we are in the constitutional end game. They may even hope or believe it to be so. But the lack of clear red lines in the debate and the continuing availability of incremental adjustments, together with the fact that solutions at the indistinct margins between independence and interdependence can be interpreted differently on either side, means that both the opportunity and the political energy and motivation for constitutional re-engagement are likely to persist.

In part, however, unsettlement is also a matter of complex interdependence, and the multi-actor and multi-level quality of new constitutional processes and sequences. Where bright-line solutions are unavailable and constitutional arguments are likely to turn on the relative attractiveness and plausibility of differing calculations of the balance between autonomy, capacity and influence, the ability to develop a compelling narrative of constitutional sustainability or progress is at a premium. Yet, when all constitutional projects become vulnerable to forces and agent beyond the control of their authors, precisely this kind of narrative confidence can prove elusive.

The EU is an obvious case to illustrate my point. The last months of 2013 witnessed controversy over how and on what terms an independent Scotland might retain or resume its membership of the supranational club. Yet the debate proved inconclusive. Even after the intervention of the European Commission, it remained uncertain whether an independent Scotland should have continuing membership alongside the rest of the UK, or whether Scotland would have to re-apply like any new candidate, either because it would be deemed to have seceded from the larger UK entity or, more radically, because the UK itself would be treated as dissolved – in which case each successor state would have to rejoin. This lack of clarity stems from the fact that, as with so many constitutional conundrums of a post-sovereigntist age, we are entering virgin territory. There is no precedent for the devolved part of an existing EU state becoming independent, and no definitive answer to be drawn from historical practice. What *is* absolutely clear, however, is that Scottish independence would require substantial renegotiation of the terms of EU membership. Questions of representation in European institutions, of budgetary contribution, of participation in the programme of justice and home affairs, and, of course, of membership of the Euro, would have to be addressed anew, as would many other important issues. Whether done in the context of the accession negotiations of a new state, or through the amendment of longstanding Treaty agreements amongst existing states, tough choices would have to be made and difficult compromises struck. Certainly, there would be no unilateral right for Scotland to dictate terms, regardless of whether their international law position was treated as one of new or of continuing membership. Whichever route was taken, the terms of Scotland's membership would depend on what all existing members could be persuaded to accept – including members such as Spain concerned about secessionist movements in their own sovereign backyard.

Yet if this speaks to a near future of profound uncertainty, matters look not dissimilar from the other side of the debate. In a context of rising Euroscepticism in and beyond the Conservative Party, the prospect looms of a referendum in the next Parliament, whether on retention of core status or, as seems ever more likely, on the very principle of continuing UK membership of the EU. The outcome of such a referendum is difficult to call. If a favourable vote depends upon a looser compact, there is no guarantee that the EU will be receptive to negotiation, and even if the UK renews its European vows the vicissitudes of the Euro over the last three years remind us that European membership, even on favourable terms, is hardly today a condition of copper-bottomed stability.

What is true of the EU is also true of other exclusive international organisations such as the Security Council, or the G8, or the Nuclear Club. Given the volatility of many such international regimes, the constitutional projection is one of uncertainty on both sides of the question. The stubborn prospect of multi-faceted constitutional unsettlement, therefore, is one that afflicts all positions, and which is emerging as one of the defining conditions of the debate.

(d) Reframing political identity

Sovereign statehood, typically endorsed in a foundational constitutional text, has traditionally supplied not only a vehicle of authority but also a focus of political identity. It expresses and affirms the self-determining status of a community of affinity. But what becomes of the identity dimension of constitutional statehood when its accompanying authority, as a matter of both fact and prospect, becomes divided, qualified, pooled or is otherwise rendered precarious in the ways discussed above? If state sovereignty is not what it used to be, what does that imply for the aspirations of political belonging and self-realisation of those who either do or do not identify with that state? Translated into local terms, if political authority in these islands is now split and shared between and beyond their various seats of government, and will continue to be regardless of whether the Scottish pathway stops at 'independent interdependence' or proceeds towards 'interdependent independence', does this alter how constitutional self-government is likely to be perceived and pursued as a badge of political identity?

Two contrasting possibilities suggest themselves. One would envisage the expressive dimension of nationalism declining in importance, while the other would see its importance elevated. From one viewpoint, identity should track and shadow actual political capacity and influence. In that perspective, the diffuse quality of political authority is likely to be reflected in the multi-layering of political identity and belonging – a tendency encouraged by the fact that a majority of Scots already embrace dual British and Scottish identities. Scottish independence, from such an angle, would become ever less a vindication of a categorical sense of political identity. It would be pursued, if at all, primarily on the basis of an instrumental calculus – as a platform for better achieving the optimal mix of autonomy, capacity and influence on behalf of a preferred (but, for many, not exclusive) community of attachment than would be available from a UK point of departure.

From the other viewpoint, the symbolic affirmation of a *distinctive* political identity might instead come to operate in inverse relation to the *indistinctive* character of multi-level, interlocking authority. It may become more important, either as a reaction against the compromised possibilities of self-government, or, at least, as a form of cultural compensation for the trend towards global interdependence.

That the contemporary SNP has consistently stressed the instrumental worth over the cultural expression of political nationalism is underlined by its recent emphasis upon the continuing importance of the bonds of Britishness, and its affirmation of a residual Union – both social and monarchical. Yet nothing is simple in the politics of identity. Any conception of political nationalism, in truth, needs both dimensions – instrumental and expressive – to operate in close tandem. It does so if it wishes to avoid becoming either a claim to authority that cannot be won, or even if won, cannot be fully exploited, because it lacks the mobilising power of strong collective identity; or, conversely, an insular culture of frustrated common destiny. This has often been a difficult balance for nationalist movements and projects to find and sustain. In today's constitutional politics, the relationship between the two dimensions, given the divergent tendencies just described, may become more volatile, more difficult and less easy to predict or to cultivate.

An unsettled Scottish constitutional prospectus, in conclusion, is not only the product of the realignment of local and global forces into a more complex and less predictable pattern of political authority. It is also a matter of deep political culture. For in consequence of that realignment of authority, the very meaning of nationality as a primary frame of political identity, and the very significance of the constitutional form of self-expression as the symbolic link between the two, no longer readily conform to earlier understandings.

References

Armitage, D. (2007), *The Declaration of Independence: a global history,* Harvard: Harvard University Press.

Rokkan, S. and Urwin, D. (1982), *The Politics of Territorial Identity: Studies in European Regionalism,* London: Sage.

The Defence of the Union: Ironies and Ambiguities

COLIN KIDD

THE DEBATE OVER THE future of the Anglo-Scottish Union is far from straightforward; at times, indeed, it exhibits a strange infirmity of purpose which verges on the wilfully perverse. While nationalists and unionists happily attack one another at every opportunity, so much so that the Scottish media is often repellently sulphurous, the respective policy positions of the two camps seem far less differentiated than the casual observer might imagine. There is a bizarre and conveniently unacknowledged convergence at the policy level, which tends to go unnoticed in the din of rhetorical battle. The leading defenders of the Union with England appear as enthusiastic as any nationalist about the prospect of greater autonomy for the Scottish Parliament within a much-looser Union – what is colloquially known as 'devo-max' – and ostensible nationalists champion a continuing 'social union' with England, the British monarchy and a shared sterling zone.

The gulf between nationalists, such as Alex Salmond, for whom independence amounts seemingly to a process of gradual disengagement from England, rather than a fixed destination of full sovereign separation, and unionists who are themselves diffident about pressing the case for the status quo short of further constitutional reform, might not be as wide as their rhetorical flyting would suggest. On either side of the debate furious partisanship coexists with caveat and qualification, vitriol and indignation with double-talk and subtly triangulated positioning. Undoubtedly there are high stakes involved for Scots in assessing the pros and cons of union and independence, but the bitterness of contemporary debate is also compounded by what Freudians call the 'narcissism of small differences', the sense, in this case, that both unionists and nationalists are laying claim to some of the same emotional space. These surprising features of constitutional debate in contemporary Scotland provide an obvious point of departure for anatomising Scottish unionist argument, and in particular its apparent spinelessness. For, it is perhaps unsurprising that Unionists should so obviously lack spirit, forcefulness and what Scots traditionally called 'smeddum', when their very raison d'être, the Union itself, seems so infuriatingly to elude their grasp. Such indeed is the crooked timber of contemporary Scottish politics that the nationalists have decisively appropriated the catchphrase, if not the cause, of a British 'social union'.

How did things come to such a pass? This essay examines the factors that have inhibited or delayed – until very recently – the emergence of an articulate Unionism. Why did Scottish unionism take so long to develop as a coherent response to the long-term rise of the Scottish National Party [SNP]? It examines the phenomenon of 'banal unionism' – the instinctive acceptance of a Union so uncontroversial that, ironically, it elicited little in the way of positive support. Rather the Union was simply taken for granted as part of the rarely noticed background, the wallpaper as it were, of Scottish political life. Moreover, the essay also addresses the ways in which the Anglo-Scottish Union was eclipsed in Scottish political culture by the more controversial Union of Britain with Ireland of 1800 (and then the continuing connection with Northern Ireland since 1920). In modern Scottish history, strangely enough, the most articulate Unionism has concerned itself with the Irish Question, not with the Union of 1707.

Other problems spring from the fact that in Scotland nationalism is a decidedly fuzzy opponent for its unionist opponents to target. Not only is there the irony that Scottish nationalism has always enjoyed a curiously ambivalent relationship with Unionism, whether the Union of the Crowns (1603) or the recent idea of a 'social union'; in addition, nationalism has had a range of different goals from the time of the National Party of Scotland's [NPS] creation in 1928, including dominion status for Scotland, a co-partnership with England in the running of the British Empire, home rule within some kind of devolved settlement, independence within the European Union, 'independence-lite' within a British social union, and outright independence. Behind these significant policy variations, however, the big idea of Scottish nationalism – and the emotional resonances it was capable of generating – remained broadly the same, namely some form of Scottish self-government; but the shifting register of constitutional preferences which accompanied the central idea has left unionists chasing shadows.

It's all rather reminiscent of the old Sellar and Yeatman joke, that whenever Gladstone came close to answering the Irish Question, the Irish changed the Question (Sellar and Yeatman: 116). Alex Salmond is similarly slippery. At the signing of the Edinburgh Agreement on the holding of the single question independence referendum with Prime Minister David Cameron on 15 October 2012, Salmond navigated away from the rhetoric of outright independence in order to court (otherwise unionist) supporters of devo-max, hailing the Agreement as 'a major step forward in Scotland's home rule journey.' But what does Home Rule – often taken to be a synonym for devolution – mean in this context? If the nature of the nationalist project which unionists opposed kept changing, then it made it harder for them in turn to articulate exactly what kind of Union it was they were defending – a centralised unitary state; a union-state partnership; a looser devolved polity; or even an evolving Union heading towards some kind of semi-detached 'sovereignty-association' under devo-max?

Unionists also have to cope with another fog of confusion, a disorientating mist which forms because the British state and the Union are not quite synonymous, though they might seem so to the wider public. Although opinion in favour of Scottish independence has tended to peak at around 30 per cent of the Scottish electorate, this substantial minority in favour of breaking up the Union has tended to drown out the electorate's quiet unionist majority. A passive, as often as not lukewarm and even disgruntled acceptance of the Union has been the norm in modern Scottish political culture. Yet the majority that dislikes – or rather perhaps fears – the prospect of Scottish independence tends, naturally enough, to have its own gripes with the British state and with governments of either stripe. Clearly, there are difficulties in pressing the case for the Union with uninhibited enthusiasm as a Labour-leaning Scot under a Tory government, or vice versa, as a Conservative-minded Scot under a Labour, or New Labour, administration. Loyalty towards the British-state-in-theory is compromised by one's immediate feelings towards the British-state-in-practice: what is the impact of British government policy at any particular time on one's own family, its finances and its prospects? Unsurprisingly, it is rare that loyalty to the British state rises to affection for the Anglo-Scottish Union, as such.

The focus of British belonging tends to be the monarchy, the armed services, the 'Union Jack', possibly even Parliament or the wider Commonwealth; but almost never a loyalty to the Union of 1707 per se as a revered founding charter. While Britishness can, on occasions, stir the emotions, Scottish unionism – unlike its more strident Ulster Unionist counterpart – does not. Scottish nationalism, by further contrast, is based precisely on the notion that a warm affection for Scotland should trump other political considerations and should indeed operate as the point of departure for a democratic system of self-government. Clearly there is a truth in the received assumption that while unionism speaks to the head, nationalism engages the heart. However, the situation is more complicated than that. Nationalism and unionism, it should be clear already, are far from mirror opposites but lie on different sides of a strange asymmetry; yet there is also the curious predicament that even in comparison with Britishness – surely, one might reason, a kindred form of identity? – Scottish Unionism can seem cold, robotic, unfeeling and negative.

Oddly, despite its deep roots in early modern Scottish history, going back to the union of the Crowns and even beyond, the Scottish Unionism of today is a product of the very recent past. Before the 1970s, at the very earliest, there was no such thing as a Scottish Question in politics. In so far as there had been irritants in the Anglo-Scottish Union these had been ecclesiastical rather than political. From the Patronage Act of 1712, by which the new British Parliament restored lay patronage in the Scottish Kirk against its wishes and the apparent terms of the legislation securing the privileges of the Church of Scotland which accompanied the Articles of Union in 1707, by way of the Disruption of 1843 when the Free Church of Scotland liberated itself from the authority of the British state connection, through to the Church of Scotland Act 1921, which resolved these tensions and long-standing grievances, it was ecclesiastical issues which had hampered the generally smooth processes of Anglo-Scottish integration. Ecclesiastical issues excepted, there was no Scottish Question.

Even the birth of the NPS in 1928, followed by the right of centre Scottish Self-Government Party in 1932, and the amalgamation of these two groups to form the SNP in 1934 did not – even in the medium term – give rise to a pressing Scottish Question. The SNP won its first parliamentary seat at a by-election during the closing stages of the Second World War in 1945, and its first seat at a general election only in 1970. As there was no Scottish Question to answer, there was no need for an aggressive, proactive or even reactive unionism. For much of the Union's history, Scottish unionism existed in a state of passivity and quiescence as a kind of banal, 'wallpaper' unionism. Yet if the Anglo-Scottish Union was uncontroversial, the same could not be said of the British-Irish Union of 1800.

Unionism in Scotland has traditionally thrived as a full-throated and uninhibitedly negative response to the *Irish* Question (Macdonald 1998). Indeed, the dominant party in Scotland during the middle decades of the

20th Century was the Unionist Party, a party founded on the rocks of the Irish Question – the same Irish Question which had wrecked the Liberal Party and split it asunder. Gladstone's first Irish Home Rule bill in 1886 had created a schism between Liberals and Liberal Unionists, who were allied with the Conservatives in their opposition to Irish Home Rule. In time this alliance was cemented with the formal integration of Conservatives and Liberal Unionists into the Conservative and Unionist Party; at least that was how the party was known in England. In Scotland the formal amalgamation, which occurred in 1912, was known as the Unionist Party, until in 1965 it changed its name to the Scottish Conservative and Unionist Party. At each stage, however, the Union to which the party name referred was the Union with Ireland (or Northern Ireland), not the unquestioned Anglo-Scottish Union. It might occasion some surprise that the Scottish Party of 1932 emerged out of the Glasgow Cathcart branch of the Unionist Party, and that the early SNP included among its leading figures former Unionists, until one remembers that Unionism here referred to the Union with Ireland. Unionists perceived a need to assert traditional *Scottish* Protestant values against the immigrant culture of Roman Catholic Ireland, and, given this nativist emphasis, the ideological walls between Scottish Unionism and Scottish nationalism – some of whose loudest proponents shared the same concerns – were unexpectedly porous. Scottish Unionism of this sort was lively, articulate and engaged. Its vigour was predicated upon an umbilical link between Presbyterianism in Scotland and its kindred offshoot in Ulster.

By contrast this strain of unionism had very little concern with the Union with England, which was, of course, simply taken for granted. If anything, the reverse was the case. Anglo-Scottish relations make little sense historically without some appreciation that Unionism, or, to be more precise, distinct Anglo-Scottish and British-Irish Unionisms, belong to a triangular set of relationships among England, Scotland and Ireland, of which the Scottish-Irish connection was during the late 19th and early 20th centuries decidedly more vexed than the slumbering marriage between England and Scotland. While there was, of course, some overlap between the Unionism of the Unionist Party (essentially a form of conservatism inflected by Presbyterian politics and a generous measure of old-fashioned anti-Catholicism) and the lower-case non-partisan unionism of those who defended the Anglo-Scottish Union, Unionism and 'unionism' were, it is clear, far from congruent. Nevertheless, the very rich hinterland of partisan associations which lurked behind the term Unionism long served to inhibit – though never fully stifle – the expression of unionist sentiment outside the ranks of the Scottish Conservatives.

Ireland has remained an uncomfortable spectral presence in Scottish unionist politics. Since the 1970s the most vivid and emotionally-charged brands of Unionism in the United Kingdom have been found neither in Wales, nor in Scotland, notwithstanding their arguably closer institutional and cultural relationships with England, but in Northern Ireland. Although a considerable distance separated the integrationist Official Ulster Unionism of Enoch Powell from the Protestant-state devolutionism of the Reverend Ian Paisley's Democratic Unionists, such was the influential – and disturbing – media presence of these two gifted and enthusiastically illiberal spokesmen, that their distinctive versions of Unionism tended to be conflated by mainstream British opinion; and, in turn, the very term 'Unionism' became a dirty word in British political culture, contaminated by association with these Ulster bogeymen and their reactionary hostility to the progressive values of the British mainland.

As Iain McLean and Alistair McMillan note, 'primordial unionism' – an enthusiastic embrace of the historic traditions of Union – flourished only in Ulster as the outlandish, folkloric culture of illiberal Unionists, while unionists in Scotland were left with a drab and defensive 'instrumental unionism', which rarely aspired to anything more poetic than a cost-benefit analysis of the Anglo-Scottish connection (McLean and McMillan 2005). Notwithstanding the persistent sectarianism in some quarters of Scottish society, Unionism of the Ulster variety has no political purchase in contemporary Scotland. Indeed, the lingering risk that Scottish unionism might be linked to its Ulster counterpart came into focus in the spring of 2012 when David Trimble, the former leader of the Ulster Unionists, visited the Scottish Conservative conference at Troon to stir the Scottish Unionist campaign out of what – to an Ulsterman like Trimble – seemed its all-too-apparent apathy. Nevertheless, the vigorous Ulster Unionist activism which Trimble lauded and recommended that unionists in Scotland copy, had itself contributed to the historic diffidence and prudent reserve of Scottish Unionism, ironically and indirectly, perhaps, as an unwelcome example of an overzealous unionism which Scots had little desire to imitate. For the very term 'Unionism' – so pregnant with Irish associations – has not been one with which Scottish unionists, other than a few diehard Orangemen, feel at all comfortable.

Yet over the course of the 20th Century – inevitably perhaps – the distinction between the non-partisan case for the Anglo-Scottish Union of 1707 and the partisan Unionism of the Unionist Party and its successor, the Scottish Conservative and Unionist Party, became blurred. This confusion was exacerbated by the fact that since Labour's enforced conversion to devolution in 1974, it has been the Conservatives who in the run-up to the devolution referendums of 1979 and 1997 made the case for the unitary state. As a result, unionism became in large measure a partisan issue. Nevertheless, during the mid-1970s the first explicitly pro-unionist campaign in Scotland, the Scotland is British [SIB] campaign of 1976–8, was in good part the creation of a Labour politician, tellingly a *former* MP, George Lawson, who had been Deputy Chief Whip in 1966–7 and had sat for Motherwell from 1954 until his retirement in 1974. The SIB campaign celebrated 'our common nationhood with the rest of the people of Britain', but was confronted by various awkward strategic problems. Notionally cross-party, it nevertheless lacked a heavyweight presence from the Labour side, though Tam Dalyell ran his own maverick campaign against devolution (Dalyell 1977).

Moreover, the perceived Conservative appropriation of the Union Jack as a party symbol made it very difficult for the SIB campaign to wrap itself in the flag. As Graham Walker has shown the SIB faced the problem of celebrating the wide measure of *administrative* devolution Scotland already enjoyed within the British union-state, while opposing the proposed *legislative* devolution on offer from the Labour government. It was especially tricky to accentuate the positive aspects of existing devolution, not least as it was administered after all by the Scottish Office which seemed grey and remote, when visible at all to the general public. What seems to have held the campaign together was the guile of a former Whip, but with Lawson's death in July 1978 the cross-party SIB campaign lost its moorings, its membership drifting into separate 'Scotland Says No' and 'Labour Vote No' campaigns (Walker 2007).

Two decades later the devolution referendum of 1997 was a more straightforward battle between a cross-party popular front which favoured devolution (Labour, Liberals and – more ambivalently – the SNP) and a rump anti-devolutionist campaign centred on the Conservative Party which had just lost all its seats in Scotland at the 1997 general election. Dalyell remained opposed to devolution, but was largely silenced by Labour pressure, and the feeble and unimaginative anti-devolutionist Think

Twice campaign had trouble reaching out beyond the embattled and shrinking Tory laager. To all intents and purposes, there was very little in the way of a serious 'unionist' campaign in 1997, for devolution already appeared to be the 'settled will' of the Scottish electorate, which simply needed the unproblematic ratification of the required referendum. At this point, unionism seemed shrill, partisan and pointless (and, from the vantage point of today, strangely opposed to the very scheme of devolution which unionists – not only Labour and Liberal but Conservative too – *now* defend).

Think Twice was perhaps the nadir of Thatcherite unionism. Ironically, the Thatcher era saw the emergence of three distinct visions of Union, two of which existed *within* the Conservative Party, which was fast shrinking as a potent electoral force north of the border. The three ideas of union were, first, the Liberal-Labour idea of Scottish devolution as a means of both protecting Scotland from the perceived ravages of an alien, predominantly home counties, Thatcherite conservatism and, ultimately, preserving the Union-state; second, the Thatcherite interpretation of Britain as a unitary state, run according to the universal dictates of the free market; and, third, the union-state unionism of an older Conservatism, which recognised the diversity of political traditions and institutions within the United Kingdom. Unfortunately for the long-term prospects of unionism as an ideology, the first, the Lib-Lab vision of John Smith, Donald Dewar, David Steel and Charles Kennedy was couched in the rhetoric of Scottish popular sovereignty and home rule, so that it appeared to sound like a version of Scottish nationalism, which, in a way, it was – but a form of nationalism under the umbrella of the Union.

The effects of the second form of unionism – the Thatcherite version – were to produce in the minds of the Scottish electorate a distorted caricature of what unionism meant (Stewart 2009: Ch. 6). To most anti-Thatcherite Scots, unionism had come to mean the imposition of the perceived loadsamoney, get-rich-quick ethos of the City of London and the southeast on the hard-working, but downtrodden, manufacturing regions of Scotland and the north of England. After all, Thatcher's Chancellor of the Exchequer between 1983 and 1989, Nigel Lawson, complained in the course of a speech he gave in Glasgow in November 1987, only months after the Conservative and Unionist presence in Scotland had been reduced to a rump of ten seats, that 'large areas of Scottish life are sheltered from market forces, and exhibit the culture of dependence rather than that of enterprise.' The Scottish edition of the *Sun* translated these far from euphemistic broadsheet sentiments into a lilting music hall tabloidese, which left little room for misunderstanding: 'Will ye stop your snivelling Jock?' (Mitchell 1990: 113) By a series of ironies, Thatcherite unitarism generated a spiral of unintended consequences: Scots were alienated from Thatcherism and rejected it at the ballot box, but when Thatcherite governments were re-elected at the UK level with paltry Scottish support, the obvious democratic deficit in Scotland led to a further degree of estrangement from an illegitimate British state and its unreformed constitution (Hassan 2012: 80). Thatcherism stood, of course, for the liberation of the individual from the trammels of state dependency, but it had little to say about communities or regions, and seemed oblivious of the United Kingdom as a multi-national state – except from the cheese-paring perspective of a parsimonious Treasury. There was no scope here for devolution, nor even for regional policies or the promotion of cross-subsidies from richer to poorer parts of the United Kingdom.

If so, it seemed to those on the Left, then what was the point of the Union? It was left to Conservative moderates – the fifth column of those deemed 'not one of us' – to articulate a more capacious and unthreatening form of unionism. The clearest enunciation of this union-state unionism came in a speech delivered by the then Secretary of State for Scotland, Malcolm Rifkind, to the Aberdeen Chamber of Commerce on 15 April 1988. Rifkind was something of a subversively traditionalist Tory within the upper echelons of the Thatcher-era Conservative Party, having resigned Shadow ministerial office a decade previously over Thatcher's decision to oppose Labour plans for devolution in 1976. By the late 1980s Rifkind had necessarily trimmed his position for the sake of political advancement, but still remained at a considerable remove from the narrow dogmas of Thatcherite unionism. Instead Rifkind identified four core pillars of unionism. There was, of course, an 'unshakeable belief that the peoples of these small islands share a common destiny and that both their shared and their distinctive social and economic interests require and justify a common Crown, Parliament and economic structure.' However, the union was not simply about commonalities, reckoned Rifkind, who contended, somewhat daringly for a member of Thatcher's Cabinet, that 'the unity of the kingdom is strengthened by diversity and does not require uniformity' and that 'the Union neither requires, nor would benefit from, the Anglicisation of Scotland'. The fourth pillar of Rifkind's unionist wisdom was the idea of 'partnership, that 'the Union must remain a partnership of its constituent territories and Scotland must enjoy all the benefits as well as the responsibilities of full partnership' (Rifkind 1988).

Of course, the nuances of the Rifkind version of Union tended to be drowned out by the roaring Thatcherite tide. However, this tide turned out to be ebbing, in Scotland at least. John Major and his Scottish lieutenant, Ian Lang, tried to refurbish something of the Rifkind-style unionism, but it was too late. The retreat of Conservatism in Scotland left both the Thatcher and Rifkind interpretations of Union high and dry by the time of Tony Blair's huge election victory of 1997. It transpired, by a further twist in the cunning of history, that from henceforth only the old rhetoric of devolution – which until 1997 had been considered a *nationalist* idiom – was politically credible with the electorate as a foundation for Scottish Unionism.

References

Dalyell, T. (1977), *Devolution: the End of Britain?*, London: Jonathan Cape.

Hassan, G. (2012), 'It's only a northern song: the constant smirr of anti-Thatcherism and anti-Toryism', in Torrance, D. (ed.), *Whatever happened to Tory Scotland?* Edinburgh: Edinburgh University Press.

Macdonald, C. (ed.) (1998), *Unionist Scotland 1800–1997*, Edinburgh: John Donald.

McLean, I. and McMillan, A. (2005), *State of the Union: Unionism and the Alternatives in the United Kingdom since 1707*, Oxford; Oxford University Press.

Mitchell, J. (1990), *Conservatives and the Union*, Edinburgh, Edinburgh University Press.

Rifkind, M. (1988), 'Speech to Aberdeen Chamber of Commerce', *The Scotsman*, 16 April.

Sellar, W.C. and Yeatman, R.J. (1976, orig. edn. 1930), *1066 and All That*, London: Methuen Paperbacks.

Stewart, D. (2009), *The Path to Devolution and Change: a Political History of Scotland under Margaret Thatcher*, London: I.B. Tauris.

Walker, G., (2007), 'The Scotland is British Campaign, 1976–8', *Scottish Affairs*, 61, 74–100.

Varieties of independence

JAMES MITCHELL

'When I use a word,' Humpty Dumpty said in rather a scornful tone, 'it means just what I choose it to mean – neither more nor less.' 'The question is,' said Alice, whether you can make words mean so many different things.' 'The question is,' said Humpty Dumpty, 'which is to be master – that's all. (*Through the Looking Glass, Ch. 6*)

THE DEBATE ON Scottish independence is primarily a debate amongst supporters of liberal democracy. The debate is about whether people living in Scotland should be part of a Scottish or a UK liberal democracy. At one level this limits the debate but it means that the debate takes us to a contradiction at the heart of all liberal democracies. As Hannah Arendt noted, liberal democracy is informed by Enlightenment thinking, believing in universal individual rights, but simultaneously its supporters accept that the world is organised into sovereign states, each having autonomy within its own boundaries to provide or deny rights to individual or categories of individuals and the right to decide who should receive such entitlements. In Arendt's terms, these are the 'rights to rights' and the 'rights to belong' (Arendt 1986: 295–296). How a state chooses to define and limit these rights will determine what kind of state it is.

This does, however, presuppose that independence provides an ability to determine rights and who should have these. In its most basic sense, independence is the capacity to determine such matters but while each state may claim equal 'sovereign' status, no two states are equally capable of providing the same rights to the same breadth of people, let alone likely to choose the same rights for the same people. Even having the capacity to deliver rights does not mean that states (or, rather, peoples) will choose to deliver these rights to the same breadth of people. In essence, independence is about capacities and choices. This debate is not about which flag should fly over government buildings so much as what kind of society and state is envisaged and whether these can be delivered. There are, of course, diehards on each side who, even if they do not admit it to themselves, are more concerned with the flag – *my country right or wrong*. These are the real nationalists (British and Scottish) who will probably make up a large proportion of those campaigning for and against independence but they will articulate themselves in instrumental terms because they know that this is the key to winning this debate. Part of the difficulty for unaligned voters is that there are many imponderables on both sides of the argument: what kind of state and society will we have under the existing constitutional arrangements in, say, a generation and would a Scottish state be any different? The largest part of the problem will be identifying substantive evidence and reasoned argument amidst the fug of battle conducted in very British adversarial terms.

The SNP's Independence

Capturing the essence of independence may not be difficult but does not take us far. The Scottish National Party (SNP) define independence as, 'the restoration of Scottish national sovereignty by restoration of full powers to the Scottish Parliament, so that its authority is limited only by the sovereign power of the Scottish People to bind it with a written constitution and by such agreements as it may freely enter into with other nations or states or international organisations for the purpose of furthering international cooperation, world peace and the protection of the environment.' Independence only became the formal constitutional objective of the party in 2004. This change in 2004 was more symbolic than real. The SNP has diluted its understanding of independence over many years even as its language hardened. From its establishment three quarters of a century before until 2004, the SNP objective was 'self-government' but for many years this was defined in broadly the same way as it now defines independence. The party had long since abandoned the language of 'self-government' in favour of 'independence' and it made sense that this should be reflected in its constitution. 'Self-government' reflected the distinct political grammar of the early/mid part of the 20th Century and it helped bridge the divide between more hardline and pragmatic elements, acceptable to all because of the ambiguity of its meaning. For most of its history, the SNP did not have to clarify what it meant by independence or self-government as it was a distant prospect. Its constitutional objective motivated its activists, ensured that the SNP was united around this objective. It offered great rhetorical opportunities captured in Winnie Ewing's 'Stop the world Scotland wants to get on' and demanding 'a seat at the UN between Saudi Arabia and Senegal'. In this sense it resembled clause 4 socialism for the Labour Party of old: an objective that was imprecisely defined, on which members were in fact divided but had symbolic, mobilising value. But what does this independence amount to?

The SNP's view has changed over time, reflecting changes in the international order. At one stage early in its history, an element within the party saw Scotland within an evolving Empire and Commonwealth. In the 1950s, it saw opportunities in being part of the emerging European community though it became hostile for a mixture of opportunistic reasons and concerns about the creation of a centralised European with policies inimical to Scottish interests. Its activists have had an ambivalent view of NATO due to the issue of nuclear weapons. While the United Nations and its agencies were favoured this was as much to do with the symbolism of Scotland joining the world and an idealism, sometimes naivety, regarding some ill-defined role for an independent Scotland in world peace and third world development. But the SNP's pro-European stance, forged in the 1980s, was much more than a means of 'killing the separatist bogey' and was arrived at after considerable debate. Its debates on Europe over the decade and more prior to adopting 'Independence in Europe' involved coming to terms with the inter-dependent world. It may not have abandoned the language of independence and sovereignty but it had abandoned its underlying thinking. All states have wrestled with these matters and most parties across liberal democracies have had to do so too. This new thinking informed more than its attitude towards Europe. It made it easier to accept devolution. Understanding that power was not concentrated in one source opened opportunities as well as understandings for the SNP. Quite simply, this allowed the SNP to join the world.

Nonetheless, the party has struggled to articulate a clear and consistent view of how an independent Scotland would relate to others parts of the United Kingdom. Though it has consistently supported the monarchy, it has failed to take full electoral advantage. It might have insisted, for example, that the United Kingdom would, quite literally, be unaffected by independence. It might, for example, have argued that Scotland and England are 'two nations, under one Queen', as Prime Minister Cameron recently described UK-Canadian relations, taking more than rhetorical form with proposals to share embassies across the world. Part of the SNP's problem, of course, is that any relationship with the rest of the UK could not be decided unilaterally and, publicly, no UK government would ever admit to the possibility of Scottish independence. Any ideas emerging from the SNP or others on relations with its immediate neighbours could be an enforced monologue with the deaf before a vote on independence.

However, we have some sense of what is likely to emerge from various statements issued by the SNP over many years. In the mid-1970s, the SNP proposed a 'new partnership' while 'preserving the social harmony of the United Kingdom'. This early articulation of a social union came at a time when the SNP were riding high in the polls, when scrutiny of the SNP was at its height with the apparent prospect of independence. It has advocated something akin to a Council of the Isles at various times. In the 1970s, it argued for a consultative convention of up to 30 delegates from each part of the UK, with committees preparing reports on matters of mutual interest but with decisions being made by 'sovereign' states. It also argued for an inter-governmental council, again modelled loosely on the Nordic model and maintained that economically close relations would be maintained through either common membership of the European Economic Community or through a free trade agreement. In recent times, the British Irish Council has been seen as offering potential opportunities for some emerging new institutional structure. On close inspection, the SNP's independence involves the maintenance or redesign of many unions.

Ironically, for a party with constitutional change as its central objective, the SNP is clearer in its non-constitutional objectives than it has been in defining independence. The reason is simple. The SNP has been obliged to vote on everyday public policy concerns so long as it has had members elected to local councils, Parliament at Westminster and Holyrood. It has long styled itself as a 'moderate left of centre party' and though this is vague, this along with its behaviour gives us a reasonably clear idea of the kind of state it supports as any party. While it must be acknowledged that the SNP is only one part of the independence movement, it is by far the most important and its policies and ideology can be expected to reflect consensus in Scotland as a party that aspires to be a genuinely national party. These policies have given us a better understanding of the kind of rights likely to exist in an independent Scotland and for whom, assuming the SNP either articulates mainstream Scottish thinking on these matters. Leaving aside constitutional arrangements, we have a reasonably clear idea of the nature of citizenship that would, at least, be favoured and aimed for.

Independent Statehood

Defining independence in terms of sovereignty often becomes circular: independence means national sovereignty and sovereignty means having independence. However, if it means creating a state then we need to understand what is meant by a state. The definition of a state as the institution with a monopoly on the legitimate use of physical violence offered by the German sociologist Max Weber conveys the all-powerful nature of the state, at least within its own borders. This suggests that power ultimately resides within the state (though there may be a dispute as to where within the state) and no external body has such authority within that state. But the notion that power ultimately resides in any single place or that extra-state bodies have no authority or power within a state is difficult to take seriously. Independence has often been a rallying call focused on a desire to be freed from a particular foreign power. In many instances, winning constitutional independence has not provided much in the way of substantive independence. Even as one foreign power is swept away some other external powers – not necessarily states or even a tangible power – emerges to undermine the new state's autonomy. Across large parts of the world, states have gained their independence only to discover a very limited degree of autonomy in practice. The distinction is often made between internal and external sovereignty, the ability to control events within and outside a state's boundaries but this distinction often breaks down in practice. Sovereign statehood does not necessarily mean having meaningful independence. Equally, lacking recognised sovereign statehood does not mean lacking meaningful independence.

The growing number of states in the world serves to highlight the great diversity of capacities and choices involved in being an independent state. The United Nations has 193 members, almost four times its original membership in 1945. There are states which remain outside the UN system and not all states are recognised by all or, at least, some others. Sovereign statehood in this sense describes the status enjoyed by a growing number of polities across the world from China and the United States of America to San Marino, the Marshall Islands and South Sudan. Switzerland has chosen not to join but is acknowledged as a state while Taiwan is now outside the UN, recognised by only 22 states, but a member of the World Trade Organisation and is a formidable trade and economic power. Other states that are not UN members and with contested status include Abkhazia, Kosovo,

Nagorno-Karabak, Transnistria and Palestine. So, what do the wide range of polities calling themselves independent states have in common? What is the basic characteristic of being independent? Gaining recognition is important but there is debate on the recognition of independent states, whether this requires formal recognition by other states or by meeting certain criteria (clearly defined territory; permanent population; an established government; and an ability to engage with other states and international organisations). Independent statehood may not be recognised because of disputed boundaries and territory. Indeed, some of the most bloody conflicts have arisen over such matters. This is not an issue in the Scottish debate as none of the criteria involved are disputed. However what remains disputed is not whether Scotland would be recognised as an independent state but its relations with international organisations (discussed below).

Many formally recognised states are dysfunctional by almost any definition and hence we find references to 'weak' and 'failed' states in the literature on international relations. Scotland would clearly not fall into such a category. But even strong states and superpowers are limited in what they can do both internally and externally. Despite being described as the world's only superpower, the USA is dependent in many important respects. A key objective of successive American Administrations has been 'energy independence', the aim to reduce/eradicate American dependence on foreign energy sources. Every American President has proclaimed this aim since the energy crisis of 1973 though only recently moved much beyond rhetoric. Having formal status as independent tells us little about the capacity and choices available to any state. Independence is a relative rather than absolute idea other than in its (very limited) formal sense.

Independence from Whom or What?

In 1976, at the bicentenary of American independence, a leading American historian remarked that what independence meant to the revolutionary generation had received surprisingly little attention. Though this was not in any sense a liberal democratic debate, it was a debate about the kind of state and society which would be possible with independence. The meaning of independence was assumed rather than explored or contested. What became clear on close examination was that independence had many meanings. Thomas Jefferson, the author of the Declaration of Independence, had little time for any mystical notions of nationalism. For him American independence was an opportunity to develop notions of the independence of the individual beyond what had previously been known within a new state (see Morgan 1978). Independence was conceived in terms of the kind of place America should become in contrast with the kind of state it was leaving behind. But what united each of the different American ideas of independence was agreement on what it should not involve.

All entities are defined in contrast to some *Other* or *Others*. Being Scottish or British means not being something(s) else. This does not preclude the possibility of having two or more identities either simultaneously or consecutively. While being Scottish means not being American or Chinese, these more distant *Others* are less relevant because the *Other* that defines an identity is, in some sense, proximate. Whether geographic, ideological or other, proximity is important. We define ourselves not in terms of what is most distant but what is closest to us. What is significant is not only how imprecise the *Other* may be but also how malleable this *Other* can be. Additionally, this relationship need not be symmetrical. England may be the *Other* for Scots but Scotland need not be England's *Other*.

What is true for identities applies to independence. Being independent means not being dependent on or unduly influenced by some *Other* or *Others*. States of independence may vary over time. Scotland has rarely been England's *Other*. England's *Other* has been France, Germany but today for many in England it is some variation of *Europe* or *Brussels* despite Scotland's *Other* being some variation of England, London, Westminster. Being geographically contiguous but perceived to be unthreatening makes a neighbour less relevant in forging an identity or inducing demands for independence. Geography is only relevant because neighbours are more likely to impinge upon or limit independence. But this need not be the case. During the Cold War, America defined itself and its independence in contrast to the Soviet Union which, other than in its outermost territory on the fringe of Alaska was geographically far from the USA. It also meant that America's understanding of its independence had an ideological dimension, defining itself emphatically in contradistinction to Soviet Communism. Canada, though in the same ideological camp as the USA, has long felt the presence of its larger southern neighbour, captured well by Pierre Trudeau's comment about being 'in bed with an elephant'.

Scottish independence has come to mean more than constitutional independence and Scotland's *Other* is not understood in strict constitutional terms. It is taken for granted that it involves some variant of liberal democracy and a mixed economy which makes it appear thin compared with that against which it defines itself. The key relationship is not England, London or even Westminster but citizenship. Scots voted for devolution in the 1997 referendum because they wanted to protect an understanding of citizenship perceived to have been under threat by UK Government policies. This thinking may have been inchoate, conservative and sometimes mythical but it was such ideas of social citizenship more than some mystical notion of Scottishness that brought voters to the polls to vote for a Scottish Parliament. Much has been written on the nature of *Thatcherism* (a conviction style of politics, an ideology rooted in beliefs in a free economy and strong state, or governing in sectional interests) but such distinctions are irrelevant in understanding support for a Scottish Parliament. Thatcherism was not viewed as an existential threat to Scotland but a threat to an understanding of Scotland shared by many Scots. Despite being a society deeply divided by inequalities, these may have amounted more to shared misunderstandings, *Thatcherism* or some variant became a powerful mobilising agent. Thatcherism was Scotland's *Other*.

It might be contended that the need for a Parliament disappeared with the return of the Labour Government and that the establishment of the Scottish Parliament was Scotland's insurance policy against the day when the Tories were returned. This instrumental interpretation of Scottish nationalism should not be exaggerated but what united Scots in favour of a modest form of independence was negative, conservative and mythical at that the time of the 1997 referendum. The experience of a decade of devolution at a time when Labour was in the ascendancy across Britain and during a period of massive public expenditure growth gave Scotland the opportunity to experiment and diverge in significant ways from the path pursued by New Labour in London. Divergent policies were possible through a combination of devolution and increased expenditure.

Changing Nature of Debate

There are, of course, people who would support or oppose an independent Scotland regardless of the kind of state it was capable of and chose to become. These core loyalists will stick with their constitutional preferences regardless of any evidence that the kind of society they would prefer to live in would be more likely under another constitutional arrangement. There are ample examples in human nature of the heart ruling the head though it is not always easy to know when this occurs. Rational decision-making is more easily understood in theory than in practice and who is to say that a decision of the heart lacks a rational foundation? But in any political debate, rational foundations are sought to justify decisions whatever their basis. Impartial evidence can be hard to come by and some impartial evidence turns out to be from a partial and suspect source, though that alone does not make it suspect.

An aspect of this debate that has changed considerably over time has been the greater degree of consensus over Scotland's capacity to be independent in more than the formal legal sense. The lack of impartial data previously hindered analysis and undoubtedly favoured supporters of the status quo. Given that much data was sourced back to one of the key protagonists for the union, UK central government, care had to be taken with data and claims in the past. It has become more difficult to argue conclusively either way as more data, and more refined data, has become available. There is the added issue of how independence might affect Scotland's potential as compared with the status quo. Even if it is accepted that the welfare state is undergoing significant changes and may end up being almost unrecognisable in a decade or more under the current constitutional arrangements, what is likely to happen in an independent Scotland? But making a judgment on the nature of citizenship will play its part in the referendum.

Another key change has been the number of precedents of secession. Until the dramatic changes following the fall of the Berlin Wall in 1989, the only successful secession since 1945 was the creation of Bangladesh as an independent state in 1971. From 1947, Bangladesh had previously been East Pakistan. The two parts of Pakistan were not contiguous but over 1,000 miles apart with northern India in between. There was too little in common between the UK and Pakistan for comparisons. Since 1989, there have been a number of examples of secession provided precedents, procedures and of course different forms of autonomy and independence. There is still no single authoritative 'road map' to independence but it is now clear that each secession will follow its own path but can draw on others' experience where appropriate and acceptable.

When is Independence?

Given the varieties of independence and range of continuing relationships, even unions, it might prove difficult to know when independence exists other than in some formal and/or symbolic sense. A referendum vote in favour will, no doubt, feature as a significant date but there will be a period of negotiations, interim arrangements and staged agreements on transfer of powers, creations of new and alterations in existing institutions. It is conceivable that some interim arrangements may prove attractive and become acceptable on the grounds that a decision could be made at any time, within reason, to bring such arrangements to a conclusion. It is a common enough feature of institutional change to find radical changes still involve considerable continuities.

These considerations apart, there is the wider and far more significant matter of whether any state can ever really claim independence, even ignoring the obvious inter-dependencies, given constant changing pressures that arise challenging the authority and autonomy of states. What supporters of independence are becoming increasingly aware of is that as that goal appears in sight, it proves to be more elusive. Knowing that is helpful. Supporters and opponents on Scottish independence need only observe the illusion of independence evident in the metropolitan capitals including that of the United Kingdom. It is difficult to avoid the conclusion that independence becomes less clear the closer are to it.

References

Arendt, H. (1986), *The Origins of Totalitarianism*, Andre Deutsch.

Morgan, E.S. (1978), *The Meaning of Independence*, University of Virginia Press.

The Size of States –
An Economic Analysis

JOHN KAY

THE UNION OF PARLIAMENTS between Scotland and England took place in 1707. The triggering event was the failure of Scotland's Darien expedition, an attempt to colonise a strip of land in what is now Panama. This was a good idea, but an idea considerably ahead of its time: world trade would indeed grow, and Panama would became a pivotal location although still an inhospitable one. The Company of Scotland did not have the skills and resources that would enable the US government to realise the vision two centuries later.

The financial impact of its collapse on the aristocracy and leading merchants of Scotland paved the way for Union – this was the first great bailout of failed Scots financial institutions. But some were prescient enough to realise the much longer term implication of these events: that Scotland could not expect to take a major role in the development of global trade except through union with a neighbour which was fast becoming the principal naval power.

The outcome in Scotland was one of the most extraordinary transformations in economic history. A poor country on Europe's periphery became, within a century and a half, one of the richest areas in the world. The contrast between Edinburgh's old and new towns makes the point in stone.

Entrepreneurial capabilities gave the Scots a disproportionate role in the trading – and looting – opportunities created by the growing British Empire. An extraordinary constellation of intellectual talent in Edinburgh, led by David Hume and Adam Smith, advanced the Scottish Enlightenment. Technological advances propelled Scots to leadership in the development of steam engines, and hence in locomotives and shipbuilding, and in textiles.

The economic success of Scotland in the 18th and 19th centuries through union with England presaged a more general trend. In the 19th Century, states became larger. That century began with Napoleon's failed attempt to establish a European empire for France. But Bismarck and Cavour and the Royal Navy, which won control of the seas and the pioneers who settled America, would be more permanently successful in forging political structures with economic power. The dominant political events of the remainder of the century were the expansion of empires, the unification of Germany and Italy, and the emergence of the United States of America as a global political and economic power.

In the 20th Century, states became smaller. The century began with the collapse of the faltering empires of Turkey and Austria-Hungary and ended with the collapse of the last European empire, that of Russia. In the second half of the century, the membership of the United Nations grew from 50 to 200. A majority of the current members of the European Union are countries that have only recently become independent. Several small, peripheral, European states – such as the Nordic countries and Switzerland – moved within a century from being among the poorest of states to being amongst the most socially and economically successful societies in the world.

A primary motive of 19th-Century expansionism was the belief that economic prosperity was founded on securing political control over natural resources. There was something in this notion, but much less than was thought. Those who subscribed to that view greatly overestimated the importance of resources in economic development. They had not recognised how large would be the military costs of securing resources, and of maintaining control over the associated territory without the consent of the local population. These costs would come greatly to exceed any economic benefits. Moreover, while the economic benefits of empire mostly accrued to private firms and individuals, the costs of administering and defending territory fell on the public purse. Democracies were reluctant to sustain this imbalance.

By the end of the 19th century, new technologies – railroads and steamships, cables and telephones – were transforming transport and communication. These innovations facilitated trade in goods and services and allowed easier movement of capital across borders. Market access became possible without political union as the world became more economically connected. As a result, small states became able to achieve prosperity on the basis of narrow specialisation in a global economy.

Small states also benefitted from the greater capacity of homogenous communities to reconcile economic dynamism with social cohesion. Scandinavia benefited from these factors in the 20th Century, but Scotland did so earlier because the Union of 1707 gave the country free access to the world's largest military and economic alliance while allowing it to retain some of the social attributes of a small state.

Scotland's relative economic position deteriorated sharply in the 20th Century. This was part of a rebalancing which occurred in the UK, and subsequently in other European countries which had been early industrialisers. In the 19th Century, the northern part of the UK had been the focus of industrialisation and economic growth, while in the 20th Century the South would become more prosperous. But Scotland's manufacturing sector, taken as a whole, is a story of spectacular failure. At the beginning of the century, J & P Coats, the textile conglomerate, was Scotland's largest industrial company and one of the largest companies in the world. In the hundred years that followed, the company would decline into oblivion. Scotland dominated the world shipbuilding industry, and 'Clyde-built' was a symbol of quality.

Textiles and transport were not the best industries to have specialised in – heavy capital goods industries generally suffered during the interwar period, and competitive advantage in the products of commodity ships and clothing would slip away to lower wage locations on the opposite side of the world. But there was nothing inevitable about the scale of Scottish industrial decline, and Scots today wear Italian suits, travel to England in French trains, and cruise in Scandinavian built ships.

A specialism in engine technology that comprehensively fails to make a shift from steam to internal combustion is a particularly narrow one. There was a general failure in imagination, innovation, and investment, the production of weak management abetted by obstructive labour militancy which resisted change in the organisation of production. Family control can often be positive – as it mostly has been in similar industries in Germany – but in Scotland such control seemed to be associated with arrogance and complacency, and a reluctance to recruit able managers from outside the family. History records a long list of successful industrialists of Scottish origin, from Andrew Carnegie in the late 19th Century through John Reith in the first half of the 20th to Alex Trotman in the second half of the 20th, who would build their careers outside Scotland.

Scotland's role in the economic exploitation of the British Empire would, however, be translated into a continuing strength in financial services. Banking, insurance and asset management were areas of competitive advantage, and while the imperial role would diminish as the empire itself did, Hong Kong had always been as much a Scottish colony as a British one and Scots and Scottish dominated institutions would play a principal role when the island became a centre of trade and finance for the Asian region. In the 20th Century, white-collar activities – including public administration – principally based in Edinburgh prospered while blue-collar activities, mainly located in and around Glasgow, did not.

In the 20th Century, it became possible to build a prosperous economy based on mobile phones, on speciality chemicals, precision engineering – even to build an economy based on fish. Iceland learnt that if your principal product is fish, you are poor as an autarchic state, but rich in a global trading environment. Some of the greatest economic success stories of the 20th Century have been built on Adam Smith's greatest insight – that the division of labour reflects the extent of the market.

Switzerland and Finland, for example, were among the poorest countries in the world in the 19th Century (Maddison 2001). In the 21st Century, they are among the richest. Inhospitable terrain, adverse climate, and absence of minerals, are no longer disadvantages. Indeed the resourcefulness and mutual support that such unfavourable physical factors engendered is a positive boon.

These changes in the nature of economic power went hand in hand with changes in the nature of political authority. The primary role of the state was once coercive – to main social control at home and confront foreigners abroad. Max Weber famously defined the state as the body which sustains a monopoly of coercion within a defined geographical area Weber 1919). And the nature of 19th-century government followed that definition. Military expenditure was the largest component of government spending. Typically the next largest component was debt interest, which mainly represented the costs of past wars.

This view of the state was associated with what Norman Angell would term 'the Great Illusion' (Angell 1913): the idea that nations could best increase their prosperity by gaining resources through territorial conquest. In a world of little or no economic growth, where the principal means of enhancing wealth was to steal it from someone else, there is much sense in that view.

The associated rise of specialisation and world trade, the industrial revolution, which made sustained economic growth within national borders possible, and the rise of democracy, which required that national wealth be widely shared, would comprehensively undermine that analysis of the sources of prosperity (although it would only change perceptions more slowly). Wealth creation within the framework of security of property and stability of institutions would provide a larger and more enduring source of opulence than grabbing land, resources or treasure. The Great Illusion would, at least for Europeans, be finally dispelled in the ruin of Europe in 1945, and the collapse of overseas empires that followed. The rapid recovery of European economies from the destruction of their infrastructure would provide a vivid demonstration that in the modern world wealth is the product of people not things. The Japanese co-prosperity sphere that had not been achieved by conquest would be established through trade.

And so the influence of economic forces on the size of states has changed radically. Many people will resist this economic thesis, preferring to explain the events I have described in political terms. Yet the units that nationalism defines have changed. Nineteenth century nationalism sought to establish attachment to larger units. 'We have created Italy,' said reunification hero Massimo d'Azzeghio, 'now we must create Italians.' (and with the aid of railways and mass education, that is what happened in Italy, as it did in Britain, Germany and France). But since the Treaty of Versailles, global politics has favoured the claims to nationality of smaller units, even to the emergence of microstates such as Montenegro and Kosovo. This is because nationalism is as much servant of economics as master.

Nationalism is a potent force in defining social and political identity, a complex mixture of ethnic and cultural affinities, rooted in a shared history. Individuals have an evident need for these group identities, but the identities they emphasise change. The Scots have been British when it suited them, and Scottish when it suited them. In the 19th Century, Scots as Britons gained access to the British Empire and the apparently necessary protection of a great military power. Today, Scots no longer attach much store to these advantages and are, once again, primarily Scots. There is nothing reprehensible about this opportunism, which is by no means unique to Scotland. To think otherwise is to believe that national identity is somehow innate, perhaps genetic, rather than a social construction which is the product of a particular time and place.

And to ignore the changing expectations of the things the state should do. Modern Europeans rarely want their governments to kick ass. Nor do they want to spend much on preparations for that activity. As a proportion of overall public spending, defence is now well behind social security, education and health. What modern Europeans expect their government to do is to provide schools and hospitals, and to assure their physical and economic security. The notion of government as a hostile, coercive force, still widely encountered in the United States, has very little resonance in Western Europe. Services such as education, health and social welfare, are the predominant functions of government and larger states have few advantages and significant disadvantages relative to smaller ones in these activities.

European government is an economic agent, like a supermarket. The ideological content is steadily draining from European politics: European leaders proclaim their competence rather than their convictions. As with supermarkets we judge government mainly by the quality of its output and the perceived competence of its management. And in general, we judge it less favourably than we judge supermarkets.

And, as in a world dominated by supermarkets, smaller units succeed by finding niches to which they are well suited and developing these niches on a global scale. Extensive trade is key to the prosperity of small states, and the key development making such growth possible has been the dissociation of trading alliances from military alliances. So long as the belief that prosperity depended on control over resources was prevalent, such an association was inevitable. A war-going nation needed to be self-sufficient in resources, food and industrial capacity. But this military requirement for autarchy has disappeared.

The prosperity of small states is a direct consequence of globalisation. Finland and Switzerland manufacture no cars, though they consume many. They do make textiles, but as high end speciality products for a world market. In the modern global environment, economic success depends not on scale but competitive advantage. Such competitive advantage may be held by individual firms – the Disneys and Coca-Colas. More commonly in Europe, groups of related firms exploit local competitive advantages – southern Germany's strengths in precision engineering, Korea's high quality low cost production work force.

Scotland's economic future should be seen in these terms. The lesson from the success of other small European countries is the opportunity to develop growth and prosperity on the basis of quite narrow sources of competitive advantage. Modern consumers increasingly want services rather than goods, and the goods and services they want are increasingly differentiated products tailored to their individual needs. That is why firms like BMW have prospered, and in the richest economies such niche firms have won sales from global mass producers. Their global success is a reminder that niche doesn't necessarily mean local but it frequently does, especially in services. And services, to repeat, are what we now seek from govern-

ment. Welfare, health, education: then we find defence: followed by transport, internet security, environmental services.

With privately produced goods and services the organisation of production adapts to the nature of the market. Boeing and Airbus assemble
aeroplanes for the world from single facilities at Seattle and Toulouse: hair-
cuts are, and always will be, locally produced and delivered. The adaptation of the location of production to the needs of the customer is equally
relevant to public consumption. The level of organisation appropriate for
elementary education is lower than the level of organisation appropriate
for higher education; most environmental issues, like river quality, are
best dealt with at very local levels, but some, like carbon emissions, at
very aggregate levels. And so on.

Trade policy needs to be handled at a high level. And so does monetary policy. In an era of global finance small states need to be part of a
trade bloc and an actual or de facto monetary union. The experience of
governments everywhere is that the levels at which it is most efficient to
collect taxes are higher, on average, than the levels at which it is most
efficient to make expenditure decisions. Even for large states, jurisdictional and enforcement problems for corporation tax and the taxation of
income from capital are becoming increasingly severe. The mismatch
between efficient tax raising and efficient expenditure allocation is why
federal states generally have a system of distribution of centrally collected
revenues to state or provincial governments (see Oates 1999).

That matching of service delivery to efficient scale changes in what we
mean by sovereignty. Weber's definition emphasised the coercive role of
the state: along with coercion went monopoly. But if coercion is no longer
the defining characteristic of state action, the requirement for monopoly
falls away also. We can envisage multiple layers of government operating
within a single local area, each delivering the services in which they have a
competitive advantage. And that is what, increasingly, we observe (Alesina
and Spolare 2003).

The word sovereignty derives from the word sovereign. Nobles exercised authority at the authority of the king and governed their territories
through that authority. The analogy in a world of many governments
requires that both supranational and subsidiary governments operate under
licence, as it were, from sovereign government. But this constitutional
analysis is without economic relevance.

If sovereignty is the capacity to act without the agreement of other governments, then every government, even that of the United States, faces serious limits on its economic sovereignty. The concept of sovereignty is a distraction from the issues of economic debate, whether the debate is about Scotland's relationship with the United Kingdom or the United Kingdom's relationship with Europe. The EU is a layer of government which appropriately wields authority on issues for which the appropriate level is the European. There are not many such issues, but internal and external trade policy are at or near the top of the list.

That view of the economic role of the EU sees it for what it should be, and substantially is – a bureaucracy with limited, well-defined functions. Not everyone wants to see it that way: officials and politicians who operate at the EU level naturally try to seize what powers they can from other levels of government, with modest success. They often seek to create the appearance of a traditional Weberian coercive state at European level. That means European involvement, and ultimately control, of fiscal and monetary policies and foreign and defence policies. These advocates make little progress in these areas, and are likely to continue to make little progress.

But in Philip Bobbitt's words, 'it is a failure of imagination, however, to assume that the only thing that will replace the nation-state is another structure with nation-state like characteristics. It is in some ways rather pathetic that the visionaries in Brussels imagine nothing more forward-looking than the equipping of the EU with the trappings of the nation state' (Bobbitt 2002; see Cooper 2003).

Many people in Britain are still wedded to the concept of the modern democratic nation state as it developed through the 19th Century. That modern state used democratic institutions to legitimise its monopoly of coercion. The post-modern state which is succeeding it is primarily an economic agent which gains legitimacy through its effectiveness in the delivery of services. Many people in Britain remain hostile to the European Union and many of those who support the EU count themselves among Bobbitt's 'pathetic visionaries' who want to reproduce the nation-state at a European level.

But economic competition in the 21st Century is not about capacity to mobilise divisions and dreadnoughts, but about the capacity to achieve high living standards by selling mobile phones and speciality chemicals. Economic success is not achieved by armies fighting political enemies on broad fronts, but predicated on the development of relatively narrow competitive advantages in firms and groups of firms. In this modern competition, some of the major winners have been small states whose economies have been able to pursue their strengths without the paralysis created in larger countries by conflict between large, established vested interests: the paralysis the Thatcher government partially destroyed in the UK but which is so evidently persistent in Europe's other large economies in France, Germany and Italy.

In 2011, the Scottish Social Attitudes Survey asked Scots how whether they would support independence for Scotland if it would make them £500 a year better off, and found a two-to-one majority in favour. The survey reversed the question – suppose you would be £500 a year worse off – and found that this would reverse the plurality. It is hard to imagine a similar finding in Ireland in 1921, or India in 1945. Patrick Henry's cry to the American colonist of 'Give me liberty or give me death' lacks the same resonance when reframed as 'Give me liberty or give me £500'.

Yet perhaps this represents a realistic advance. The modern debate about political structures is appropriately cast as a debate about economic efficiency, not about a concept of sovereignty which has little meaning in the economically interdependent world which, to our great benefit, we have created.

References

Alesina, A. and Spolare, E. (2003), *The Size of Nations*, MIT Press.

Angell, N. (1913), *The Great Illusion*, G.P. Putnam's Sons.

Bobbitt, P. (2002), *The Shield of Achilles*, Knopf.

Cooper, R. (2003), *The Breaking of Nations: Order and Chaos in the Twenty-First Century*, Atlantic Press.

Maddison, A. (2001), *The World Economy: A millennial Perspective*, OECD Development Centre Studies.

Oates, W. (1999), 'An Essay on Fiscal Federalism', *Journal of Economic Literature*, vol.37, No.3.

Weber, M. (1919), 'Politics as a Vocation', at sscnet.ucla.ed

Concepts and Challenges Relating to the Economics of 'Self-Government'

STEPHEN BOYD AND KATHERINE TREBECK

Introduction

SHOULD THE AUTUMN 2014 Scottish referendum yield a positive result for the Yes campaign, it is likely that the new independent Scotland will enter a global economy still struggling to cope with fallout from the great financial crisis of 2007/08. It is possible that Scottish output, (full-time) employment and exports will, at best, be only marginally higher than pre-crisis levels. Unemployment will almost certainly be higher and a greater proportion of that unemployment will have become structural. For many, work will be less rewarding and less secure. Any reform of the financial sector will be almost inevitably prove inadequate and leave serious, long-standing structural weaknesses. A new independent state will be paying the costs of previous failure for some time to come.

An ostensibly 'independent' Scotland will do well to learn from the failures of the economic and social model that shattered so spectacularly in the latter part of the last decade. It seems all too apparent that the crisis represented the inevitable implosion of a failed economic and social model. The 'financialised' economy, pursued with particular vigour in the US and UK, didn't lead to greater prosperity for all: it generated moderate GDP and productivity growth, an exponential rise in income and wealth inequality and a decline in social mobility.

The financial crisis *should* have blown away many of the orthodoxies (particularly around deregulation and the role of the state) that have underpinned economic policy for far too long. Constitutional change in Scotland therefore provides an opportunity to create a new economic architecture that reconnects a strong, flexible economy to the living standards of all, not just to residents of the penthouse. Attaining self-government in the fullest sense of the term means doing the economy differently. It means reconceptualising the economy and the purpose of economics so that they are the means to a different ends, an ends defined by the people of Scotland, rather than rating agencies, unaccountable corporations, or the narrow, but powerful vested interests who have most to lose from a new economic model that puts people first.

This chapter will examine the failure of the prevailing economic model to deliver sufficient benefits for enough people or even to work on its own terms to deliver sustained and sustainable economic growth. It will critique the economic system and assess whether there are any signs that it would be more closely aligned to what Scots want under alternative constitutional scenarios as currently proposed. It then sets out, by way of example, some indicative changes required to create a truly self-governing economy. The challenges of pursuing such shifts under any constitutional configuration are noted in a concluding 'reality' check.

Bringing Democracy back to Economics: Reconceptualising 'Self-Government'

Widening the concept of 'self-government' beyond the parliamentary to its real political meaning presents a more challenging goal. It implies people determining objectives and the means to attain them. Self-government means an economy that serves the needs of the people, rather than the other way around. No matter what constitutional scenario is pursued, without an end to dominant economic orthodoxy taking precedence over people's interest, self-government in the true, democratic sense of the term, will remain elusive.

Yet government action often does not reflect values held by a majority of its citizens (let alone those of disadvantaged minorities), constituting a democratic deficit. As Charles Lindblom, in his article *The Market as Prison* identified, in capitalist states the objective of being economically competitive often takes precedence, aligned political and corporate interests and undermining democracy (1982). Part of the problem is the understanding of 'competiveness' in Scotland, the UK and elsewhere. It is approached in a manner that yields destructive short-termism and prioritisation of capital to the exclusion of all other stakeholders, despite evidence that other forms of capitalism – such as that pursued in Nordic countries, north-western Europe and Japan – produce much better outcomes. The results suggest government by an elite, rather than self-government for the many.

A Critique of Current Economic Model

Real self-government thus means self-determination: community control, economics for social outcomes, rather than kowtowing to powerful economic forces. Yet to a great extent the current economic model has not delivered – not for enough people, nor has it delivered enough social justice or sustainability – and the failings of the current economic model arguably manifest themselves profoundly in Scotland's growing health inequalities.

The current economy and its disconnectedness from socially desired outcomes needs to be understood with reference to Scotland's recent economic and social history which is characterised by a shift from production to an economy based on services and consumption. Tellingly, where Glasgow was once the second city of the British Empire, manufacturing the means by which the global economy expanded, it has in recent years laid claim to be the second largest shopping destination in the UK.

Policies accompanying this shift (encouraging it and also purporting to ensure people benefit from the new economic structure) reflected assumptions that a process of 'trickle-down' will address social disadvantage. How and what wealth is created and distributed has largely been ignored in efforts to simply increase it. Competitive cities, it was argued (for example in the Scottish Executive's 2002 Review of Scotland's Cities), would drive growth: urban areas thus needed to become more attractive to 'ideal' residents – namely, aspirational young people (that is, consumers) who worked in the service and 'knowledge' sectors. Actions to make urban areas more flexible and friendly to businesses were vigorously pursued. Consequently, 'regeneration' has often been conceptualised as construction of luxury housing, shops, and privatised spaces in which local people are expected to engage as consumers and as customers. Simultaneously, pursuit of labour market flexibility foisted most risk onto individuals: individuals must increase their employability, be more flexible, more mobile, and participate whole heartedly in the consumption-based economy.

Under these policies social goals (such as community cohesion, strong relationships between people, a sense of empowerment, and sustainability) are rarely ends in themselves. Instead, as Crawford *et al* (2007) highlight, strong communities seem valued because they enable the economy to 'exploit the widest range of talent across the population'; good health is 'a way of improving the performance of the Scottish workforce, while ill health would impose significant costs'. The hierarchy of respective goals is clear: strong communities and healthy citizens as ingredients of a growing economy – poignantly, not the other way around.

Growth reliant on retail and consumption imposes a materialistic mode of socio-economic inclusion, based almost exclusively on consumerism, image and superficial relationships. This has narrowed social, economic and participatory 'space', crowding out space for other goals, values and relationships. Locations where people congregate give way to retail spaces, while workplace relationships become increasingly superficial as human connections are reduced to one-sided market transactions. This leaves little room for consideration, let alone valuing, of non-economic activities and objectives (such as care for family or community). The result is a society and economy in which many social problems stem from alienation – from each other, from the economy and even from our own aspirations and sense of identity. One could argue that an extreme manifestation is high levels of liver disease and suicide amongst young men in the West of Scotland, which suggest a link between lacking a sense of hope and having anxiety about one's perceived 'place' in society, resulting in despair, even violence.

More of the Same? The Continuation of the Dominant Economic Orthodoxy, No Matter What the Constitutional Scenario

The economic model behind these processes has not enabled real self-determination. It has reduced autonomy, reduced community led development and reduced the economy's role in supporting health and strong communities. It has not delivered what communities want. Instead, it has vested power in markets and remote elites, away from the people most impacted by their decisions.

Even in purely economic terms, seeking to compete for mobile investments through business tax cuts and deregulation is bound to fail in the longer-term. These 'race to the bottom' policies do nothing to build and sustain advantages that cannot easily be replicated. But they are guaranteed (see Wilkinson and Pickett, 2009) to lead to a more unequal and unstable society, which in turn undermines economic performance.

Such agendas have been described as the 'new conventional wisdom': prioritisation of flexible labour markets, deregulation (particularly of finance), privatisation, competition as the default solution, elevation of the private sector as key to regeneration and re-branding of locations to render them attractive to incoming buyers. Wealth-creation is the paramount goal, with insufficient heed to equity, cohesion or poverty reduction – these are currently described as 'characteristics of growth', rather than the ultimate goals that the right sort of growth should deliver.

If an independent Scotland is to nurture an economy that is fairer, more equal and democratic, more stable and less prone to systemic crises, then a thorough reassessment of policy and institutions is required. Politicians must begin to question the orthodoxy that has dominated for the last three decades and delivered only modest growth and productivity increases, alongside a collapse in social mobility.

What Might an Alternative Model Look Like for Social Justice and Environment Sustainability?

Utilising mechanisms to achieve a more equal Scotland requires creating an economy that serves the people of Scotland, not the other way around. The failure of policy making processes as currently manifested and the market as it currently operates to deliver equality and real prosperity in our most deprived communities suggests that profound and substantial changes are required. Drawing on Oxfam's recent Our Economy and other papers, below are just some suggestions as to what a new model might entail; an economy that can be described as 'self-governing' (Trebeck, 2013).

Finance for Collective Prosperity

Deregulated labour and product markets practically beg 'race to the bottom' business strategies. Hitherto policy makers have rarely engaged in creative, radical thinking about corporate governance, the functioning of equity markets or pension fund regulation. Most importantly, there has been a persistent refusal to intervene directly to seriously tackle Scotland's longest standing structural failure: the inability or unwillingness of private finance to allocate capital efficiently by providing patient, committed finance to growing firms.

Hence a thoroughly restructured and more effectively regulated financial sector is required alongside a programme to reinvigorate sustainable manufacturing and services. As shown in STUC's *Future of Manufacturing in Scotland* report (2011) manufacturing, for example, offers potential benefits to society via local supply chains; driving innovation; enlarging the pool of skills and good jobs; spreading benefits beyond cities and bolstering communities with middle income/middle status jobs. Robust local economies will help communities resist imposed agendas, resist the judgement of remote economic actors and develop in the manner they wish – real self-government.

The exports, direct and indirect employment and research and development provided by manufacturing continue to support the Scottish economy. Sustaining manufacturing at current levels and growing its share in the longer-term can be achieved through provision of patient, committed capital, creative public procurement, effective skills development and a new approach to ownership and control. Government is not powerless to prevent the decline of manufacturing employment and lessons must be learned from, amongst others, Germany and Sweden: high wage economies with a recent track record of successful investment in manufacturing.

Pro-social Business Models

Scotland suffers from a severely skewed distribution of ownership and control in the private economy. Even sectors lauded as driving growth, exports and jobs – oil and gas, whisky – are largely owned and controlled beyond Scotland's borders. Inability to make investment decisions within Scotland's borders and the flight of profits helps explain low investment in, for instance, research and development. Boosting indigenous ownership, particularly through socially beneficial organisational models, can be a key component of more effective, let alone self-governing, economic development policy.

Reconceptualising and reorientating economic activity is needed to link the economy to the needs of communities to advance social and environmental sustainability. This requires new models of business and new models of production in which ownership and management is more widely shared; social and environmental returns take priority; and in which economic decisions are democratised.

For example, collective business models such as community or employee ownership can be used to share prosperity, allowing communities and employees to own and control their assets. Collective ownership impacts community identity – increasing cohesion, confidence and assertiveness. Ownership of assets also generates income that bolsters the local economy (as opposed to being siphoned off by remote corporate headquarters). Crucially, the community (or employees) decides where surpluses are spent, so money is retained locally (leading to further investment and multiplying benefits), distributing resources more fairly than other business models as the wealth received by employees flows into local economies – directed as employees or communities themselves decide. Cooperatives give individuals greater influence in economic transactions where individuals – as employees, as communities, as consumers or as producers – would otherwise be unable to exercise any market power. The presence of cooperatives in local economies is associated with lower levels of inequality.

Such models need to play a central role in Scotland's economy for it to be described as 'self-governing'. The taxation system should positively discriminate in favour of socially beneficial business models, rather than incentivising debt driven private equity as is currently the case. State agencies must support different organisational models with sufficient resources to do so.

Progressive Taxation for Equality and for Social Protection

Creating a self-determining economy necessitates that Scotland's taxation system ensures all taxes are levied in a progressive manner for a fairer distribution of Scotland's resources. Tax should be used as a redistributive mechanism to ensure economic development benefits the most vulnerable in society. A sufficiently resourced and rigorously enforced progressive taxation system requires individuals and companies with most opportunities to sustain their livelihoods and enhance their assets to pay a fair amount of tax. Sanction and reputational weight should be brought to bear on those who avoid paying: public procurement, business support, corporate social responsibility awards and government plaudits should be contingent on companies meeting their tax obligations.

Tax can also help create the sort of Scotland we want – it is a mechanism for self-determination. Shifting the tax base to environmentally and socially harmful activities (such as pollution and overwork) means that entities undermining the collective good pay more. The public health levy on large retailers selling alcohol in Scotland is a good example of this. Its principles should be extended to other activities that harm Scotland's prosperity – such as businesses that pollute, speculate on land and those which do not provide decent work.

Sharing Work and Quality Employment

Work provides an income and often skill development, and social status that imparts esteem and self-worth, which is in turn linked to mental and physical health. Yet work is a realm where power is currently exercised by the few at the expense of the many. Unfairly distributing the 'wellbeing returns' to employment, through polarisation of the labour market, means that such benefits are not enjoyed by everyone, and the economic returns from quality work are only derived by some people. Too many workers are compelled to work long hours, while others are left to languish out of work or in jobs they would not choose if they had the choice, while others have insufficient hours to make ends meet. In Scotland, around one in six people of working age are not in work, while many more are in low quality and low paid work. Yet Scotland and the UK tolerate 'hoarding of work' (the UK was alone in opting out of the EU maximum working hours legislation). For those in work there is a growing divide between the hours worked by high and low paid workers. Polarisation is thus growing; between the highly paid and those relegated to the lower paid, insecure end of the labour market; between professional and managerial workers (who retain considerable bargaining power) and those who lack the education and skills to be 'competitive' in the labour market. The systematic legislative undermining of trade unions and collective bargaining has exacerbated these trends.

The simultaneous existence of overwork, underemployment and unemployment in Scotland demonstrates that work needs to be better shared for greater equality and poverty reduction. Doing so will create more self-determining individuals; individuals less at the whim of a labour market that currently treats people as mere factors of production. Better sharing work is important to manage lower levels of growth without the increasingly high levels of unemployment currently evident. Greater socio-economic equality demands radical rethinking of how work is allocated across society, between age groups and how individuals assess their own employment needs – a high employment, low carbon labour market. Clearly, current conditions (high unemployment, real unemployment rate of around 11 per cent) demonstrate the need of getting more people back to work and building a stronger, more stable and sustainable labour market.

Sharing work better means limiting overwork that deprives others of employment and reprioritisation of paid and unpaid time. This will require changes to regulation and remuneration, and new social norms celebrating work-life balance above long hours. This could include wider implementation of flexible working practices and perhaps a shorter working week in Scotland. Of course, decreasing employment for those currently working too much will require a significant change in the collective mindset – away from narrow conceptions of individual value premised on high income and consumption, towards recognition that individual value derives from relationships, contribution to community, mutuality and so on. It also requires sufficient security of income through strong collective bargaining and social protection mechanisms. Indeed, it is difficult to envisage a Scottish labour market radically reshaped to support good work and economic security that does not have a strong, centralised and co-ordinated system of central bargaining at its core.

In addition, the imbalance between remuneration and social value and the way that the market undervalues activities of greatest social value needs correcting. Scotland needs to properly value activities that increase prosperity and enhance wellbeing. This entails redeploying remuneration so activities that are most socially beneficial are prioritised. Such redeployment would signal which roles are most important in Scottish society and alter associated incentive structures. Recalibrating reward to social value also means recognising that useful and socially valuable 'work' need not mean 'jobs' in the sense of paid work. Work in the home and in the community are fundamental to our collective prosperity and individual wellbeing, and need to be encouraged and enhanced for an economy that serves the people of Scotland and their interests, rather than the interests of the economy as an end in itself.

Limits to Growth as Currently Defined

In order to achieve this sustainable, socially just and self-governing Scotland, politics needs to be re-framed so Scotland's economy nurtures what matters to Scotland. This should encapsulate a better measurement of our collective prosperity, beyond just narrow economic growth, in order to reconceptualise what constitutes the 'success' of the economy and the 'success' of communities and individuals. Pursuing real prosperity, encapsulated by a consensual measure that captures what is important to people, would help shift our attention and the efforts of our policy makers so that they sustain our society, and do not simply kowtow to the economy.

New measures (such as Oxfam's Humankind Index for Scotland) will help Scotland prioritise good growth, not simply growth at any cost in the hope that it will naturally 'trickle down'. Instead good growth should be prioritised, including re-balancing of economic activity to support communities that need economic activity most. Gross Domestic Product, in its consumption orientation and blindness to distribution, is clearly incapable of representation these goals (nor was it ever designed to do so).

Reality Check

Scotland is – and whatever the extent of constitutional change, will continue to be – a small open economy on the periphery of Europe trying to make its way in a globalised economy. Whether progressive voices wish to admit it or not, there are constraints on the development of policy challenging prevailing orthodoxy.

These might be compounded by the nature of the independence settlement with the rest of the UK. The space is not available here to discuss detailed scenarios for the division of assets and liabilities, but it is worth noting the following:

- It seems likely that the Scottish Government will promote a model of independence that concedes monetary policy and financial regulation to the rest of the UK, hence some kind of fiscal compact will probably be required. This will constrain management of the business cycle; structural and regulatory reform of the financial sector; and, potentially, the degree to which the taxation system might be used as a tool of redistribution and economic development.

- Prevailing economic orthodoxy has proved very resilient. Progressive policy development will undoubtedly be constrained by uncritical iteration by media, commentators and many politicians of the axioms continuing to underpin economic policy: flexible labour is an unmitigated good, business tax cuts drive investment and everyone benefits from growth that trickles down. Similarly, economic debate will continue to be infantilised by claims of significant benefits of big lever policy change, namely that cutting corporation tax will dramatically increase Scotland's rate of growth.

- The elevated status afforded by Scotland's political class to certain economic actors, particularly profoundly regressive and unrepresentative employer organisations. Economic development should meet the needs of all. Employer bodies have persistently promoted policies detrimental to workers, communities and the environment, and the mantra of creating a context conductive to business growth seems to take precedence in policy making circles, rather than the goal of an economy that serves the people of Scotland.

- Economic development has been characterised by what has been described as 'non-intervention interventions', refusing to see the state as a dynamic and essential economic actor. Somewhat stunningly, and certainly dangerously, propping up the collapsing financial sector in 2008/09 has not precipitated new thinking in this regard. A new model will require the state to play a direct role in, for instance, access to finance through a State Investment Bank and innovation policy through investment in early stage technologies too risky for private capital.

- Building new institutions of economic development requires change that is planned and managed, including acknowledgement of any gaps in capacity.

- Challenges designing and enforcing an effective taxation framework are significant. A considerable proportion of activity in the legal and accountancy professions is sustained by design and marketing of legal tax minimisation schemes (see Shaxson, 2011). There are issues too, of carbon leakage: if Scotland levies heavy tax on polluting enterprises activity might be simply exported to low regulation jurisdictions with related human and environmental damage (and heavily polluting transportation costs).

Conclusion

This chapter has highlighted serious flaws in the current economic model. It has cautioned that current constitutional change scenarios do not offer much hope that a new, more socially just and environmentally sustainable economic model can be achieved, even were it to be vigorously sought. Discussion has set out some suggested characteristics of a new economic model in order to keep 'our eyes on the prize'. It is clear that a self-governing economy is about much more than the (relatively simple!) transfer of powers from Westminster to Holyrood. It is about a fundamental rethinking of the axioms of economic development. It is about challenging the influence of vested interests and ascendance of economic goals at the expense of quality work, robust local economies and environmental sustainability.

Any claim that independence in and of itself will deliver more self-government in the true sense of the word is over optimistic. Real self-government is about self-determination, and an economy that is positioned as a mechanism to deliver what the people of Scotland determine they want.

Note

Both authors are writing in a personal capacity and the views presented here do not represent Oxfam, nor STUC policy.

References

Crawford, F., Beck, S. and Hanlon, P. (2007), *Will Glasgow Flourish? Learning from the Past, Analysing the Present and Planning for the Future,* Glasgow: Glasgow Centre for Population Health.

Lindblom, C. (1982) 'The Market as Prison', *Journal of Politics,* 44: 2, 324–336.

STUC (2011), *Future of Manufacturing in Scotland,* STUC: Glasgow.

Trebeck, K. (2013), *Our Economy: Towards a New Prosperity,* Oxford: Oxfam GB.

Wilkinson, R. and Pickett, K. (2009), *The Spirit Level: Why More Equal Societies Almost Always Do Better,* London: Allen Lane.

The Continuing Battle for Scottish Tax Powers

JAMES AITKEN

Introduction

IT IS IMPORTANT in the context of the wider independence debate to remind ourselves how the UK Government, its institutions and its supporters in Scotland have considered the idea of devolving substantial tax powers to the Scottish Parliament. Tax powers are important to any central government, particularly UK Government and Scottish tax powers. If they lose the tax powers debate they lose Scotland. It is often forgotten that there were two votes in the 1997 referendum. The first was for the establishment of a Scottish Parliament and the second for the Scottish Parliament to have tax-varying powers. 74.3 per cent voted in favour of a Scottish Parliament and 63.5 per cent in favour of tax-varying powers.

My renewed interest in Scotland's constitutional debate, and in particular the tax and fiscal powers debate, began on my return from the USA in 2000. Serious tax powers were not even considered in 1997. The Scottish Parliament simply gained control of the matters that were for the most part already controlled by the Scotland Office despite the vote in favour of tax-varying powers in the referendum.

The view I adopted then, articulated in a number of articles, was that it was easy improve the administration of tax in Scotland. Although these articles generated a great deal of comment nothing happened. I then accepted an invitation to join the tax committee of the Law Society of Scotland. Serious tax powers for the Scottish Parliament were still not on the political agenda. That led me and a few others to set up the think tank Reform Scotland which gave us the chance to add some substance to this debate.

A Brief History of Tax in Scotland in Recent Times

The Scottish Parliament was given control over the two local authority taxes: council tax and business rates. It was also given partial control over income tax. The Scottish Parliament is responsible for approximately 60 per cent of government spending in Scotland but only has control over, and again approximately, seven per cent of all tax raised in Scotland. The income tax power was never used and even the ability to use it lapsed a number of years ago. A great deal was made of the income tax power at the time of the 1997 referendum. This included having a specific question was devoted to it.

There were no significant developments on tax and the Scottish Parliament until the Liberal Democrat *Steel Commission* report was published in March 2006. Even though the report did not receive a great deal of publicity at the time of publication it was generally well received. This report shows how far the Liberal Democrats have retreated on devolving substantial tax powers for the Scottish Parliament. I will come back to this point.

The real game changer happened in 2007 when the SNP become the largest party in the Scottish Parliament and formed a minority government. The response of the Labour, Liberal Democrat and Conservative parties was the *Commission on Scottish Devolution*, more commonly referred to as *Calman*. Why did they do this? These parties felt they had to be seen to doing something. They thought the SNP victory was a blip and that there was nothing really to worry about. Normal service will be resumed in 2011. The remit of *Calman* was also clear: '... to secure the position of Scotland within the United Kingdom'.

The first Reform Scotland *Fiscal Powers* report was published in November 2008. The report got a great deal of coverage. The authors, including myself, looked at this issue from the position of the present constitutional arrangement i.e. a devolved parliament. Our proposal was that the Scottish Parliament should be given the tax powers to enable it to raise approximately the amount it spends. Under this proposal control over the vast majority of taxes would have been devolved to the Scottish Parliament.

In contrast to the Reform Scotland report was *Calman*'s interim report published in December 2008. This report made no specific recommendations regarding tax powers and was probably an effort to test the water. The difference now was that there was something to compare *Calman* with.

Calman's final report was published in June 2009. The report appeared to offer as little as they thought they could get concede. It included four miscellaneous taxes (Stamp Duty land Tax, landfill tax, aggregates levy and air passenger duty) and a very restricted income tax proposal. *Calman*'s membership, which included Iain McMillan of CBI Scotland, meant this was the most likely outcome. The main report even suggested that a number of powers including parts of Scottish charity law be re-reserved. Reform Scotland updated its *Fiscal Powers* report in October 2009 to take account of *Calman*.

The reaction of the UK Labour and then coalition Governments to the *Calman* proposals was particularly telling. They could not even countenance legislating for the powers recommended by *Calman*. This involved what I then termed *Calman minus*. The coalition Government's Scotland Bill was published in November 2010 and only included two minor taxes (Stamp Duty Land Tax and landfill tax) and partial control of the income tax bands. The arguments put forward for not including the two other minor taxes are revealing. Air passenger duty was not included as it was under review and aggregates levy was omitted because it was subject to a European court action by a trade body. The recommendation that 50 per cent of income tax on savings and distributions was to have been assigned to the Scottish Parliament had simply been dropped.

In response to the coalition Government's Scotland Bill the Scottish Government produced papers on adding excise duty, corporation tax and control over the Crown Estate to the Scotland Bill. None of these suggestions were taken up enthusiastically by the UK Government. In addition the UK Government ignored recommendations made by both the present and previous Scottish Parliament Scotland Bill Committees (chaired by Wendy Alexander MSP and Linda Fabiani MSP respectively) and even Westminster's Scottish Affairs Committee for including some or all of these powers. Reform Scotland's third fiscal powers report, *Devolution Plus*, was published in September 2011, of which I was one of the authors. There were two main changes. Control over income tax was to be given entirely to Holyrood and the devolving of substantial welfare powers to the Scottish Parliament was recommended but these met with little support.

The Devo Plus campaign was formally launched in February 2012 and its fiscal power proposal is based on the Devolution Plus paper produced by Reform Scotland. Devo Plus was set up by Reform Scotland, although it is not supported by everyone associated with Reform Scotland, and includes representatives of each of the main unionist parties. Neither the Devolution Plus paper nor the Devo Plus campaign has had any discernible effect on the Scotland Act 2012 which received Royal Assent in July 2012. The latest devolution paper is called 'devo more', from the Institute for Public Policy Research, was published in January 2013. This proposal does not go nearly as far as 'devo plus' and only goes slightly further than the Scotland Act 2012.

The Wider Context

It is worth noting that Westminster has already refused to devolve control of a range of taxes, duties and charges to the Scottish Parliament. Those listed below are the main taxes but there are a number of others. In bold are the additional powers the Liberal Democrats would devolve under its *Home Rule and Community Rule Commission*. The figures in *italics* are mostly from the Government Expenditure & Revenue Scotland 2010–1 (GERS). The figures are included to give an idea as to the level of revenue produced by a particular tax and are a number of millions of pounds.

1   Full control over income tax including the underlying law dealing with reliefs etc (**some additional powers but not complete control**) *10,634*
2   National insurance contributions *8,018*
3   Corporation tax (**assignation of revenue only**) *3,114*
4   North Sea revenue *7,951*
5   Fuel duties *2,339*
6   Capital gains tax (**partial control only**) *244*
7   Inheritance tax (**to be devolved**) *159*
8   Other stamp duties – stamp duty and SDRT on shares (estimated) *265*
9   Tobacco duties *985*
10 Alcohol duties (includes spirit, wine, beer and cider duties) *895*
11 Betting and gaming duties *113*
12 Air passenger duty (even though included in *Calman*) (**not clear if to be completely devolved**) *183*

13   Insurance premium tax *210*
14   Climate change levy *61*
15   Aggregates levy (even though included in *Calman*) **(not clear if to be completely devolved)** *54*
16   Vehicle excise duty *470*
17   Bank levy (estimate as no separate Scottish figure) *200*
18   Licence fee receipts *325*
19   Crown Estate revenue **(not clear if to be completely devolved)** *10*
20   VAT cannot be devolved but VAT revenue could be assigned *8,560*

Taxes Devolved or Being Devolved under Scotland Act 2012

1   Income tax (still only partial control over tax bands and will cost Scottish Parliament millions of pounds a year to administer even if not used) (estimated partial control over) *5,000*
2   Council tax *1,986*
3   Business rates *1,891*
4   Stamp duty land tax (Scottish Parliament control by April 2015) *330*
5   Landfill tax (Scottish Parliament control by April 2015) *99*

The Scotland Act 2012 also does not resolve the imbalance between the amount the Scottish Parliament is responsible for spending and which it raises. The Scotland Act 2012 only takes us to about a third.

Likelihood of Additional Powers being Devolved if Scotland Votes 'No'

Let us begin our examination with the Liberal Democrats who published their *Home Rule and Community Rule Commission's report: 'Federalism: the best future for Scotland* in October 2012. There are a number of problems with this report. The first is the likelihood of the Liberal Democrats being part of and having a major influence in a future UK Government. At best the Liberal Democrats will again be a junior partner in a UK coalition government. Even if they were to persuade the senior party to implement their plans the Scottish Parliament would not see any new powers until at best 2020.

Then there is the accusation: why should anyone take the Liberal Democrats seriously on devolving substantial tax powers to the Scottish Parliament? The Liberal Democrats are in power just now at the UK level but have had remarkably little impact on the coalition in this area: all we have is *Calman minus*. The Scotland Act 2012 does even devolve control of the Crown Estate in Scotland to the Scottish Parliament even though the Liberal Democrats have campaigned on this issue for many years. Then there is the report itself. The report barely goes beyond *Calman*. Inheritance tax is to be devolved and also some parts of capital gains tax and the Crown Estate.

The Liberal Democrats have historically been willing to go further than the other main UK parties on devolving powers to the Scottish Parliament. The *Steel Commission* for example goes much further. What this report shows is that the Liberal Democrats are moving away from devolving substantial tax powers to the Scottish Parliament.

It is unlikely that the Liberal Democrats will come up with much more. Scottish Labour has a 'further devolution commission'. There is little prospect of this commission coming up with a proposal close to 'devo max' or even 'devo plus'? The UK Labour Government's response to *Calman* did not go any further than the UK coalition Government's recent Scotland Act. The fact that the leader of the 'No' campaign, Alistair Darling, refuses to say anything constructive on this issue simply suggests that the UK Labour Party will only even consider devolving substantial tax powers if forced to do so. Then there is the Conservative Party. The idea of a 'Constitutional Convention' is questionable. The Conservatives have consistently adopted a policy of prevarication, kicking the matter into the longest of long grass for another generation.

In her much trailed speech, Scottish Tory leader Ruth Davidson promised no new tax or fiscal powers, no timetable for even considering the issue and no confirmation that she had moved on from saying that corporation tax and welfare powers should not be devolved. That is what Davidson said as recently as October 2012. All that has been hinted at is that they will consider setting up a new commission to examine the devolution of more powers to the Scottish Parliament.

No Second Question

The campaign for a 'second question' to be included on the ballot paper in 2014 failed. So what does that mean for those arguing for 'devo max' and 'devo plus'? Devo Plus did not argue for a second question and its supporters have confirmed that they think Scotland should vote 'No'. They also think that Westminster will devolve substantial tax powers to Scotland if Scotland votes 'No'. This is not a realistic position to take. *Calman* only existed because Scotland elected an SNP Government. If Scotland votes 'No' in the referendum the Unionists will simply assume the pressure is off. It is not surprising that the Devo Plus campaign has failed to gain any traction. It is also not surprising that people like Jim McColl who supported 'devo max' have declared that they will vote Yes.

Arguments Put Forward Against a Scottish Tax System

So how have the opponents of substantial tax powers for the Scottish Parliament been able to ensure that substantial tax powers are not devolved to the Scottish Parliament? A template can be seen from *Calman*, what might be called the *Calman doctrine*. Make a huge fuss about having someone look at the issue, take your time, offer as little as possible, exaggerate any problems, minimise or ignore any advantages and ensure HMRC and HM Treasury remain in control. It seems that HMRC and HM Treasury cannot help but react negatively to any policy proposed by the Scottish Parliament that deviates from or impinges on reserved matters. An example of this was how HM Treasury withheld the attendance allowance funds when the Scottish Parliament introduced free personal and nursing care. Another example was the reaction when the Scottish Government proposed and then set up the Scottish Futures Trust. And yet a further example was the reaction from both HM Treasury and HMRC when the Scottish Government wanted to introduce a local income tax.

Memo to Treasury and HMRC: Scotland Has Its Own Legal System

It has been well documented as to how much of a shambles the introduction of Stamp Duty Land Tax (SDLT) in Scotland was. The HMRC has openly said they did not realise that Scotland's property law was different to English and Welsh property law. They also made it clear that they did not have time to change the legislation. 'Don't worry we will have plenty of time to sort things out later', they said. The only reason that SDLT worked in Scotland was due to the goodwill and pragmatism of the Scottish legal community. This experience confirms the lack of awareness and interest in Scotland and its institutions. Even though the UK does not have a unitary legal system, the UK tax system uses English and Welsh legal principles. This occasionally causes problems, for example where the underlying law, Scots law, differs from the law of England and Wales. In the SDLT example above HMRC did not take into account the fact that Scottish property law is different.

It is not just the lack of awareness of Scots law, but the centralisation in England of the administration of certain taxes that has caused problems for us in Scotland. Two examples: Birmingham for SDLT and Nottingham for inheritance tax. The centralisation of the administration of these taxes has meant increasing problems with getting expert advice on particular Scottish legal issues. In addition the Edinburgh Stamp Office has been under constant threat of closure and the Trusts and Estates office in Edinburgh is being run down. Then there was the proposal for a UK wide planning-gain supplement before the recession and the debate was all about how much developers should contribute.

Again the level of knowledge of Scots law and the extent of the powers held by the Scottish Parliament was disappointing. The main argument against a UK planning-gain supplement was a simple one. This was a matter for the Scottish Parliament as planning and housing are devolved matters, a point so obvious that they said it had never occurred to them. This debate went on for many months but finally the proposal in Scotland was dropped.

There was also the Scottish Government's local income tax proposal. It was unclear why anyone expected HMRC to cooperate and work to Scottish Government deadlines. Similarly, with respect to Council Tax

Benefit. HM Treasury have withheld attendance allowance funding since the Scottish Parliament introduced free personal and nursing care. The attitude of the UK Government and its institutions meant there was little likelihood of this proposal being implemented.

What about Northern Ireland?

A similar pattern emerges when considering VAT and the proposed new Scottish national police and fire services. These forces will have an annual VAT bill of approximately £30m. Under the current structure police and fire services are treated like local authorities and are exempt from VAT. However on merger they may be subject to VAT. HM Treasury has rejected the Scottish Government's request that these new bodies should be able to recover VAT. It has, of course, been pointed out to HM Treasury that the Police Service of Northern Ireland is exempt from VAT.

The 'just because it happens in Northern Ireland' is not likely to work with HMRC and HM Treasury. Northern Ireland already has borrowing and welfare powers. Anyone involved in the Scotland Act deliberations knows how hard HM Treasury resisted calls for borrowing powers to be included. They succeeded in ensuring that only restricted powers be included. Welfare powers were simply not even considered. It does not seem to matter that Northern Ireland is also to get partial control over air passenger duty and also possibly corporation tax although not any time soon. Nick Clegg has indicated that the UK Government will not devolve corporation tax to Northern Ireland in the short term due to the 'knock-on effects' in Scotland.

The argument does not just stop with Northern Ireland. The Scottish construction sector would like to see a reduction in VAT for building repairs and renovations. The UK Government has so far refused this request notwithstanding that it allows a similar reduction in the Isle of Man.

This Would Complicate the Tax System

The UK has one of the most complicated tax systems in the world. Each UK Budget adds further complications. Tax simplification is simply not taken seriously by the UK Government. A Scottish tax system could actually simplifies the UK system though this is rarely considered. As mentioned above, the UK does not have a unitary legal system. Therefore a Scottish tax system would simplify the system for the rest of the UK. For example, when SDLT is devolved there will be no need for the guidance and the forms to explain the differences in Scotland due to our different system of property law. The same applies for the inheritance tax guidance and forms.

This also applies to Scottish charity law. As previously mentioned, *Calman* recommended re-reserving parts of charity law. A more sensible proposal would have been to agree that when the Office of the Scottish Charity Regulator (OSCR) registers a charity it automatically becomes entitled to the tax reliefs associated with charitable status. At present, to gain charitable status and the various tax benefits it is necessary to apply to OSCR and HMRC. There may be a lot of talk about tax simplification but an obvious opportunity was missed.

Tax Competition is Bad

This argument that tax competition is bad is made fairly regularly. Gordon Brown made this claim last year. He claimed devolving tax powers to the Scottish Parliament automatically means a 'race to the bottom' for tax rates and in particular business tax rates. One major problem with this statement is that tax competition already exists. Not just within the European Union but throughout the world. Why is the UK Government reducing the rate of corporation tax to 20 per cent by 2015? In short, to ensure competitiveness. Why does the UK Government object to a Financial Transaction Tax? Because it thinks it will affect the competiveness of the City of London.

Always Stay in Control

Tax reliefs are just as important as tax rates to businesses. Business does not just consider the headline rate of tax when deciding where to locate. Many other factors are analysed, and not just tax. The underlying law that allows for the creation of reliefs or to vary the tax base as well as connected legislation that affects the tax legislation, for example the tax residency rules or employment legislation for income tax. This makes the case for tax being devolved in its entirety. On its own, the ability to vary a rate of tax is not much of a power. By not devolving a tax in its entirety, control is retained. That is why the Scottish Parliament is not being given complete control of income tax. The argument that any such changes would be in breach of 'state aid' rules used to be a favourite of the opponents of substantial tax powers until the European Court of Justice ruled that tax powers can be devolved if certain conditions are met. These conditions are easily met.

Westminster Always Knows Best

The UK Government does not consult the Scottish Government or Parliament on issues such as whether to introduce a Financial Transaction Tax. Westminster would not think twice about amending the income tax legislation without consulting the Scottish Parliament. It is no coincidence that HM Treasury is opening an office in Scotland with a 'Head of Scotland Analysis and Stakeholders Engagement', in other words someone to argue against independence. The appointment, only runs to the end of 2014.

What Could Have Been Done?

Westminster could have relatively easily devolved substantial tax powers to the Scottish Parliament but it did not want to. A number of taxes are closely associated with the responsibilities already devolved to the Scottish Parliament which would have given the Scottish Parliament a substantial number of economic levers and the chance to develop policy more effectively.

Below are some examples:

- Property law is devolved but SDLT and the property parts of capital gains tax are not.
- Succession law is devolved but inheritance tax is not.
- Environmental law is devolved but the environmental taxes are not.
- Health is devolved but alcohol and tobacco duties are not.
- Transport is devolved but transport related taxes are not.

Much could have been done during the last few years if even some of these powers had resided with the Scottish Parliament.

It Will Cost Too Much

The Scottish Government recently announced the creation of Revenue Scotland. Revenue Scotland will be responsible for collecting the two miscellaneous taxes being devolved. The Scottish Government is in no doubt that Revenue Scotland will be able to administer the two new Scottish taxes at a lower cost than HMRC. Those arguing against substantial tax powers for the Scottish Parliament disagreed with this. That is all the more surprising given the problems HMRC are having with matters such as tax avoidance and tax evasion just now.

The Scottish Parliament will need an Exchequer that ideally combines the functions presently undertaken by HMRC and HM Treasury. During the *Calman* deliberations, it was claimed by the Scotland Office that the cost of administering a separate Scottish tax system would be the same as the present UK system. But Scotland does not need a separate Stamp Office, Registers of Scotland, Trusts and Estates Office and Companies House. It could create a one stop shop to combine these and other government tax, legal and registration services. By doing this we could also have sub-offices throughout Scotland, just as London is not the UK, Edinburgh is not Scotland.

Conclusion

If Scotland votes No we will not see substantial tax powers devolved to the Scottish Parliament. The actions of those arguing against such powers speaks for itself. Creating a Scottish tax system is a once in a generation chance to create a simpler and more progressive tax system. Scotland literally has a blank sheet of paper. Let us not waste this opportunity.

Scotland and the UK: Public Finances and the Economy

GRAEME BLACKETT

Introduction

In the debate about Scotland's future, the main economic and financial questions should be about how a Scottish Government with additional fiscal powers could use them to improve Scottish economic performance. Independence or greater fiscal powers would not automatically lead to better or worse Scottish economic performance; it is what will be done with those powers that will make the difference. However, it is also necessary to understand how the Scottish economy has performed within the UK and the current state of UK and Scottish public finances.

The Size and Performance of the UK and Scottish Economies

The Scottish economy is often benchmarked against the UK economy as a whole. The long-term rate of economic growth in the Scottish has lagged UK economic performance. Over the four decades leading up to the on-set on the current economic recession the annual rate of growth in the Scottish economy was 0.2 per cent less than the UK for economic output per capita and 0.5 per cent less for economic output in total (see Table 1). This growth gap may seem like a small difference; however, it makes a big impact over time.

The UK economy has experienced a century of relative economic decline, being left behind by international competitors. Historic analysis of economic output (measured in GDP per capita) shows that the UK over-took the Netherlands in the 1830s to become the richest country in the world in GDP per capita terms and retained this position for several decades. The UK had lost its leading position to the United States by 1913, marking the start of a century of relative decline from the richest to only

Table 1 — UK and Scottish Economic Output Growth 1970–2007 (Gross Domestic Product, GDP)				
Output per capita % Annual Change	'70s	'80s	'90s	'00–'07
Scotland	+1.5%	+2.1%	+2.2%	+2.4%
UK	+1.8%	+2.6%	+2.6%	+2.4%
Population % Annual Change	'70s	'80s	'90s	'00–'07
Scotland	-0.1%	-0.2%	0.0%	+0.2%
UK	+0.1%	+0.2%	+0.3%	+0.5%
Output % Annual Change	'70s	'80s	'90s	'00–'07
Scotland	+1.4%	+1.9%	+2.2%	+2.6%
UK	+1.9%	+2.8%	+2.9%	+2.9%

the 22nd richest country in the world according the International Monetary Fund rankings for 2012, behind other large developed economies and well behind small European economies like Norway, Sweden, Denmark and Ireland.

The IMF database only provides statistics for nation states and so Scotland is excluded from the list. However, data from UK National Statistics show that in 2011–12, GDP per capita in Scotland was 118 per cent of UK GDP per capita. This would mean that Scotland would rank as the tenth richest country in the world, just ahead of the Netherlands.

Regional and National Economies in the UK

At the centre of the economic case for independence and for greater fiscal powers for the Scottish Parliament is that decisions made in Scotland are more likely to benefit the Scottish economy than decisions made in London, where a wider range of interests also needs to be considered. The case is not that there is some conspiracy against Scottish interests; rather that UK decision makers need to consider the interests of the UK as a whole and these may or may not be the interests of the Scottish economy.

Given this argument, it is worth giving consideration to the economic history and geography of the UK. The UK's economic success in the 19th Century was based on trade and from the high value added manufacturing products that came with the industrial revolution. The North of England and Scotland were both central to the UK economy at this time, with a significant proportion of both manufacturing and the ports that were at the centre of global trade. However, the decline in the UK's relative economic performance over the last century has also seen a shift south of the UK's economic centre of gravity. More than half of the UK's economic output is associated with the South of England (that is London, the South West, the South East and the East). In this context it would be irresponsible for the UK Government to formulate UK economic policy without taking full regard to the needs of the South of England. A UK Government that formulated economic policy to meet the needs of the Scottish economy (ten per cent of UK output) or the Welsh (four per cent) or Northern Irish (two per cent) economies would not expect to last long in office.

UK economic and industrial policy over the last two to three decades is often simplified as favouring the service sector, in particular financial services, with less focus on the needs of manufacturing. While the whole story is probably more complex than this, an examination of the trends and location of the UK's financial and manufacturing services is illuminating.

In the decade to 2008 the number of financial sector jobs in the UK grew to 1.2 million, an increase of around ten per cent (although a large proportion of this increase has been lost as banks have cut employment since 2008). While there are centres of expertise in some sub-sectors elsewhere (notably fund management in Scotland), the financial services sector is overwhelmingly based in the South of England, which has two-thirds of the UK's financial sector jobs, despite accounting for only 44 per cent of the UK's population (see Figure 1).

However, 40 per cent of the manufacturing jobs that existed in the UK as recently as 1996 had been lost by 2012, a reduction of 1.7 million jobs to a total of 2.6 million jobs. Proportionately, the biggest losses of manufacturing jobs were in Scotland, the English Midlands and the North of England.

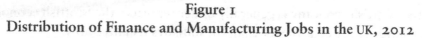

Figure 1
Distribution of Finance and Manufacturing Jobs in the UK, 2012

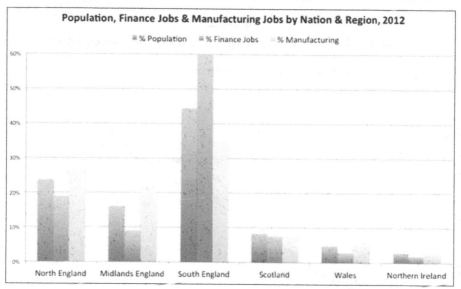

Source: ONS Workforce Jobs by Region and Industry, Q3 2012

Given the geographic distribution of financial and manufacturing jobs, it is not surprising that there have been regional differences in economic growth rates. As Figure 2 shows, the South of England has experienced by far the highest rates of growth. Scotland has been the next fastest growing; part of this can be attributed to the oil and gas sector, when it is excluded the Scottish growth rate falls well below that of the South of England. The growth gap between the South of England and the rest of the UK, demonstrate the effects of policy that has delivered growth in financial services and decline in manufacturing.

Contribution of the Oil and Gas Sector

The Scottish figures in the charts above include Scotland's share of the North Sea oil and gas sector. In UK national accounts and statistics, the oil and gas sector is usually allocated to 'extra-regio', a hypothetical UK region. Given that Scotland's geographic waters account for around 65–75 per cent of the oil and gas sector as a whole (and 85–90 per cent of taxation revenues), this approach means that the size and performance of the Scottish economy is generally under-reported; the Scottish economy is around 20 per cent bigger than UK statistics usually show.

Figure 2
Economic Growth in UK Regions and Nations since 1997

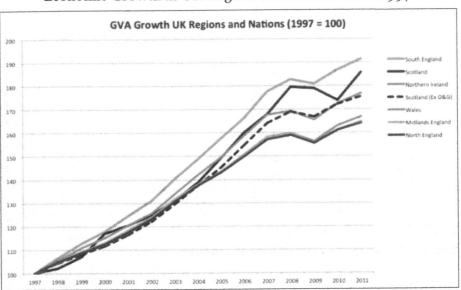

Source: ONS Regional GVA Statistics, Government Expenditure and Revenue in Scotland

In order to make like-for-like comparisons, it is reasonable to include the oil and gas sector as part of the Scottish economy (excluding it makes no more sense than excluding the financial sector from the London economy). Excluding oil and gas, GVA per head in Scotland is just below the UK average. However, including the oil and gas sector, increases Scottish GVA per head to 18 per cent high than the UK, giving Scotland the highest GVA per head in the UK, marginally higher even than the South of England.

While the long-term future of the Scottish economy will be based on building competitive advantage in growth sectors (for example, renewable energy and life sciences), North Sea oil and gas is important in the shorter term, not least because it makes a significant contribution to tax revenues. In 2010/11 oil and gas tax revenues collected from Scottish geographic waters contributed £10.6 billion to the UK Treasury, around 19 per cent of all taxes collected in Scotland and the longer term trend in oil and tax revenues is still upwards.

The large contribution of the oil and gas sector to the Scottish economy would have implications for economic management of the economy in an independent Scotland or in a Scotland with significantly enhanced financial powers since the sector is volatile, with large changes in output and tax revenues possible from one year to the next. However, this volatility could be described as up-side volatility since the volatility is between being slightly richer and much richer than the UK.

Oil is of course a non-renewable resource and so has been 'running out' since the first barrel of oil was produced. However, Professor Alex Kemp of the University of Aberdeen has undertaken work on scenarios for future production, with a range of estimates from 16.5 to 23.1 billion barrels. If the future oil prices projected by the UK's Department of Energy and Climate Change of $115–135 per barrel to 2030 are applied to this, at current exchange rates, this implies that future oil production could be worth between £1.3–1.8 trillion. The UK (or Scottish) Treasury could expect to receive at least a third of that in tax revenues, which means that future oil and gas tax revenues could be worth more than the £300 billion that has been collected over the last 40 years.

Public Sector Spending Across the UK

In addition to the wide variations in economic performance across the UK, there are also significant differences in public sector spending per head, with spending one-third higher in Northern Ireland compared with the South East of England. Scotland has higher public spending per head (£12,134) than the UK average of £10,937. However, public sector spending per head in Scotland is lower than Northern Ireland, London and Wales.

While the debate in Scotland often focuses on the differences between Scotland and the UK average, from a UK perspective the differences between regions are perhaps a bigger issue. The differences between the North and the South of England are partly a result of relative economic performance. However, the figure for London stands out as much higher than might be expected. Being at the centre of the prosperous South of England, it would be difficult to justify such high levels of public spending on the basis of the social and economic needs of the population. Indeed, London has benefitted from UK economic policy with its focus on the financial sector at the expense of manufacturing and yet is receiving high levels of public sector spending.

Moreover, official statistics tend to understate the real levels of public sector spending in London. Public spending in the UK includes identifiable spending (where the geographic location of spending can be identified, for example education, health and social security) and non-identifiable spending (where the benefit is considered to be for the population as a whole regardless of where the spending might take place, for example defence). Around two-thirds of this non-identifiable spending is accounted for by defence and debt interest payments, both of which are discussed further later in this chapter. Around a third of the non-identifiable spending, more than £30 billion per year is accounted for by items like 'public and common services' (the administration of central government), 'international services' and 'recreation culture and religion', where a significant proportion of spending takes place in London.

Details of where the non-identifiable spending actually takes place are not readily available. However, if the conservative assumption were made that just a half of the non-identifiable spending (excluding defence and debt interest) took place in London (benefitting the economy of London and the South of England as a result of salaries, demand for commercial property and other bought-in goods and services), that would increase the public spending per head in London by a further 10–15 per cent, which would make London by far the highest recipient of public spending in the UK, receiving more than a quarter more per head than the UK average.

UK *and Scottish Tax Revenues and Public Spending*

Since the early 1990s a National Statistics publication called *Government Expenditure and Revenue in Scotland* (commonly known as GERS) has been published each year, setting out taxes collected in Scotland and public spending in and on behalf of Scotland. The initial motivation behind GERS was clearly political, to demonstrate that Scotland benefited financially from being part of the UK.

The quality of the publication has improved considerably over the years and it is now an official National Statistics publication. While politicians of difference persuasions usually pick out different statistics to suit their own position, the evidence that has come from the GERS publications, and the more recent Scottish National Accounts Project that provides figures going back as far as 1980, is robust. The statistics tell us that if Scotland's geographic share of oil and gas revenues are included, Scotland has contributed greater sums to the UK Exchequer than have been returned to Scotland in terms of public spending.

The 2011–12 GERS showed that Scotland, with 8.4 per cent of the UK population, accounts for 9.3 per cent of public spending, which means that public spending per person in Scotland is about ten per cent higher than the UK average. However, it also showed that tax revenues collected from Scotland were also higher than for the UK as a whole, accounting for 9.9 per cent of UK taxes.

Over the last three decades for which figures are available the share of UK tax revenues collected from Scotland has tended to exceed Scotland's share of UK public spending. Revenues exceeded spending by a considerable margin in the 1980s while more recently revenues and spending have been closer, with Scotland making a small net contribution to the UK some years and receiving net spending from the rest of the UK in other years.

Public Spending and Value for Money

Overall, government spending in Scotland is around £64.5 billion per year. In 2010–11, the Scottish Government was responsible for £38.6 billion of this (for example, on the NHS and education) and the UK Government spent £25.8 billion (for example, on defence, pensions, social security benefits).

While the spending of the Scottish Government is regularly debated in Scotland, little attention is paid to the UK Government's spending. This is very relevant to the constitutional debate since smaller countries often take different decisions on spending compared with larger countries, in response to differing needs and preferences. Any Scottish Government which inherited responsibilities related to the UK Government's £25.8 billion annual spending in and on behalf of Scotland would be well advised to consider whether this spending delivers value for money for the Scottish taxpayer and is appropriate to Scotland's needs and preferences.

An obvious example would be defence spending. The UK's annual defence spending is currently £39 billion per annum, of which Scotland's population share is £3.3 billion. Even with cut-backs in some areas of defence, this could increase in future with commitment to a replacement for Trident nuclear armed submarines, with an estimated capital cost of

Figure 3
Scotland's Share of UK Tax Receipts
and Government Spending since 1980

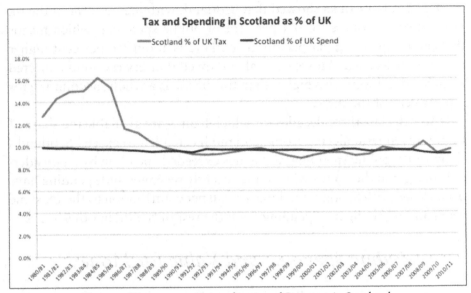

Source: Government Expenditure and Revenue in Scotland,
Scottish National Accounts Project

£15–20 billion according to a 2006 White Paper (with Greenpeace estimating a 30 year whole life cost of almost £100 billion).

Incidentally, while the future of the Trident nuclear weapons system is primarily a strategic and defence issue that is beyond the scope of this chapter, claims have been made that the UK spending on Trident delivers economic benefits for Scotland, because the submarines are based on the Clyde. This is a claim that does not stand up to much scrutiny. Scotland's per capita share of the capital costs for Trident replacement would be £1.3–1.7 billion but, if the experience of previous procurement is any guide, it is unlikely that many, if any, of the construction work would take place in Scotland. The Clyde naval bases do, of course, provide employment. Analysis by the STUC estimates that, of the total 6,700 military and civilian jobs at Faslane, those directly and indirectly supported by Trident amount to 1,536 jobs. With total annual running costs of some £1.8 billion, this gives a cost for each job supported of £1.15 million per year (excluding the capital costs of Trident). To put this in context, the economic output required to support one job in the Scottish economy generally is around £60,000. If the objective of Trident were to support employment, it would be the most expensive job creation scheme in history.

On defence spending more generally, UK spending is high by international standards, more than twice as high as a proportion of public spending compared to the average for small European countries. If Scotland decided to cut defence spending by 40 per cent, spending would still be well above the average for small European countries and there would be a saving of £1.3 billion per year. To put that in some context that is the total cost of Disability Living Allowance in Scotland or 40 per cent of total Corporation Tax revenues collected in Scotland.

Public Sector Deficit and Debt

In common with almost every country in the developed world (with notable exceptions such as Norway), the UK is currently running a deficit. This means that tax revenues collected are less than are required to meet public spending commitments, with the balance met by borrowing.

In 2011/12, the deficit between spending and tax in Scotland (net fiscal balance) was equivalent to 5.0 per cent of GDP (Gross Domestic Product, a measure of the size of the economy). The comparable figure for the UK as a whole was 7.9 per cent of GDP. As Figure 4 shows (figures are shown as a proportion of taxation revenue), over the last 30 years, Scotland's net fiscal balance has generally been healthier than that of the UK.

One of the recurrent themes of the Referendum debate has been whether an independent Scotland would inherit a proportion of the UK's accumulated debt.

Information on the net fiscal balance for Scotland relative to the UK is available as far back as 1980. That shows that during the 1980s, Scotland had a substantial public sector surplus. Had that surplus been retained in Scotland, a stabilisation fund could have been set up in order to provide funds to cover those years when Scotland had a public sector deficit (and so avoid, or at least limit, borrowing). In the period since 1980–81, Scotland's public sector has, on average, a surplus equivalent to 0.2 per cent of GDP while over the same period the UK average position was a deficit of 3.2 per cent of GDP.

On that basis it could be argued that Scotland has not contributed to

Figure 4
Net Fiscal Balance, Scotland and UK, since 1980

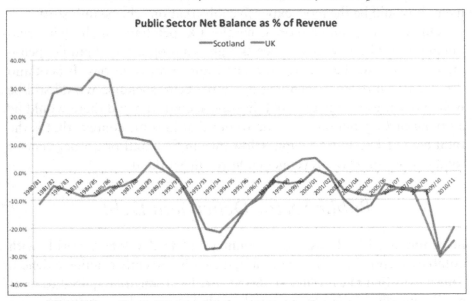

Source: Government Expenditure and Revenue in Scotland,
Scottish National Accounts Project

the public sector debt that has been built up in the UK over the last 30 years. The outcome of negotiation on Scotland's share of UK could have significant public finance consequences for an independent Scotland. The Office of Budget Responsibility puts current UK debt interest payments at around £45 billion per annum and forecasts that this could rise to £68 billion in 2017–18. Scotland's per capita share of that would be almost £6 billion, if Scotland is still a part of the UK in 2017–18, equivalent to around ten per cent of current public spending. An independent Scotland without this debt burden would have far stronger public finances, providing scope for a wide range of policy options from reversing public spending cuts to targeted tax cuts aimed at boosting economic growth.

Conclusions

The central economic question in the context of the Scottish constitutional debate is how future Scottish Governments could use the economic levers that come with independence or substantial greater fiscal powers to formulate policy that meets Scottish needs and preferences. However, it is also necessary to understand what the starting point would be, including the performance and focus of UK economic policy and the state of UK and Scottish public finances.

The UK is in long-term relative economic decline, from the wealthiest country in the world a century ago to 22nd now. Over the last two or three decades UK economic policy has focused on the development of the financial services sector (two-thirds of which is based in the South of England), widening the divergence in economic performance across the UK nations and regions, particularly between the North and South of England.

Scotland (including the oil and gas sector) has the highest economic output per person in the UK, on a par with the South of England and an independent Scotland would be in the top ten wealthiest countries in the world. However, there is potential for Scotland to do better; Scotland's long-term economic growth has lagged that of the UK and other small advanced economies.

The oil and gas sector makes a significant contribution to the Scottish economy and, while other emerging growth sectors like renewable energy and life sciences are likely to be the drivers of longer term growth, oil and gas remains important. The oil and gas sector could still contribute £1.3–1.8 trillion in future economic output and the future tax revenues could be greater than the £300 billion that the sector has contributed over the last 40 years.

There are significant variations in public spending across the UK. London stands out, particularly when 'non-identifiable' spending including the costs of running the UK Government are included. London benefits from both the focus of UK economic policy on the financial services sector, and from high public spending. Scotland also has higher than the UK average public spending. However, tax revenues collected from Scotland are also well above the UK average and so Scotland makes a modest net financial contribution to UK public finances.

More than 40 per cent of public spending in and on behalf of Scotland is still undertaken by the UK Government and its agencies. If the Scottish Government were to assume responsibility for this spending, there could be opportunities to make savings that could then be directed at other priorities. For example, UK spending on defence is higher than most other advanced economies; if a Scottish Government with control of defence policy were to reduce spending to levels closer to the average for small advances economies, this would free up £1–2 billion per year in public spending.

Scotland's net fiscal position is healthier than the UK as a whole. Indeed it can be argued that surpluses of tax revenues over public spending in Scotland over the last three decades, particularly during the 1980s, mean that Scotland has not contributed to the UK's accumulated public sector debt of £1.1 trillion. If Scotland was not required to service its per capita share of that debt, there would be a saving of almost £6 billion in debt interest payments from Scotland's public sector budget, equivalent to around ten per cent of current spending levels.

Taking potential savings in defence spending and debt interest together would turn Scotland's net public sector budget from a deficit to a surplus, providing scope for a Scottish Government with full fiscal powers to provide a growth stimulus to the Scottish economy, through tax rises, increased public sector investment or some combination of the two.

Arguing for a Citizen's Basic Income in a New Scotland

AILSA MCKAY

The Future of Social Security Policy: A Scottish Debate?

WELFARE REFORM IS currently high on the political agenda. In the wake of a global economic recession the affordability and effectiveness of current state welfare arrangements has become a focus for attention across Europe. Proposals for reform have been framed within a context of a focus on austerity and a subsequent need to cut costs or at least to constrain future growth in expenditure. At a UK level, the Department for Work and Pensions is the government's biggest spending department and the majority is spent on benefit payments. Thus, social security policy has come under attack and reform measures have been designed to restrict eligibility and reduce entitlements. Benefit spending has become a regular news item with headlines highlighting the problems associated with a 'something for nothing' welfare culture and the need to deal with 'benefit scroungers'.

Given social security policy remains the reserve of Westminster, the reform debate in Scotland to date has been dominated by a focus on mitigating the impact of measures introduced by the UK government. However, the constitutional change debate provides an opportunity to consider the options for social security in a new Scotland. In that context perhaps the opportunity exists to discuss and subsequently shape a distinctively Scottish welfare scenario that would meet the challenges associated with demographic change, the dynamics of modern labour markets and the need to secure equality as well as efficiency objectives. In embracing that opportunity the following questions should act in framing the subsequent debate; what makes a good society and what kind of welfare system would support that good society? Of course issues relating to costs are crucial with respect to implementation. However, focusing on 'what can we afford' type questions before we agree on what we want our welfare system to achieve is limiting. Furthermore, questions of affordability will be influenced by how we define and treat social security benefits and tax reliefs within our national accounting frameworks. Tax reliefs or credits are in effect a benefit but presentationally they are not regarded as such and, in a system that prioritises labour market participation – that is a welfare system built around a 'something for something' culture – they will be favoured over more traditional forms of social security payments. Engaging in debates on cost thus involves closer examination of practical process issues relating to how we view tax reliefs in the context of income maintenance policy and how we need to transform our fiscal institutions to better reflect transparency in what we want our welfare system to do.

So what do we want our welfare system to do, what values and principles will inform investment in state welfare support and how will that translate in policy terms? This chapter considers those questions from the perspective of an overall gender equality objective and argues for reform along the lines of an unconditional tax-free income to be paid to all individuals a citizens' basic income (CBI). The collapse of the world's financial markets in 2008 effectively marked a crisis in capitalism. However the response to that crisis has not been the generation of new ideas on how to *transform* our economic and financial institutions. The focus rather has been on addressing the more immediate problems, such as failing banks, with approaches that appear to be driven by a notion of supporting and preserving the existing order. With respect to social security policy this is particularly apparent. Writing in 1984, Francis Blanchard the then Director General of the International Labour Office argued that:

> ... the sudden concentration on social security, in particular on the legitimacy of state protection, is above all a reaction to current economic difficulties (increasing unemployment, declining industries, monetary chaos and so forth); and on these grounds, many people have not hesitated to accuse social security of aggravating the word-wide economic crisis.

(ILO, 1984: preface)

Those comments are equally pertinent today. The attack on social security policy throughout Europe has been consistent since at least the early 1980s and policy developments have contributed to a withering of employment-related insurance-based benefits in favour of income targeted benefits. In a UK context, within an environment of fiscal restraint, income transfer systems have undergone considerable reform resulting in greater reliance on means testing and targeted benefits rather than universal provision and a general shift in emphasis away from benefits to tax credits. The current welfare reform agenda indicates more of the same – wide-ranging cuts, a focus on promoting paid work wherever possible and a subsequent favouring of tax credits. It would seem that contemporary welfare reform debates are therefore lacking in 'new ideas'. A CBI is not perhaps a *new idea* but it does require a fundamental rethink of the justifying principles informing state supported income transfers and as such it can be considered a *radical idea*.

What is a Citizen's Basic Income – A Reform Proposal or a Radical Idea?

The concept of a minimum income guarantee paid to all citizens on an individual basis, without means test or work requirement, is simple and appeals to a wide range of political and economic perspectives (see for example Van Parijs, 1992). A CBI would replace all existing income maintenance benefits, including all reliefs set against income tax liability and the amount paid would be tax-free. The proposal would involve full-scale integration of the tax and benefit system thereby potentially reducing administration costs associated with current structures of delivery and eroding any disincentives to work that can arise from the interaction of separate tax and benefit structures. A CBI would ensure that the financial gains from paid work were always positive and would provide a more secure base for individuals to opt in and out of the labour market, thus promoting greater flexibility with respect to individual life choices. Furthermore, the universal aspect of the proposal protects against discrimination, thus providing the foundations for a more equitable system of state welfare provision. The CBI proposal presents as a new and fresh way of approaching state supported income maintenance policy in terms of justifying principles, design and delivery mechanisms. Adopting a CBI would not simply imply tinkering with existing systems in response to identified inadequacies or inefficiencies. The concept itself involves the acceptance of a whole new way of thinking about social security policy in terms of the functions it *can*, *should* and *does* perform. If understood in these terms, a CBI is more representative of a radical idea than a welfare reform proposal. However, the tendency is to view a CBI within the confines of rather narrow and limiting debates on the future of social security policy. Furthermore, no modern welfare state has fully endorsed and subsequently implemented a scheme for the provision of social security that could be described as a CBI. Thus, a CBI remains a *reform proposal*, considered as a possible alternative to current measures, but failing thus far to translate into reality.

In arguing for welfare reform along the lines of a CBI it is generally assumed that the issues being discussed relate exclusively to the reform of social security policy. This is mainly the result of two associated assumptions regarding the nature of a CBI. First, a CBI involves a transfer of monies from the state to individuals and therefore by definition falls within the realms of state managed income transfer schemes. Second, a CBI presents as an income source unrelated to earnings and as such is categorised as a social security benefit, that is, cash received outwith the formal labour market. However, a CBI has the potential to promote individual autonomy and allow for the development of social and economic relationships, negotiated outwith the confines of traditional market oriented transactions. Thus a CBI provides the basis for creating *space* to rethink our notions of work, income and citizenship rights within modern capitalist economies. However, an assessment of the literature indicates that arguing for a CBI displays a long established tradition of adherence to a socially constructed analytical framework that favours the traditional work and pay relationship and an assumed vision of how the economy *should* operate. Policy therefore *should* be designed and delivered in ways that support, indeed prioritises active labour market participation. The focus given to highlighting how a CBI could enhance greater labour market flexibility assumes that formal labour market participation is the desired end result, as opposed to providing the space to consider any benefits of alternative end results.

In trying to move the debate beyond such confining parameters it seems appropriate to try and locate a CBI within the context of a focus on *crisis, cuts and citizenship*. That is, perhaps we need to consider the CBI proposal in the context of the perceived crisis in capitalism and the current economic recession as an opportunity to reshape our thinking on *what makes a good society, how do we value and who do we value in that society*. Crucially, in doing so we need to develop a better understanding of how the structures and processes associated with our economic systems can better serve the needs of *all citizens* across all of our communities.

Thus, in the context of the current economic recession, and the policy responses to it, this is precisely the time to be considering radical ideas. The inadequacies of our current welfare system, operating alongside and in conjunction with contemporary labour markets, are obvious when evidence is presented of increasing income inequalities, the persistence of widespread poverty and the associated problem of social exclusion. Furthermore the social justice case for the promotion of equality has been strengthened by a heightened awareness regarding the negative impact inequality has on overall economic performance. Existing social security policy can therefore be criticised for failing to deliver both as an effective social policy that promotes 'security' for all citizens, and simultaneously as a mechanism that acts in supporting the efficient functioning of a modern capitalist economy. A strategy involving 'more of the same' – albeit a little less of it – is hardly likely to alter that criticism. From a gender equality perspective this is particularly the case.

The current position of women in Scotland's economy is a cause for concern at a number of levels and the constitutional futures debate provides a platform for raising and discussing issues relating to gender inequality. With specific reference to social security policy, gender concerns should be central to the debate as state intervention in the field of income redistribution will have very differential impacts on men and women. In fact, formal social security arrangements have traditionally served men more favourably than women. This is, in part, due to the direct relationship between insurance-based benefits and the labour market but is also an indirect consequence of policies that fail to recognise the diverse role of women as wives, mothers, carers and workers. Thus, a key consideration of any proposal for the future of social security policy should be how does it support greater gender equality by providing for all citizens on a fair and equal basis:

> Many regard the fight for gender equality as largely a 'women's affair' requiring perhaps some concessions here and there. If women are emerging as a key axial principal in the new socio-economic equilibrium, it follows that the quality of our future society hinges on how we respond to their claims on men, on the welfare state, and on society at large. For good or bad gender equality becomes therefore a 'societal affair', a precondition for making the clockwork of post-industrial societies tick. Gender equality is one of the key ingredients that must go into our blue prints for a workable new welfare architecture.
>
> (Esping Anderson, 2002: 69)

The Scottish constitutional futures debate provides the space to consider new ideas and proposals that will transform our welfare system into a 'workable new welfare architecture' that will meet the needs of the Scottish economy and the women who live and work in that economy.

Crisis, Cuts and Care Work: Who is Paying the Price?

The global financial crisis, the resulting economic recession and the response to it by the UK government have resulted in very bleak outcomes for women in Scotland's economy, particularly with reference to the labour market. Women's unemployment has almost doubled over the period from 2007 to 2012. Over the same period a rise in the number of part time jobs against a fall in full time jobs amongst women indicates that women may be 'under-employed' in a stagnating economy. In addition reform to the welfare system has resulted in wide ranging reductions in benefits, an increase in pension contributions and an increase in the age at which pensions can be drawn. This comes on top of a two-year wage freeze for the majority of workers in the public sector in Scotland. Thus, the terms and conditions of public sector workers, the majority of whom are women in Scotland, are deteriorating. Furthermore, as the public sector continues to contract, a consequence of increasing austerity measures, more women will lose their jobs and at the same time will find their eligibility and access to social security payments significantly restricted.

A further cause for concern in considering the impact of the crisis on women's position in the Scottish economy relates to the changing face of the public sector. The unique feature of this recession and subsequent *limited* recovery is that rather than serve as a natural buffer against the impact of the downturn, public spending has been the focus of an austerity policy with long lasting implications for the nature and purpose of the public sector in modern economies. It is this reconfiguration that presents as a real 'threat' in considering the impact on women and families. Cuts in state support in care services, alongside restrictions in benefit entitlement, pay and recruitment freezes in the public sector and pension reform have dominated the policy agenda since at least 2009. The combined effect has been to expose women to greater risks of job losses, real reductions in income over the longer term and managing increased pressures on limited household budgets. Furthermore, reductions in spending on state supported care services do not imply a subsequent reduction in demand for those services but rather a transfer of responsibility from the public to the private sector. With no guarantee that the private sector will pick up the slack, and given what we know about the gendered division of labour within households, it is safe to assume that women will absorb this activity. Thus women will find that their opportunities for formal labour market participation are further restricted due to the demands placed on their time performing necessary work at home, without pay. The gendered impact of the current economic recession, and subsequent austerity measures, highlights how women are now disproportionately paying the price. Given that there appears to be no let up in the implementation of austerity measures the conclusion to be drawn perhaps is that this particular gender inequality is a price worth paying? This question is essentially a question of what do we, as a society, value?

Despite the changing position of women in the labour market in recent decades, women continue to assume responsibility for the majority of unpaid household tasks, including care work. Accordingly women are more likely than men to work part-time or have some form of flexible working arrangement. Furthermore, the types of jobs undertaken by women are often distinctly different from that of men. This is a direct result of an array of different social pressures and burdens influencing the employment opportunities and decisions of both men and women, including most significantly stereotypical assumptions about their respective interests and capabilities. That is, female and male employment tends to be concentrated within occupations traditionally related to their gender, and views on their role within society. As a result female employment clusters around the 'softer' caring, teaching and cleaning sectors. These perceived 'lower status and subsequently lower paid jobs tend to be viewed as 'feminine' work and not suitable for the greater part of male employment. Thus occupational segregation features as a key characteristic of modern labour markets and with an associated tendency for the market to consistently and persistently undervalue the jobs that women do.

Within a Scottish context, occupational segregation is a significant and persistent feature of the labour market. The actual distribution of workers by gender across sectors indicates the influence of gender-based stereotypes in informing occupational choices and career paths. That is, women will pick jobs that fit around their family life. For instance, in the

Scottish labour market, at the time of writing, 85 per cent of workers in the personal caring services are women, 77 per cent of workers in administrative and secretarial occupations are women and eight per cent of those employed in skilled trades are women. Given these patterns of occupational segregation and the types or work women find themselves clustered in it is not surprising that women are around twice as likely as men to work within the public sector in Scotland and around 70 per cent of the local government workforce are women (WiSE Facts, 2012-2013). Thus women's position within the labour market is more precarious, primarily because they work flexibly, are more likely to be in temporary or part-time employment and/or are segregated in low-pay sectors and occupations. Women, therefore, are less likely to have built up any savings, resulting in less resilience to weather tough economic conditions and putting them, and their families, at greater risk of increased poverty. Conversely, however, patterns of gender based occupational segregation serve to protect women in times of economic recession where the impact of the downturn is normally felt in male dominated industries, such as manufacturing and construction. Ironically that same segregation is now exposing women to far greater risks than their male counterparts in the labour market due to their position in public sector. Prolonged and deep-seated public spending cuts will impact significantly on women as *workers* in the public sector but also as *users* of public services.

Evidence relating to occupational segregation, the gender pay gap and the gendered division of labour within the household indicate that many of our community assets are going unrecognised, in particular the skills and knowledge of our women workers both in the paid and unpaid economies. The majority of provisioning, caring, nurturing and managing activity that supports, and indeed drives our local communities, takes place outwith the market and remains invisible in our formal frameworks of measurement of economic activity. Thus it would seem that traditionally there is a tendency to undervalue women and the work they do and or want to do. A CBI may provide a framework to build a welfare system that moves away from that tendency, providing a blueprint for a 'workable new welfare architecture' that effectively recognises the *totality* of women's contribution to the economy and wider society. The question remaining is – in the new Scotland is there a desire and/or political will to do so?

Gender Equality in a new Scotland – A Question of Values?

Within a Scottish context a commitment to the promotion of equality has been a defining feature of the post devolution political and policy frameworks, made explicit via high-level strategy and processes. The Scottish Government's economic strategy – focused on a single overarching purpose to promote sustainable economic growth – makes explicit a commitment to ensuring *opportunities for all citizens* to benefit from Scotland's economic prosperity. Thus, the implication is that the promotion of equality is integral to the government's economic strategy. Recent policy documents appear to support this claim by indicating an acceptance of the interdependence of economic performance and equality goals:

> We recognise that equality is an important driver of growth and that inequality detracts from our economic performance and our social wellbeing. We make clear in our Economic Strategy, the importance of increasing participation in the labour market, removing the structural and long standing barriers which limit opportunities and harnessing diversity and wealth of talent we have available to us as a nation.
>
> (Equality Statement: Scottish Spending Review 2011 and Draft Budget 2012–13: 10)

Thus the current policy agenda in Scotland is framed by an overall objective of ensuring patterns of public spending contribute positively to securing the overarching purpose of sustainable economic growth, whilst simultaneously addressing structural inequalities, with particular emphasis on the labour market. As a result the position of women in Scotland's economy has become a focus for attention:

> There has been considerable progress made in addressing inequality and in improving people's life chances. However, Scotland continues to carry deep rooted and structural inequalities which limit opportunities and hold people back. These are evident in labour market participation, income and health. Women are particularly disadvantaged in terms of unequal pay and occupational segregation resulting from stereotypical assumptions about the roles of men and women in society.
>
> (ibid: 14)

However, perhaps more crucially in considering the opportunity and the space to transform our thinking and embrace radical ideas, *recognition* of the issue appears to be accompanied by a more fundamental criticism of how we understand that issue;

> In September 2012, the first Minister hosted, with the Scottish Trades Union Congress (STUC) the first Women's Employment Summit. This highlighted the importance of women's role in Scotland's labour market and in the economy. It flagged the current pressures on women's employment and the limitations of economic models which fail to reflect the contribution of women's paid and unpaid employment. It signalled the opportunities to extend women's employment in emerging industries and sought continued efforts to address the longstanding issues of occupational segregation, child care and the value attached to women's role in the economy and labour market.
>
> (Equality Statement, Scottish Draft Budget 2013–14: 6)

It would appear then that the current political climate within Scotland provides real opportunity to move beyond the confining parameters of mainstream economic analysis in attempts to understand the role of women in the economy. The door is ajar, creating a space for new thinking that more accurately accounts for a whole range of economic activity that is welfare enhancing yet remains invisible within a policy framework focused on the world of paid work. In the context of social security policy the open door allows for consideration of the CBI proposal and how it presents as an invaluable opportunity for reshaping welfare policy in accordance with a goal of promoting opportunities for *all* of Scotland's people.

This brings us full circle to our initial question – what kind of welfare system do we want in a new Scotland and what part does social security policy play in that? That is what function *should* social security perform and what outcomes should be employed in any evaluation process? Considering the role a CBI could play in providing the basis for a more gender equal and socially just 'welfare state architecture' it is essential to initially agree on *what* social security policy is and *what* it is intended to achieve:

> Social security – broadly, a system of social transfer benefits – represents one of the most effective tools to combat poverty and vulnerability that any society has at its disposal. It should also be seen as an instrumental investment in the social peace that is an indispensable condition for sustainable economic development and, furthermore,

as one that is essential to unlocking the full productive capacity of individuals. Social security is a social and economic necessity.

(ILO, Social Security for All, 2009: 1)

Accepting this definition of 'social security' implies an ideological goal of ensuring and maintaining the protection of all citizens from economic insecurity and recognising the importance of the desire of all citizens to be secure in the knowledge that such public protection exists. A CBI could meet these goals.

In contrast to current social security measures, a CBI does not explicitly link income provision with work. In this sense it can be regarded as an emancipatory measure in that it serves to free individuals from the economic necessity of *toil* and provides the basis to support a range of welfare enhancing activity undertaken outwith the confines of market based exchanges. A CBI is not merely an alternative to existing social security provision but rather a *philosophy* aimed at enhancing individual freedom and promoting social justice. In essence providing the basis for securing 'real freedom for all'. However, the arguments posed against the proposal mainly focus on costs and the impact on work incentives and disincentives and to date those arguments have won over the very diverse and convincing arguments in support of the proposal. That is, paying people in exchange for what is *perceived* to be doing nothing is highly unlikely given the value modern society attaches to work. The word *perceived* is used deliberately here as what is it we understand by 'doing nothing'? This kind of statement indicates a very narrowly confined notion of what we as a society currently value as economic activity.

What do we mean by economic activity and how do we define/measure it? For the mainstream/traditional economist the answer would be that kind of activity that takes place within a regular production/consumption exchange pattern and the value is reflected in the market price. If this line of thinking is influential in determining how we conceptualise a CBI then we are missing the opportunity to recognise the truly radical nature of the proposal. Indeed this line of thinking implies that what we value is a particular set of socially constructed norms about how we *should* behave rather than how we could behave or how we could respond to new policy ideas and proposals. In reviewing the relevant literature it is clear that there are two routes in arguing for a CBI – the commodification route and the non-commodification route. It would seem that the CBI literature displays a bias in favour of the commodification route. That is, the predominant focus on paid work and labour market impacts indicates the privileging of a socially constructed analytical framework that is in turn dominated by mainstream economic analysis about how a capitalist-economy *should* operate. The challenge then becomes one of trying to locate the CBI proposal within a different analytical framework – one that encompasses broader range of economic activity.

In rising to this challenge a number of questions immediately come to mind – how do we go about reconceptualising what we consider to be 'work'?; how do we deal with the free–rider problem when we consider the third party effects resulting from the energy and effort some individuals expend in building local communities and/or staying at home to care for others; how do we deal with the vulnerability of certain groups and the institutions they rely on as a source of economic and social welfare and how do we manage the social costs associated with increasingly unequal societies? If we continue to rely on and promote welfare schemes that have an overarching purpose to promote paid work exclusively we fail to account for the experience of that work for many vulnerable individuals, including most significantly women. Finally if we think what, how and who we value in the context of assessing the gendered impact of austerity measures on overall economic performance a further set of questions come to mind. Who was bailed out and why; how was the bailout financed and who will continue to pay the price; why the impact on pay and jobs in the public sector; and how can we justify the level and scope of the current public spending cuts evident across Europe? Policies to encourage private sector investment may lead to positive outcomes in terms of boosting aggregate demand. But this is by no means guaranteed due to the uncertainty and volatility inherent within global financial markets as Keynes so eloquently argued in the 30s. In accounting for gender difference it may be that we can conclude that the best way to boost aggregate demand is to effectively target resources towards meeting the needs of women and their families. However this would require a fundamental shift in thinking. In particular it would require an acceptance of the centrality, and indeed the superiority, of public sector expenditure and the care sector in supporting economic and human development. Perhaps it is time to make that fundamental shift, and to consider a different set of values as the defining feature of our 'good society'.

Maybe a CBI provides us with just the platform for doing so in a new more gender equal Scotland.

References

Esping-Andersen, G. (2002), 'A New Gender Contract in Gaillie, D., Memerijck, A. and Myles, J. (eds), Why We Need a Welfare State', Oxford: Oxford University Press.

International Labour Organisation (ILO) (1984), Into the Twenty First Century: The Development of Social Security. Geneva: ILO.

International Labour Organisation (ILO) (2009), Social Security for All. Geneva: ILO.

Report of the Consultative Steering Group on the Scottish Parliament (1998), 'Shaping Scotland's Parliament' Presented to Secretary of State for Scotland, December 1998. The Scottish Office: Edinburgh.

Scottish Government (2012), Scottish Budget Draft Budget 2013–14. Edinburgh: September 2012.

Scottish Government (2011), Equality Statement Scottish Spending Review 2011 and Draft Budget 2012–13, Edinburgh: September 2011.

Scottish Government (2007) The Government Economic Strategy. Edinburgh: November 2007

Van Parijs, P. (ed.) (1992), Arguing for Basic Income: Ethical Foundations for a Radical Reform, London and New York: Verso.

WiSE Facts (2012–2013), 'Women in Scotland's Economy', Glasgow Caledonian University, http://www.gcu.ac.uk/wise/wisefacts/

Public Service Reform In Scotland

COLIN MAIR

Introduction

'PUBLIC SERVICE REFORM' has been a hot topic for all Scottish governments since devolution, for fairly obvious reasons. The vast majority of
public spending governed by the Parliament supports the delivery of
health, education and other public services across Scotland. These services
were previously governed directly by Westminster so showing 'devolution
was working' involved showing those services were different and better
as a consequence. As macro-economic, fiscal, social security and monetary
policy were *not* devolved, transforming public services was the only major
lever Scottish governments controlled to improve the lives and opportunities of people in Scotland.

This chapter explores public service reform in that context. It examines the pattern of reform and the impacts of reform. It also considers
whether the stated purposes of reform as it has evolved can be achieved
by focus on Scottish public services alone, or whether a wider range of
powers and levers would be necessary. The chapter has absolutely no
position on independence or continued union. It simply explores the conditions for effective reform and improvement.

The Pattern of Public Service Reform: 1999–2010

Across the period, four key strands of public service reform recur in
different forms and guises:

- A strand concerned with improving the efficiency and productivity
  of public services, and 'best value' in the use of public money.
- A strand concerned with 'integration' of public services though
  collaborative and partnership working, to offer better 'joined up'
  services to the public, and to cut down waste and failure due to
  duplication and fragmentation of effort.

- A strand concerned with reducing inequalities in life chances and opportunities in Scotland. Over time, this strand morphed into an emphasis on 'improving outcomes' through prevention and early intervention.

- A strand concerned with extending previously restricted service entitlements (e.g. means tested entitlements) to all citizens (irrespective of income) to maintain solidarity and support for major public services (e.g. free personal care; free tuition; free bus travel for all older people).

Stated this way, clear inter-connections seem to exist between these strands and potential contradictions (e.g. would better integrated public services not be a precondition for reducing inequalities through more effective prevention? Can inequality be reduced by extending free service entitlements to already 'more equal' sections of the community?). This is true but misses the point through retrospect. In reality, each of these strands evolved in a fragmented way over time and only gradually consolidated. It is only at the very end of the period, through the work of the Christie Commission and the response to it, that these interrelated strands were shaped into a coherent agenda. It is worth looking briefly at each strand in turn.

Efficiency and Best Value

The 'efficiency' focus evolved out of fragmented beginnings: initiatives in various parts of Government and the public service to improve procurement, to manage public assets more efficiently, to use the opportunities of new technologies to reduce costs, and to create shared services that would generate economies of scale. By 2004, this had evolved into a more consolidated efficiency programme with national co-ordination, support funding and a common reporting framework. This continued, with renewed emphasis, between 2007 and 2011 under the SNP minority government. The aim for most of this period was not to use savings to cut spending, but to redeploy monies to enhance services and extend service entitlements.

The 'efficiency' focus was augmented by the introduction of a duty of 'best value' in 2003, supported by an independent audit regime. 'Best value' linked *efficiency* to the *outcomes* achieved for service users and communities so that just cutting costs was not best value unless outcomes were maintained or improved. The core of best value was 'continuous improve-ment' driven by benchmarking and market testing, robust governance and performance management, and recurrent engagement with service users and communities. The independent audit was intended to ensure that these were in place. 'Best value' was initially introduced for local government but subsequently rolled out to Health, Police and Fire authorities and to government public bodies.

Integration and Partnership

At devolution, the inherited structure of Scottish public services was complex: 32 councils, 15 Health Boards; 8 Police and Fire authorities and a wide range of 'quangos'. This created a high risk of fragmentation with different agencies and services dealing with the same families and comm-unities without coordination and common purpose. Clearly, each agency could deliver *services* separately, but without coordination it was unlikely the best *outcomes* could be achieved in a cost effective way.

Again, this began in a relatively fragmented way and became more consolidated over time. Specific integration initiatives based on particular service areas (e.g. community health and social care) or clientele (pre-school and school age children) or geographical communities (SIPs) devel-oped, often led by different parts of government working with different parts of local public services.

The introduction of 'community planning' as a statutory duty in 2003 was intended to provide a single overarching framework for integration of service planning and delivery in each council area in Scotland. The council, and named partner agencies, were obliged to work together to develop a plan and priorities for the area and it communities (the Comm-unity Plan). In doing so, they were obliged to involve communities them-selves, and the private and voluntary sector. The 'community planning' requirement came after many other specific partnership arrangements were in place and, in effect, sat above them.

Because of the perceived slowness with which 'community planning' developed, this was strengthened by the SNP minority government in 2007 in partnership with local government. An integrated national performance framework was introduced to provide a more coherent context for local planning. The council, and its local partners, were asked to develop a 'Single Outcome Agreement' (SOA), which would be binding on local partners and signed also by Scottish Ministers. The soa was based on an analysis of the area, and its present and future needs, and expressed in terms of real world outcomes the partners were intending to achieve, rather than just in terms of services and activities they would provide. This should reflect of nationally agreed outcomes within the national performance framework, but also priorities arising from the distinctive needs and circumstances of each area. Although this was intended to make Community Planning the dominant framework, in reality service specific or clientele specific integration initiatives still tended to achieve more traction.

Reducing inequalities and Extension of Entitlements

At devolution, Scotland was characterised by significant inequalities in health, educational attainment, employment prospects, household income and risk of criminal victimisation. This understandably led to a significant focus after devolution to addressing and remedying this situation. Across the period we can identify at least 20 major policy initiatives that sought to reduce inequality or improve fairness. Again, some of these were focused on particular *service areas* (health, education, etc.); some were focused on specific clientele (preschool children, older people, etc.) and some were *spatially* focused on deprived and disadvantaged communities (Social Inclusion Partnerships, 'Fairer Scotland'). All overlap with the integration strand and imply a focus on prevention.

Two issues are apparent across this period of reform. The approach to reducing inequality was fragmented and lacked any overarching priorities and performance framework. Different initiatives developed separate performance frameworks, and separate management and budgetary arrangements. As a consequence, such approaches often resulted in multiple, duplicative and ineffective engagements with the same communities and households.

The second issue is that the highly targeted approach potentially necessary to tackle deeply embedded inequalities sat uneasily with political imperatives for offering a similar range of services and entitlements to everybody to maintain support and solidarity. At the same time as seeking to reduce inequalities, the period since devolution has seen major extension of free services, previously restricted to those on low incomes, to all people who met the relevant criteria, irrespective of income. This includes free bus travel for everybody over sixty, free personal care, free tuition, and free prescriptions.

There is argument to be made for universal service entitlements in terms of avoiding 'means testing' and in maintaining support for public services but the cost is formidable and, without budget growth, potentially limits the resources available for prevention and early intervention approaches necessary for reducing inequalities. This is clearly a question of choices and priorities, but balancing them became more difficult as rapid budget growth gave way to recession and retrenchment.

Each strand of reform became progressively integrated and consolidated over time. It was not, however, until retrenchment began to bite from 2010 onwards that the relationship between them, and the need to prioritise across them became focused.

The Watershed 2010–2012

The election of the UK Coalition Government committed to rapid deficit reduction and significant planned reductions in public spending fundamentally altered the reform agenda. An influential report by the Chief Economist of Scottish Government showed that it was likely that the Scottish budget would not return to its 2008/09 level (in real terms) until the late 2020's. A report by the Strategic Finance Review Group for local government projected a massive gap between income and demand trends through to 2018 if services, service entitlements and cost structures remained as they were. The reform agenda was rapidly redefined in terms of 'sustainability' of public services in the light of the projected cuts.

A range of practical actions followed very quickly. Significant reductions in the public workforce were initiated, largely through early retirement and voluntary redundancy (the local government workforce declined by ten per cent between 2009 and 2011). Multi-year pay freezes were also negotiated, initially in local government then across the public sector. This mitigated short-term pressures but, given the projected duration of retrenchment, two more fundamental reviews were commissioned: a rapid review of the Scottish Budget (the Independent Budget Review – IBR) and a commission to look at the future of public services in Scotland (the Christie Commission).

The Independent Budget Review

The IBR was important in two ways. First, it strongly underlined the un-sustainability of the existing level and pattern of public spending in Scotland. In particular, it raised serious questions about the sustainability of the new universal service entitlements created since devolution given projected budget constraint. Second, it linked up previously unlinked strands of the reform agenda. Efficiency initiatives of the past sort were seen as insufficient to close the projected gap between income and demand. As income was likely to be relatively fixed for Scotland (this was prior to any likelihood of an independence referendum) then the key reform target was taking demand out of the system.

This led to a forceful advocacy of *prevention*: rather than waiting for negative things to happen in peoples' lives and then reacting to them, prevent the negative happening in the first place. This was seen as more cost effective for public services and better for people. This focus on closing the income/demand gap by reducing demand integrated the reform agenda: *improving outcomes* by knowing where the risk of negative outcomes lies, and adopting an *integrated* approach to prevention and early intervention across the public service. This implicitly redefines *efficiency* as a whole system concept: *a public service that deploys the right resources in the right places at the right time to achieve outcomes cost effectively.*

The IBR had much less influence than it deserved, partly because its messages on universal entitlements were hard to process in the run up to the election in 2011. (In fact, party manifestos in the 2011 election seemed almost consciously to have ignored the findings of the review: every major party supporting every universal entitlement whilst simultaneously proposing to freeze all taxes controlled in Scotland). It did, however, shape thinking in the Christie Commission that followed.

The Christie Commission

The Commission was set up to examine 'The future delivery of public services in Scotland' in 2010 and reported immediately after the Scottish Parliament elections in 2011. A powerful report therefore coincided with the election of a majority government for the first time in Scotland. For present purposes, the crux of the report is that it builds on the IBR and integrated all elements of the reform agenda discussed in Section one.

The report re-emphasised the gravity of the financial and demand situation documented by the IBR, but linked the solution to reducing inequalities that drive 'failure' demand on public services. It reported evidence that as much as 40' of public service spending was on responding to *preventable* negative outcomes in people's lives once they had happened. Effective prevention was seen to depend on public services working more collaboratively together (and with the private and voluntary sector), and working in new and different ways with communities. On the former, the commission proposed strengthening integration by giving all public agencies a common duty to improve outcomes through working together, with a 'presumption in favour of prevention and early intervention'.

With respect to working with communities, the report rejected 'top down' approaches (doing things *to* communities) in favour of a co-production approach (working *with* communities). The report proposed giving statutory rights for communities to be involved in the planning, design and delivery of public services. The report made no specific proposals for changing the *structure* of public services, focusing more on collaborative *culture*, and noted rather than addressed the issue of universal entitlements. It does however note that prevention requires a *targeted* approach on people and communities at high risk of negative outcomes, and that the priority of *universal* entitlements needs seen in that light.

2011–Present

The Commission's report was well received and the period since its publication has seen a range of efforts to implement its major recommendations. The Scottish Government responded to the report, and its critique of the status quo, with 'Renewing Scotland's Public Services'. This emphasised a major shift to prevention and an integrated 'place' based approach to improving outcomes, particularly for vulnerable communities. This has helped shape and reshape a range of implementation initiatives to promote integration and the shift to prevention, focused on particular client groups ('Reshaping care for older people'; 'Getting it right for every child') or on particular service areas ('Health and care integration'). 'Change funds' have been put in place to support this.

It has also led to a rapid review and reform of Community Planning arrangements. The Christie Commission recommendation for a common duty on all public partners to work together to improve outcomes has been endorsed and is being progressed. The next round of SOA's between local partnerships and Scottish Government in 2013 must include an explicit prevention plan for each area with clear targets. This must be based on a detailed analysis of the pattern of outcomes at community level, and focused on where preventative action is most needed. The recommendations for empowering communities will be embodied in the 'Community Empowerment and Renewal Bill', which will also make provision for the transfer of public assets and resources to community control.

The period ended, therefore, with a much more consolidated agenda for public service reform than previously existed: virtually universal consensus about public service integration, prevention and 'letting the community in'. This, however, remains an agenda: it is not yet implemented and it has not yet been shown to work. It coincides with, and to some extent is driven by, recession and retrenchment of public spending and the perception that pre-existing models of public services are simply unsustainable under new circumstances.

The Impact of Reform

The dynamics of reform in Scotland need seen in context. An electoral system designed to prevent a single party majority necessarily led to a consensus building approach within and out-with Parliament if reform was to happen. Budget growth for most of the period allowed many strands of reform to run in parallel without the need for clear priorities to be decided. The limits of the devolution settlement, and the block funding of the Scottish Parliament by Westminster, created a politics built largely around public service spending precisely because macro-economic, fiscal and welfare levers were not devolved. Put differently, it is inconceivable that a government with macro-economic, tax and social security powers would have sought to improve outcomes and reduce inequalities solely by reforming public services.

That said, there are tangible achievements across the period. Over £3 billion of recurrent efficiency savings were achieved, equivalent to around ten per cent of the current budget. However, these savings were not taken as cuts, but redeployed to extend service standards and entitlements in ways that increased the cost of services, and the demand on services now faced. Economic, health, educational and safety outcomes improved for all sections of Scottish society across most of the period. However, entrenched and systematic inequalities of outcome continued as well. This raises again the issue of purpose and priorities.

The game changer, reflected in the IBR and Christie, was recession and cuts to public spending. Scotland, on current projections, faces real cuts in public spending of around three per cent per annum through to 2018. Reform, as we go forward, has to address the realities of this changed context and be prioritised accordingly. This also *assumes* that the powers available in Scotland are sufficient to maintain outcomes under new and adverse circumstances. These issues are explored in the final section.

Going Forward

The evidence submitted to the Christie Commission, and built into their conclusions, showed two basic things:

- There were systematic inequalities of outcome between different communities across Scotland.
- There was a very distinctive 'clustering' of positive and negative outcomes at *neighbourhood* level, i.e. neighbourhoods doing relatively well in one domain (health, education, household income, etc.) tended to do relatively well in all others and vice versa.

This led the Commission to two important conclusions. First, reducing inequalities and improving outcomes were the same agenda, not separate agendas. The biggest pay-off would come from targeting disadvantaged communities experiencing poor outcomes across all aspects of life. Second, this would require an integrated and highly localised approach to working with those communities for a prevention strategy to be successful.

A paradox not addressed by the Commission was that the Partnerships with the most need to make a sharp shift to prevention would be least able to do so because of their existing high levels of demand. For example, a partnership facing very high emergency admission rates to hospital from such communities is more or less advised to get off the back foot and prevent that happening. However, emergency admissions are very costly so how does that partnership free up resources for prevention while dealing with the demand it currently faces.

As the reform agenda has consolidated around prevention, the question of priorities and resource targeting becomes acute in the context of real reductions in public service budgets across the next five years. Are we seeking to *prevent everything for everyone, or does prevention require a selective and targeted approach?* In terms of potential pay-off, and risk, a targeted approach makes sense. The maximum potential for improving outcomes and reducing future demand (and cost) lies with a concerted focus on communities presently experiencing very negative outcomes. The risk is, if we fail to do this, we will face unsustainable patterns of 'failure' demand on services, given the financial squeeze. We will spend money on these communities: the sole question is whether we do it positively to improve outcomes, or reactively in response to negative outcomes.

There is no suggestion that more affluent communities would be denied access to public services: they do and will make extensive use of core public services. However, the implication would be that *additional* resources need targeted on prevention in the most vulnerable communities. Given the paradox noted above, partnerships facing high 'failure' demand at present would need support to enhance their prevention activities. As the IBR suggested, the priority of this needs to be honestly weighed against free bus passes for affluent pensioners, or free prescriptions for all.

The relationship between deprivation and inequality of outcome is very well established for health, educational attainment, risk of crime and employment. Reanalysis of neighbourhood level data from 2002–2011 shows income deprivation to explain 50–70 per cent of the variance in outcomes between the most and least deprived areas, even where demography, housing quality, and other economic variables are taken into account. The data shows a strong relationship between declining income deprivation until 2010 and improvement in outcomes for the most deprived communities.

This was linked to the tax credit and welfare benefit regime of the then UK Labour government which is now deemed to be profligate and unsustainable. The UK welfare reform programme will take between £400–£500 million per annum from the most disadvantaged households in Scotland across the next five years, and result in around 100,000 more children experiencing deprivation by 2020. On the evidence, this is highly likely to result in deterioration of other outcomes for these communities.

Given that, the key assumption that public service reform will reshape outcomes may be questionable. We can find no example of Governments elsewhere committed to reducing inequalities who have not given priority to economic and fiscal levers, often allied to public service reform. Neither Scottish nor international data supports a view that public service organisation and practice are the key determinants of equality or inequality of outcomes.

The focus in Scotland on public service reform as the route to better outcomes has been conditioned by the devolution settlement: what was controlled and what was not controlled in Scotland. The link between public service organisation and outcomes has probably been over-emphasised as a consequence. The recently published Audit Scotland *Audit of Community Planning Partnerships* reinforces this point. They could find no relationship between the quality of partnership organisation, and outcomes for local people.

Public services clearly matter (educating children, saving lives in hospital, etc), but outcomes are affected by a wide range of social and economic factors that are not controlled by public services. Given this, the case for being very clear about priorities within reform is even stronger: prioritising communities where economic and social factors make outcomes and opportunities poor, and mitigating and altering these. We may also have to rethink 'prevention' itself which is too often viewed as about *new types of public service*. It also needs to encompass economic intervention on employment and employability as the evidence suggests that secure employment and a decent income are the critical preventative factors.

Although this point is often acknowledged, public services have underestimated and underused their economic and employment muscle. Local Government and the NHS are overwhelmingly the biggest employers in Scotland and in any part of Scotland. Between them they spend around £26 billions per annum in local economies across Scotland with well over 50 per cent of that supporting local employment and around 25 per cent being spent on procuring goods and services. In procurement, community benefit clauses have become much more routinely part of requirements, often focused on creating training and employment opportunities in disadvantaged areas. Public services have been less good at using their own employment capacity to directly create opportunities for those with the greatest difficulties in accessing employment elsewhere. Demand from deprived communities often drives the public economy, but those communities largely get services, rather than direct economic benefits, from the public economy. This needs to change.

Public Service Reform and the 'Constitutional Debate'

The 'Constitutional Debate' is clearly linked to public service reform, if 'public service reform' is the code name for improving outcomes and opportunity in Scotland, particularly for the most disadvantaged and vulnerable communities. Even if used to the maximum possible, the current and planned devolution settlements provide relatively limited tools to Scottish Governments. The new income tax provisions that commence in 2016 share the restriction of the existing tax varying power that any variation from UK tax rates must apply equally across all tax bands. If Scottish Government wishes to increase the top rate of income tax by five per cent, it must also raise the base rate by an equivalent amount. In an economy where the average taxpayer is a low income basic rate taxpayer, this massively reduces the utility of the new tax powers.

If the UK Chancellor is able to reduce the top rate of tax by five per cent (from 50p to 45p in the pound), without the obligation to apply the same cut to the base rate, it is unclear why a Scottish Finance Secretary should not be able to do the opposite in Scotland. As importantly, there are no proposals for Scottish Governments to control the use of other major taxes such as VAT, Corporation Tax or National Insurance.

The other side of empowerment to control distribution and redistribution, social security, remains entirely non-devolved. The UK approach to Welfare Reform will have serious impacts in Scotland, and is predicated on a redistribution *away* from the poorest households and communities to improve work incentives. This, on all available evidence, will worsen outcomes for these households and communities and increase 'failure' demand on Scottish public services. The other levers of macro-economic policy remain within the framework determined by the UK Treasury (e.g. borrowing and public investment to smooth fluctuations in aggregate demand).

It is important to be clear about what this means and what it does not mean. It does not mean the case for independence is made: it is perfectly possible to envisage more developed forms of devolution that give a Scottish Government more extensive fiscal and macro-economic levers. Equally, it does not mean that, if Scotland was independent of the UK, a Scottish Government would be able to deploy all these levers as it wished (think of Italy, Spain, Greece, or Cyprus). If an independent Scotland is part of any monetary union (Euro, Stirling, whatever), it will be constrained by fiscal rules and convergence criteria that limit macro-economic options.

What it does mean, however, is that the current devolution settlement limits the ability of Scottish Government to link public service reform with other important macro-economic levers for reducing inequalities and improving outcomes in Scotland. Positive impacts in Scotland since devolution have *depended* on supportive UK Government strategy, particularly the emphasis until 2010 on raising the real incomes of the lowest income households. Strategy since 2010 has been less supportive at UK level, but strategy within Scotland has not been notably redistributive either.

It is important to emphasise that further devolution, or independence, would enhance the *capacity* to tackle inequalities and improve outcomes for the currently most disadvantaged. It does not mean that capacity would *actually be used*. That would be a matter of policy, priorities and politics for a future Scottish Government. Since the banking crises in 2007, taxes presently controlled in Scotland have been frozen, rather than increased, and all parties have been committed to universal rather than targeted entitlements. The necessarily spending focused politics since devolution have not challenged Scotland's self image as inclusive and egalitarian. Enhanced devolution or independence would force the issue of the balance of taxation and spending that the majority of Scots are prepared to accept. Without some change, however, there is not even a meaningful choice: it would remain questionable whether Scottish Government and Scottish public services could achieve the stated purpose of reform: reducing inequality and improving outcomes in Scotland.

Social Justice: Arguments on Independence and Self-Government

JIM MCCORMICK

Introduction

THE SCOTTISH POLITICAL classes talk a lot about social justice. Centre-left parties draw upon egalitarian language and ideals to contrast with conservative approaches to market dominance and/or to a broader divergence between Scotland and England. The benchmark is usually the actions of government in London – and while the focus is in this direction, Scotland's own actions can go unexplored. The evidence suggests that Scotland is *moderately* but consistently more in favour of egalitarian policies and more willing to view government as a possible ally to this end than is true in England. However, the differences are often exaggerated; trends in Scottish public opinion over time have not notably diverged from those in England; both have become less social democratic in the last decade as judged by key attitudes surveys (ScotCen, 2011a); and little attention is paid to the diversity of opinion *within* both countries. This chapter will suggest there has been a relative lack of scrutiny over how devolved powers have been used in order to advance social justice and that maximising existing powers is a necessary prelude to making the most of new powers in future.

What is Social Justice?

For all the Scottish commitment to social justice, there is a lack of clarity about what a political strategy designed to advance it would look like, particularly in an age of austerity. We can presume it would involve reducing poverty and attending to the scale of inequalities in income and wealth, and that it wouldn't involve huge welfare cuts as now being implemented by the UK Coalition government. But beyond this – what might it mean for the balance of universalism and targeted support, money versus services, contributory versus means-tested, paid relative to unpaid work? While greater conceptual clarity would be needed to map out a distinctive Scottish approach to social justice, we first need to accept that there is more than one answer to these questions. Each involves trade-offs and a mix of consequences over time. Scotland ought to be a context for rich debate on alternative approaches to social justice.

For now, a decent working definition comes from the Commission on Social Justice, an inquiry on the future of welfare set up by John Smith 20 years ago (Commission on Social Justice 1994). It framed social justice as a set of four inter-related strands:

- The foundation of any free society is the equal worth of citizens, expressed in political and civil liberties, equal rights before the law against discrimination and so on.

- Everyone is entitled, as a right of citizenship, to be able to meet their basic needs for income, shelter and other necessities. These basic needs can be met by enabling people to acquire them for themselves or by providing resources and services.

- Social justice demands more than this: improved opportunities and life chances are needed so people can fulfil their potential. How opportunities are made in the first place, as well as how they are redistributed, should be a concern for social justice.

- Unjust inequalities should be reduced and where possible eliminated.

There's a lot here that people of different political beliefs might be able to agree on. These suggest that we should be concerned about discrimination, homelessness and worklessness as well as poor experiences of education. To these elements of social justice, we might add a fifth strand – what some would call *justice between the generations*, expressed in how the decisions we make now on the environment, energy, pensions and housing for example will affect others in future.

Inequality is perhaps the most difficult element of social justice. There's plenty of evidence that Scotland remains strongly divided by income, social class and working status. In Scotland, a complex mix of economic, social and cultural factors yields a population marked by slower improvements in health than in Northern England let alone the UK or EU average; major health inequalities; and even better-off Scots faring worse than their peers elsewhere. Even if inequality isn't bad for *everyone*, it's bad enough for enough people to merit action. But what kinds of inequality offend an ideal of social justice?

The fourth strand above is helpful in pointing us towards the target of *unjustified* inequalities, not all inequality. It's not unjust that the life-time earnings of most graduates are higher than most semi-skilled workers. Nor is it unjust that some people clean offices at four am, serve burgers till midnight or do other jobs we might consider unattractive. Someone will always need to do these jobs – but it doesn't always need to be the same people. In terms of life chances, what's unjust is if people get stuck in these jobs without genuine opportunities to improve their skills and move to jobs with better pay and prospects. Within organisations, huge gaps in pay and benefits are usually bad for morale and productivity, especially where these can't be linked to performance.

We might also focus on the *duration* of experiencing disadvantage. Unemployment would still occur but we might bear down much more effectively on long-term unemployment. Poverty would still occur but would affect fewer and for a shorter period. Witness the case of Denmark having cut its poverty rate to less than half of Scotland's without having notably more economic success. Its average growth rate in the past 20–30 years has been equally modest, but it hasn't used this as an excuse to delay building a fairer society. And no-one should have to live for long without adequate resources: typically poverty would be a temporary state.

We might also aim to *disrupt patterns of inequality*. It's not inevitable that a poor start in one area – such as housing or family income – must lead to disadvantage in others, like education or health. And we should place *capacity* at the heart of our endeavour. Social justice cannot be only for government – though we shouldn't underestimate the role of public policy. It must also involve employers, service providers and citizens in developing a more resilient and capable population. This starts to touch on the theme of 'self-determination' that seems to have been largely absent from political debate about social justice, whether in terms of devolution or independence.

There are encouraging signs of this thinking in policy debates on community empowerment and asset-based approaches, Self-Directed Support and self-management of long-term conditions for example – involving greater control and autonomy within a framework of peer support. Too often, success has been at the margins of systems upon which the most vulnerable depend. That too will need to change since there can be little progress towards social justice without a shift in the balance of power between citizens, service providers and policy makers.

This chapter will look at the unfolding story of UK welfare reforms as an example of eroding social justice and at early years provision in Scotland as a potential source of progress.

Wanted: Welfare Reform to Reduce Poverty

Welfare systems have been designed with various aims. They share risks and costs across our lives, providing a level of income replacement at times of unemployment, sickness and in retirement. They meet some of the extra costs of bringing up children or living with a disability. They provide services as well as money and combine elements of social insurance based on contributions previously paid with targeted social assistance. In some countries, contributions from employers and trade unions combine with those from employees and other taxpayers.

In the UK, means-testing has expanded steadily to over-shadow the contributory principle to a degree that isn't matched in the Nordic countries, Germany or the Netherlands for example. In part this explains why public attitudes to benefit recipients have become harsher – welfare is often seen as for 'them' not 'us'.

During the decade of rising employment and public spending up to the recession in 2008–9, a series of welfare-to-work programmes and tax credit/benefit reforms contributed to a drop in poverty among families with children. Older people saw a bigger, sustained reduction in poverty (Palmer, 2010). But by the end of the period, the welfare system still created strong work disincentives, complexity and risk while the economy generated too many low-paid jobs offering few prospects of escaping from poverty.

The UK may no longer have had the tattered safety net of the 1980s, but nor did welfare provide a reliable springboard into well-paid work, or a secure floor through which no-one can fall. Under-employment is now common, many are stuck in a cycle moving in and out of low-paid work – and support for those out of work hasn't risen in real terms for a generation. So, further welfare reform is needed to address the circumstances we face – ideally when there is a buoyant jobs market and rising investment to pave the way.

Instead, the UK Coalition Government is following Labour's series of welfare reforms but at a much faster pace (increased conditionality and tougher sanctions, extended to higher numbers of lone parents and people claiming sickness benefits). A major integration of various benefits into a single Universal Credit is about to begin, while huge welfare cuts are being made at a time of weak job prospects, especially for young people. It's a toxic mix which will increase poverty substantially.

By 2020, the Institute for Fiscal Studies (IFS) expects child poverty to have returned to the level last seen in 1999, when devolution began (Brewer et al, 2011). Substantial progress in cutting child poverty in the first half of the previous decade (and even the 'flat-lining' of recent years) will be undone. Why would welfare reform aimed at simplifying the system and making work pay have this effect?

The positive features of Universal Credit – especially the lower withdrawal rate for most people moving into work– mean that poverty levels *should* fall. But analysis by the Institute for Fiscal Studies also warned this gain would be wiped out if Universal Credit rose only in line with the Consumer Price Index (CPI) – the lower rate of inflation – in contrast to the basis on which the state pension is to be raised. This decision alone would lead to poverty rising not falling – an extra 200,000 children and 300,000 working-age adults would be in poverty by 2020. However, the Welfare Uprating Bill (Jan 2013) makes matters much worse. Uprating benefits, most tax credits and then Universal Credit by one per cent each year from 2013–14 will see those on the lowest incomes increasingly exposed to rising prices. A much larger number than the IFS estimated will be poor – many of them in work.

The Treasury's limited analysis of the 2012 Autumn Statement's impact in the year from April 2013 shows the lowest-income fifth of households losing 1.5 per cent of net incomes and spending power, while a third of better-off households will be unaffected. And the negative impact of changes to indirect taxes, benefits and tax credits outweigh the gains from raising the personal tax allowance (HM Treasury, 2012). There are many design problems with Universal Credit which could be improved. But the effect of uprating below inflation is the key to why the UK including Scotland will end up so far adrift from the shared 2020 Child Poverty target of no more than ten per cent of children living in poor households.

Looking ahead, the question of *income adequacy* will have to be addressed. The annual Minimum Income Standard (MIS) measurement highlights what the public thinks is the basis of a modest but adequate income for different household types across the UK. It varies over time – for example, people's views of what is 'adequate' have tightened during the recession (Davis et al, 2012). MIS measures have been calculated for Northern Ireland, rural areas in England and will be published for remote areas of Scotland in 2013.

Consistently, the MIS programme shows that only older people can reach the level of income adequacy through state benefits (basic state pension and means-tested top-ups). Working-age households, especially single people without children, fall far short of the relevant MIS level. Benefits for workless adults range from little more than 40 per cent of adequacy (for IS, JSA and the assessment phase of ESA) to 60 per cent of it for those unable to work by reason of disability and ill-health (Kenway et al, 2010). This should focus the debate in Scotland on achieving income adequacy via an appropriate balance between earnings (including Minimum Wage and Living Wage); contributory benefits (based on social insurance principles); and means-tested support. The UK system currently falls far short not just in terms of adequacy but relative to much of the EU, the balance between these elements of income adequacy.

Welfare Reform and Mitigation

Undertaking welfare reform when the economy is growing, unemployment is falling and programmes can be adequately funded is one proposition. None of these conditions applies and an estimated £2.5 billion is due to be cut from the DWP budget in Scotland (Scottish Parliament, 2012). Mitigation responses have focused on maintaining eligibility for passported benefits that are paid or provided on the basis of low income or disability-related needs. This is needed because the qualifying UK benefits which serve as a 'gateway' to passported benefits are being rolled up into Universal Credit while others replaced (notably Disability Living Allowance). Passported benefits include free school meals, concessionary travel, blue badge permits, NHS dental treatment, optical vouchers, Education Maintenance Allowances, Individual Learning Accounts and legal aid. And the Scottish Government has committed to establishing a larger, grants-based Scottish Welfare Fund to address hardship. It will replace the Social Fund when it is devolved.

Alongside a commitment to plug the hole in the budget for discounting Council Tax which is also being devolved from Westminster, the Scottish Government can assert with credibility its desire to use new powers to reduce the impact of other welfare cuts, however limited these are currently.

We know from the Scottish Social Attitudes Survey that respondents say they want more powers devolved on tax and welfare (ScotCen, 2011b). Devolving welfare is tricky because the costs for people of working-age go up in a recession, when tax revenues go down. To fund a welfare system largely from the Scottish budget would mean devolving some of the major taxes (Trench, 2012). The *Government Expenditure and Revenue Scotland Report* (GERS) for 2011–12 shows total expenditure in Scotland on 'Social Protection' which covers payments through the current benefits system of £21.6 billion (Scottish Government, 2013). This represents 33.5 per cent of total spending compared with 34.9 per cent for the UK as a whole and is the single largest expenditure programme.

What if Scotland were designing a welfare system of its own, either as an independent state or through substantial devolution of welfare powers? Would it stick with the status quo or try to make a version of Universal Credit work?

Universal Credit: the Devil in the Detail

Some of the aims behind Universal Credit are right in principle and could help to address key problems with the current welfare system. By integrating a range of means-tested benefits – which have to be claimed separately – and smoothing transitions back into work, Universal Credit could be a step forward. Although the withdrawal rate will remain steep, with recipients losing 65p for every pound earned, this is still an improvement on the 80p or 90p marginal tax rate faced currently (Brewer et al, 2011).

However, the stakes are high: Universal Credit is an all-or-nothing reform. Getting it wrong means people will face delays, errors and cuts to their sole source of income without compensating support from other benefits. Implementing Universal Credit when the labour market is weak and when substantial cuts are being made elsewhere in the welfare budget is very different from doing it when employment and investment are growing. As well as the budget to introduce Universal Credit and the basis on which it is uprated, various design problems would need to be addressed to make it work (McCormick, 2013). Four of the necessary changes are:

- If Universal Credit is to be paid monthly and in arrears, it should continue as a guaranteed run-on payment until first wages are paid.
- Alternatively, employers should be encouraged to offer new members of their workforce the option of *weekly or fortnightly wage payments* in the first phase of employment.
- The earnings disregard should be raised to allow people to keep more of their earnings before Universal Credit starts to reduce.
- Housing Benefit should be de-coupled from Universal Credit. This would leave the door open to devolving Housing Benefit alongside Council Tax Benefit to create an integrated housing support system in Scotland (Gibb and Stephens, 2012).

Prelude: First, More within Existing Powers

Progress in reducing poverty in the last decade resulted mainly from rising employment rates and UK benefit/tax credit reforms. Both made a difference. Devolved policies also made a modest dent in poverty levels over this period, but the true impact of policies in the early years, education, skills development and public health will only be seen over a longer period. These long-term powers to address disadvantage and inequality are mainly devolved. Before new powers arrive, under any constitutional outcome, we should ask whether Scotland is making the most of the powers currently available.

The Tackling Poverty Board was convened in 2009-10 to review progress with the Scottish Government/COSLA *Achieving Our Potential* strategy. Most of the key powers to tackle income poverty are reserved to Westminster. But at least half a dozen policy areas were identified as (mainly or fully devolved and likely to have a significant impact on tackling poverty (Scottish Government, 2011). These were grouped into three categories:

- **Pockets:** Policies aimed to boosting incomes and reducing the cost of essential goods and services.
- **Prospects:** Policies to improve life chances for children and young people and for progression in the workforce.
- **Places:** Policies to improve the supply of quality, affordable housing and to regenerate neighbourhoods.

This three-dimensional approach to tackling poverty provides a sound basis for action to advance social justice. An adequate income is a necessary part of any anti-poverty strategy – and thus any effective plan for welfare reform. But it also acknowledges that poverty can't be measured just in terms of money: high quality nursery and primary school education and improving the skills of poorly-qualified adults also matter as long-term drivers of reducing poverty.

Pockets: How the Money is Raised and Spent

Mitigating the negative effects of welfare reform or taking action to reduce poverty in the longer-term must compete for funding within Scotland's devolved budget. There is some scope to raise additional revenue through local taxes. A new, time-limited Public Health Levy will generate additional income from large retailers. But the power to vary the basic rate of income tax by 3p (which would yield around £850 million) has not been used, nor has any major party proposed using it since the SNP in 1999. While provisions in the recent Scotland Act will expand flexibility on borrowing, income tax and stamp duty for example, the debate is focused for now on spending priorities within the current settlement.

Successive administrations have expanded universal services based on need rather than the means to pay. The current Scottish Government has continued to develop a social wage approach to public services. Universalism has almost every advantage over targeted provision – it avoids the problem of low take-up related to low awareness or stigma of having to claim; it reduces the transaction costs of testing eligibility; and it builds broad public support among middle-class service users with 'sharp elbows' rather than diminishing public services for the poor. But it is more expensive than targeting due to its scale of coverage. So, it's reasonable to ask whether decisions on revenue foregone (long-term Council Tax freeze and on spending (e.g. free bus travel from the age of 60) are the best choices available when each comes with its own opportunity cost. This is a debate running through 166 pages of the Independent Budget Review led by Crawford Beveridge in 2010, re-ignited by Scottish Labour leader Johann Lamont in 2012.

For example, freezing the rate of Council Tax over a period of years eases the pressure on households, but doesn't address the underlying burden of paying the full rate of Council Tax on relatively low earnings.

While the freeze is worth a significant amount to low-paid earners living in lower-banded properties, it is worth three times more in absolute terms to those living in top-banded properties. Local government taxation remains an unresolved challenge. In 2007, the SNP and Liberal Democrats pledged to replace Council Tax with a local income tax. They couldn't agree terms and by 2011 the SNP's policy had changed in favour of a long-term Council Tax freeze. Eventually a better solution will be required, probably involving some mix of property and land or income tax. In the meantime, powers to *vary the rate of Council Tax change* could be explored at the same time as a new discounting scheme is being devised alongside Universal Credit.

For example, Council Tax could rise for top-rated properties at some measure of inflation-plus, rise at a lower rate for mid-range properties and continue to be frozen for lower-rated homes. Once the power to vary annual changes has been established, the decision on how to use it should be one for local authorities. Within a reasonable limit, the Scottish Government should not impose a reduction in grant. The simplest way to reflect the continued growth of the property market for the highest-value homes is to add further bands at the top.

Targeting Beyond Means-Testing

Both universal and targeted approaches are evident in public services. Some are based on contribution, others on means-testing. It is right in principle to ask whether the balance has been struck at the appropriate level. However, there are various ways to alter this balance. Means-testing – testing income and assets to demonstrate low-income – is only one approach. Simpler and more efficient methods use income and property taxes to vary entitlements. Another would be to tax age-related benefits like Winter Fuel Allowance so that those on low-incomes retain the full payment and the better-off retain some of the payment. Another still would be to increase the premium for the over-80s as a blunt but still reasonable proxy of low-income among older people. These approaches may offer a different route to targeting that avoids the familiar problems with having to demonstrate poverty in order to receive support.

Prospects: the Case for Closing the Quality Gap in Childcare

Turning to the role of improving prospects, we know why action in the early years matters so much to any effective social justice strategy. *Analysis of the* UK *Millennium Cohort Study* (Lloyd, 2012) showed that differences in the home learning environment, family interaction, regular routines and maternal mental health have a significant impact on the cognitive gap between children by age three. These differences together explain about one quarter of the gap between children from the best-off and worst-off families. By age five, child development lagged by up to a year in poor households. And the same research found that the attainment gap continues to widen rapidly during the primary school years, until age 14 (Goodman and Gregg, 2010).

Pre-school education and childcare can have significant, long-lasting effects, by narrowing the gap in child development in the early years. From European evidence over 40 years (Melhuish, 2012), we know that disadvantaged children benefit most (France), mobility between generations is improved (Switzerland) and job outcomes are better (Norway). But the quality of pre-school provision is critical to achieving these gains. The OECD has concluded that positive impacts are higher where participation is greatest, attendance lasts longer and there is a clear focus on improving quality. North American evidence also points to the importance of family involvement. All of this suggests that the involvement of the pre-school and primary education sector in reducing poverty long-term is essential. Any reform strategy needs to focus primarily on raising quality where it is lowest.

Pre-school Care: Looking to Denmark Not 'going Dutch'

In many ways, the years of growth before the recession represent a missed opportunity for children's services. Although childcare provision grew and public funding rose, this was done in a fragmented way. The paradox of relatively high public spending on early education and care in OECD terms as well as very high costs for parents can be explained by the extent of reliance in Scotland no less than the rest of the UK on demand-led support for families to find their way in a highly fragmented childcare market where for-profit providers play a major role as in Australia, New Zealand, USA and Canada. This lacks price control and creates inefficiencies compared with directly-provided services (Lloyd, 2012). Broad-based support combining pre-school education, childcare and parenting support in communities – like the Sure Start model – largely failed to take hold in Scotland. As in the rest of the UK, net childcare costs as a share of family income increase as incomes rise. This is similar to many other countries, but even the most affluent of families in eight other European countries face lower net childcare costs as a share of their income than all but the poorest families here.

A re-appraisal of policy choices is underway in England. While the UK Government cites recent Dutch reforms which deregulate the childcare workforce and make greater use of demand subsidies to parents to purchase services from a childcare market, more critical views have emerged. In the Dutch case, a steep decline in the not-for-profit sector has occurred. The number of centre-based, not-for-profit providers located outside cities more than halved between 2000 and 2006, alongside a reduction in services in disadvantaged neighbourhoods. A similar impact on not-for-profit providers was found in Australia. In a recent study for IPPR (Cooke and Henehan, 2012), the authors conclude:

'The volatility in supply and [service] use inherent in an 'effective' demand-led funding is antithetical to long-term investment and militates against the development of a mature, reliable childcare system. Higher quality costs money, and the returns on that investment accrue beyond individual providers to the sector as a whole, not to mention wider society. It is no surprise that countries which have developed high-quality childcare systems, such as the Nordic nations, have relied heavily on supply-side funding. In these countries, parents have real choice, with funding following the enrolment of children'.

Scotland has a choice to make, within current powers and likely budgets, about the future pre-school pathway it wishes to invest in. Rather than 'going Dutch' in reforming childcare policy over the next decade, IPPR's study argues for supply-side investment directly into higher quality services in line with reforms in Denmark (see box, based on Cooke and Henehan, 2012).

Danish childcare:
national entitlement, supply-side funding, a cap on parental costs and workforce quality

The bedrock of the Danish system is a national entitlement to a child-care place for all parents, from when their child is one until they start school. Its system has evolved through supply-side funding to providers. This sustained resourcing model has enabled high-quality provision to be built up (as well as allowing for parental choice). There is a level playing field on funding and regulation, with a mix of centre-based care and childminders in operation. Parental costs are capped at a low level – a maximum of 25 per cent of the unit price – with a sliding scale of subsidies for the remaining fee. Parents pay the equivalent of £200–£300 a month for childcare, accounting for 7–10 per cent of their disposable income. In the UK, a couple earning average wages with two pre-school children spends an average of 27 per cent of their net income on childcare costs.

The high quality of the Danish childcare system is rooted in its workforce, which is well trained and decently paid. A majority (60 per cent) of the childcare workforce holds a degree-level qualification in child development compared to less than ten per cent in England. Earnings are equivalent to £25,000–£40,000 a year (10–15 per cent less than teachers).

By 2015, the Scottish Government is planning to expand provision to at least six hundred hours a year of early learning and childcare for three- and four-year-olds as well as looked-after two-year-olds, to benefit around 120,000 children. This is expected to be the highest level of provision in the UK, at least for three- and four-year-olds. The *Scottish Child Poverty Annual Progress Report* in 2012 says this will 'support parents to access improved employment opportunities, especially those in negative cycles of worklessness and low-paid work' although how employment, training and in-work support will link into provision has still to be demonstrated (Scottish Government, 2012).

The logic of expanding pre-school education to all two-year-olds is compelling. The commitment in England to expand support to under-threes is significantly greater than in Scotland. Under-investment in children's pre-school services compared with other north-west European countries, and compared with England, is a drag on social justice that Scotland can't afford. However much is invested in this area in future, resources are likely to go further if the Scottish early years approach is rebalanced towards higher direct investment in the supply of high-quality services, across all sectors.

Conclusion

Progress towards social justice can be made within existing powers – reforming local taxation and expanding high quality childcare have been considered, but we could also have looked at closing the attainment gap in schools or targeting investment in skills training towards households with few qualifications. Limited progress in these areas reveals something about Scottish political culture – hesitancy to act fully in line with stated values perhaps for pragmatic electoral reasons; a degree of complacency about the extent of inequality; a willingness to wait until more/full powers come to Scotland. But there are other signs of decisive action in the area of public health, equality law and mitigating welfare cuts which could support a more optimistic conclusion.

Either way, powers beyond the Scotland Act (2012) will be needed to make alternative choices on welfare and labour market policies. Whether these come in the shape of independence or further devolution after the 2014 referendum, greater flexibility will also be required to ensure appropriate local responses to job market and housing conditions for example. Decentralisation beyond Holyrood would enable cities like Glasgow and Dundee —among the most vulnerable in the UK to welfare cuts according to the Centre for Cities (2011) — to make different choices from Edinburgh and Aberdeen, which are among the most resilient cities in the UK. Decentralisation would also enable employment programmes in rural areas to respond better to issues of low pay and seasonal work, and how these interact with a limited supply of housing for rent.

In future, different, competing social justice strategies will be needed in Scotland. These will need to explore traditional assumptions, look outwards and shift power downwards. Further constitutional change is only the next stage of a much bigger challenge – to stand against powerful trends towards inequality.

References

Brewer, M. Browne, J. and Joyce, R. (2011), *Child and working age poverty from 2010 to 2020*, London: Institute for Social & Economic Research and Institute for Fiscal Studies.

Centre for Cities (2011), 'Cities Outlook' and 'City Tracker', http://www.centreforcities.org/outlook11.html

Commission on Social Justice (1994), *Social Justice: Strategies for National Renewal*, London: IPPR.

Cooke, G. and Henehan, K. (2012), *Double Dutch: The case against deregulation and demand-led funding in childcare*, London: IPPR.

Davis, A. Hirsch, D. Smith, N. Beckhelling, J. and Padley, M. (2012), *A Minimum Income Standard for the UK in 2012*, York: Joseph Rowntree Foundation.

Gibb, K. and Stephens, M. (2012), *Devolving Housing Benefit: A discussion paper*, Edinburgh: CIH/SFHA.

Goodman, A. and Gregg, P. (2010), *Poorer children's educational attainment: How important are attitudes and behaviour?*, York: Joseph Rowntree Foundation.

HM Treasury (2012), *Impact on households: distributional analysis to accompany the Autumn Statement*, London: HM Treasury.

Kenway, P. MacInnes, T. Fothergill, S. and Horgan, G. (2010), *Working age 'welfare': who gets it, why and what it costs*, York: Joseph Rowntree Foundation.

Lloyd, E. (2012), 'Poor children's future access to early years provision', in Judge, L. (ed.), *Ending child poverty by 2020: Progress made and lessons learned*, London: Child Poverty Action Group

McCormick, J. (2013), *Welfare in working order: Points and principles for the Scottish debate*, Edinburgh: SCVO.

Melhuish, E. (2012), 'The impact of poverty on child development and adult outcomes: the importance of early years education', in Judge, L. (ed.), *Ending child poverty by 2020: Progress made and lessons learned*, London: Child Poverty Action Group.

Palmer, G. (2010), *The impact of devolution: Indicators of poverty and social exclusion*, York: Joseph Rowntree Foundation.

ScotCen (2011a), 'Is Scotland more left-wing than England?', Special Edition No.5 British Social Attitudes 28, Edinburgh: ScotCen.

ScotCen (2011b), 'Devolution Max: United but Apart?', Scottish Social Attitudes: Devolution and attitudes to government, http://www.scotcen.org.uk/study/scottish-social-attitudes-2011

Scottish Government (2011), *Tackling Poverty Board: A summary of the evidence*, Edinburgh: Scottish Government.

Scottish Government (2012), *Annual Report for Child Poverty Strategy for Scotland*, Edinburgh: Scottish Government.

Scottish Government (2013), *Government Expenditure and Revenue Scotland 2011-2012*, Office of the Chief Economic Adviser, Edinburgh: Scottish Government.

Scottish Parliament (2012), Welfare Reform Committee 1st Report, 2012 (Session 4), Stage 1 Report on the Welfare Reform (Further Provision) (Scotland) Bill, SP Paper 125, 16 May, Edinburgh: Scottish Parliament.

Trench, A. (2012), 'Devo more, devo plus and so on: extending devolution in the UK and financing it' Presentation to PSA Territorial Politics Group, Brussels, 16 September, https://devolutionmatters.wordpress.com/2012/09/16/enhancing-devolution-presentation-at-psa-territorial-politics-conference-in-brussels/

Energy Policy, Nationalism and Scottish Independence

NICOLA MCEWEN

SINCE THE DISCOVERY of oil off Scotland's shores, energy has been an important feature of the debate over Scotland's constitutional future. Considerable reserves of oil remain embedded beneath the North Sea, offering Scotland the promise of energy security and wealth after independence. These seas also offer an opportunity to tap new sources of renewable energy, once technology is sufficiently advanced to harness limitless wave and tidal resources. Onshore, windfarms have become a notable feature across the country, from the 'dancing ladies' of Gigha to Europe's largest windfarm at Whitelee, near Glasgow. Water – an increasingly scarce resource in some countries – is in abundance in Scotland, and being used to expand the already significant capacity to generate hydroelectricity, contributing to the goal of developing Scotland into a 'hydro nation'.

This essay explores the relationship between energy policy and independence. The current Scottish government has placed energy at the heart of its policy agenda. Sitting alongside the continued desire to benefit directly from the exploitation of oil and gas reserves, the promotion and expansion of renewable energy has been the cornerstone of the SNP government's economic policy since its election in 2007. The renewables agenda combines economic and constitutional objectives. It serves the government's overall strategic objective of achieving sustainable economic growth. Marine renewables in particular have been identified as 'Scotland's second energy bonanza' and the 'the key to our future prosperity'. The powers of independence are considered crucial to fulfilling Scotland's energy potential to be the 'green capital of Europe'. From the Scottish government's perspective, independence would ensure the development of an energy policy and regulatory framework suited to Scottish interests, and would provide an enhanced presence and opportunity to exercise influence in Europe and beyond. The political implications are also clear – Scotland as an independent nation-state would be an energy-rich nation, even after the oil runs out.

But what difference would independence make to energy policy? Scotland is already a leader in renewable energy even without constitutional competence. This essay will outline some of the opportunities and constraints independence may entail with respect to energy, and consider the extent to which energy independence would be compromised by the transnational nature of the industry, the market and the policy framework.

Energy policy under current constitutional arrangements

The SNP government has embraced the renewables agenda with increasing enthusiasm since its election in 2007. In 2008, it set a target of generating 50 per cent of Scottish demand for electricity from renewable sources by 2020. By 2011, the target was to source *the equivalent of 100 per cent* of Scotland's electricity consumption from renewable sources by 2020, and for renewables to account for 30 percent of all energy demand.

One of the remarkable features of Scotland's ambitious programme in renewable energy is that it has been pursued in the face of very limited constitutional powers. The Scotland Act (1998) reserved to Westminster most areas of energy competence, including the generation, transmission, distribution and supply of electricity, the ownership, exploration and exploitation of deposits of oil and natural gas, the ownership and exploitation of coal, and nuclear energy and nuclear installations. As a result, the Scottish government could only protest about the system of transmission charging, which it has frequently argued inhibits renewable energy investment by imposing the highest grid connection charges on those generating energy in regions remote from highly populated urban centres.

Under the existing constitutional settlement, the Scottish Parliament has responsibility for promoting renewable energy and energy efficiency, as well as economic development and environmental competences, and these powers have been used to the maximum to develop a distinctive and ambitious energy policy. In addition, the Scottish government has significant executive powers, derived from the 1989 Electricity (Scotland) Act, including powers to amend (subject to UK/EU consent) the Renewables Obligation, currently the principal mechanism for promoting industry investment in renewable energy throughout the UK, as well as the power to grant or withhold consent for the construction of overhead transmission lines and new generating stations. It is the latter power which has been invoked in the pledge to prevent new nuclear power stations being built on Scottish soil.

The reservation of most aspects of energy policy – alongside most revenue-raising and tax capacities and external relations, also crucial to energy – has frequently required close co-operation and negotiation with the UK government and the energy regulator. The growing significance of the European Union in this sphere has seen the Scottish government devote a significant element of its EU engagement strategy to renewable energy, through extensive lobbying of the European Commission. The Scottish government has also invested significant efforts in nurturing relations with the regulator and the energy industry. The Scottish Energy Advisory Board, which offers strategic policy guidance at the heart of government, is a good example of the latter.

Within the UK, intergovernmental relations in this policy sphere have been cordial and constructive. Intergovernmental channels have opened up opportunities to exercise 'soft power', using informal means to influence the direction of UK policy. There have been notable achievements, for example, when negotiating banding as part of the Renewables Obligation to boost marine renewables in Scotland, or in seeking to shape Electricity Market Reform.

As with all forms of intergovernmental relations in the UK, such informal channels of influence are reliant upon goodwill and nurturing good interpersonal relationships between officials and ministers. And although relations with the Department of Energy and Climate Change are good, the latter is a relatively weak department within Whitehall, and relations with more powerful departments, notably the Treasury, can be more strained. Nonetheless, the Scottish government has some advantages in its engagement with the UK government in the energy field which it lacks in some other policy areas. The goal of increasing the proportion of energy from renewable sources is broadly shared (albeit that some recent ministerial pronouncements cast some doubt over the UK government's future policy direction). Moreover, the abundance of natural resources and the political will, reflected in a favourable policy and planning environment, to harness them to promote renewable energy makes Scotland a necessary partner in the drive to meet the UK's obligations under the EU Energy and Climate Change programme. The dependence, then, is arguably mutual.

Energy Independence

Given that the Scottish government has had the capacity to develop a distinctive and ambitious policy programme without energy self-government, and is already recognised within and beyond the UK for its leadership in this sphere, one may question what difference the transfer of energy competence, and the broader powers of independence, would make.

Ownership of oil and gas reserves, along with the transfer of competences over taxation, would of course generate significant revenues from extraction. Most revenue here would be generated not through licence fees (which produce only small returns) but through the implementation of a Scottish corporation tax, supplementary charge and petroleum revenue tax, or by their replacement should a future independent Scottish government choose alternative forms of taxing the oil industry. The direct revenue-generating benefits of renewable energy are less obvious. Potential exists to generate revenue from leasing sites for offshore windfarms (assuming revenues generated from The Crown Estate accrued to the Scottish government). However, the economic benefits that are predicted to emerge from renewable energy are broader – linked to job creation, skills development, inward investment and export potential – and don't necessarily require constitutional competence to be in the hands of the Scottish parliament and government.

At least four presumed added benefits are associated with independence. First, having jurisdictional authority over energy would, it is argued, enable the development of a regulatory framework suited to Scottish needs. This is a nod, in particular, towards frustration with the transmission charging regime regulated by Ofgem, and in particular its detrimental impact on the potential of Scotland's island communities to exploit fully the potential of renewable generation. Second, independence would transfer fiscal tools, facilitating more tailored and targeted investment and the development of a tax system suited to Scottish energy priorities. Third, independence would enable Scotland, after negotiation, to become a member-state, rather than a region, of the European Union, thereby enhancing opportunities for influencing EU energy policy. Finally, independence would raise the profile of the Scottish government among stakeholders operating in Scotland, in particular in the energy industry by making it the main player in shaping the energy policy environment. According to one senior political figure, the difference independence would make to energy in Scotland would be like 'night and day' (interview).

But independence would not be total, nor is it desired to be. The Scottish government acknowledges the ever-increasing importance of the EU in this policy sphere, which sets the parameters within which all member states must operate. Furthermore, there is a clear desire to maintain a common GB energy market, including continuing to work together to shape the system of incentivising and subsidising investment in renewable energy generation. And it supports continued co-operation between governments within the context of an All Islands Approach to energy, under the auspices of the British-Irish Council. This implies a considerable degree of interdependence that may constrain the scope for independent decision-making, and the capacity to achieve at least some of the presumed goals of energy self-government.

Independence and Interdependence

Energy is not the only area where the SNP government has emphasised continued cross-border co-operation with the rest of the UK after independence. The so-called British dimension is emphasised across a range of policy spheres. How realistic is this diluted form of independence in the energy sphere, and to what extent would it constrain self-government?

The importance of the European Union constrains the scope for autonomous decision-making within any member state. It obliges member states to accept and implement the directives set out in the third and preceding legislative packages for an internal EU gas and electricity market. Within these parameters, there is scope for some distinctiveness. A member state might, for example, choose to give greater priority to renewables, mandate a greater degree of public or co-ownership over energy production, or have stronger consumer protection and public service obligations. Member states must also work to achieve binding assigned targets allocated under the broader EU Energy and Climate package designed to ensure that the EU collectively achieves a 20 per cent reduction in greenhouse gas emissions from 1990 levels; a 20 per cent improvement in energy efficiency and 20 percent of energy demand to be met from renewable resources.

The EU may also offer some guarantees for achieving some of the continuities desired by the Scottish government. The EU promotes market integration and shared grid infrastructure, and there are sufficient examples of integrated energy markets across Europe which could set a precedent for the continuation of an integrated GB market after independence. The Spanish and Portuguese governments have been developing an integrated Iberian electricity market and the Nordic countries already share a common wholesale electricity market, with plans under way to implement a common retail market. Even closer to home, the All Island project created a common electricity market between the Republic of Ireland and Northern Ireland. Clearly, there is no impediment to creating a shared energy market between sovereign states, and positive encouragement to do so from the European Union. Indeed, the EU is working rapidly towards a single integrated market across member states.

The role of renewable energy generation as part of the economic case for independence is founded upon a belief in its export potential. If the renewables targets are met, Scotland will generate more renewable electricity than it consumes, and the assumption is that others will buy it. EU law facilitates cross-border trade and access to transmission and distribution grids, and Scottish producers of energy could not be denied the opportunity to distribute and sell their product. The challenge will be for Scottish-based generators to remain competitive so as to ensure there are willing buyers.

EU law would require the setting up of a separate regulator for Scotland, potentially permitting the creation of a regulatory regime more favourable to Scottish interests, in line with the Scottish government's objectives. However, the scope for distinctive regulation may be limited. Market integration can create pressure for common regulation, not least from the energy industry and investors, who in the main operate across borders. This may be especially the case if, as anticipated, Scotland shares with England and Wales mechanisms for subsidising and incentivising low carbon generation. It is difficult to envisage any independent Scottish Government accepting the maintenance of a system of grid charging which imposed excessive charges on those generating electricity in remote rural areas of the Highlands and Islands. But in many other areas of regulation, the scope for policy distinctiveness may be limited. The continuation of a deeply integrated energy market and shared subsidy regime would of course be subject to negotiation, and dependent upon the willingness of the UK government to share the Scottish government's view that to do so would be in their shared interest. But it would also mean imposing constraints on the degree of decision-making autonomy Scottish governing institutions would actually have after independence.

Governing Interdependence

These interdependencies and shared arrangements would require some organisational mechanism to facilitate co-operation and policy co-ordination between governments, bureaucracies, regulatory agencies and other relevant non-departmental public bodies after independence. In the case of Scottish-UK intergovernmental co-ordination, continuing current practice would seem to be a wholly unsatisfactory solution. The system of intergovernmental relations which has emerged in the wake of UK devolution is largely informal, conducted more between officials than between ministers, is very hierarchical, with power and resources concentrated in Whitehall, and is dependent upon goodwill, especially the goodwill of officials and ministers in Whitehall to permit access and provide information to the devolved administrations. It is most co-operative when governments are led by the same party and when governments share broad policy objectives. It works less well when policy differences generate intergovernmental disputes. This weakly institutionalised system of intergovernmental relations seems ill-equipped to manage relations between two sovereign states, where the informal bureaucratic links can be expected to diminish, and where more policy differences might be expected.

There are examples of intergovernmental energy forums elsewhere that might provide a model of what may be possible or desirable in managing shared energy interests and shared energy markets in a post-independence context. For example, the Irish single electricity market (SEM) is overseen by the SEM committee, an independent committee made up of three members of the Irish regulatory body, three regulators from Northern Ireland, and one independent member. It meets monthly, is accountable to the respective ministers, and indirectly to the Dáil and the Northern Ireland Assembly, and governs the operation of the single electricity market. The shared Nordic energy market is overseen by the Ministers of Energy for each of the Nordic countries, under the auspices of the Nordic Council of Ministers for Business, Energy and Regional Policy. These mostly annual ministerial meetings are supported by the Committee of Senior Officials for Energy Polices, which includes representatives from the various national energy agencies and ministries.

Some intergovernmental co-operation has already been established within the British-Irish Council, with the Scottish and UK governments taking the lead in developing an energy workstream. This may form a basis upon which to build in the event of independence, but it is a rather flimsy one; the BIC lacks the resource capacity to manage intergovernmental summitry on a significant scale, and the commitment of all partners to its broader development is uncertain. In a letter to Ed Davey, Secretary of State for Energy and Climate Change, in May 2012, the First Minister suggested that the devolved administrations' statutory right to be consulted on electricity market reform may be served by setting up a JMC Energy as part of the regular calendar of joint ministerial committees. Even if this were to be established, it is unlikely that such a hierarchical structure as the JMC would be the most effective forum for managing intergovernmental co-ordination in the event of independence. Then, as now, it is likely that bilateral communication and co-ordination may be more important than these more formal multi-lateral forums.

Whatever forum or processes were to be adopted, intergovernmental co-ordination of the services that may continue to be shared after independence, including in the field of energy, will create significant challenges for an independent Scottish government. Although Scotland would share a formal equality of status with rUK as a sovereign state, this would be alongside an informal inequality of resources, given the differences in size, status, political strength, international standing and bureaucratic capacity. This does not mean that an independent Scotland would be without influence in the intergovernmental – or indeed the international – arena. Rather, like small states elsewhere in Europe, it would need to choose its issues carefully, nurture expertise in niche areas, and build alliances with others sharing similar objectives. And even with the full complement of constitutional powers brought by independence, a Scottish government would still require non-constitutional powers of persuasion.

Scotland in the Wider World: Does Size and Sovereignty Matter?

GEORGE KEREVAN

WOULD INDEPENDENCE MAKE Scotland more or less vulnerable compared with the current constitutional arrangement? Would sovereignty give Scotland greater economic and political sway in the world, as nationalists contend? Or leave her, as a small nation, at the mercy of the vast forces unleashed by globalisation? To put the question in more populist terms: does size matter?

An independent Scotland would rank 117th by population among states and autonomous territories. Even inside the EU, 19 of the current 27 member states have a population that is greater than Scotland's. Size is also related to land area. An independent Scotland would come 118th among nations by area, though still ahead of the Netherlands, Belgium and Denmark. However, economic muscle – while related to population and area - counts most in size stakes. Here an independent Scotland rises in the league tables. Measuring GDP per capita, including a geographical share of North Sea oil and gas revenues, Scotland easily ranks among the top 20 economies, though somewhere in the bottom half. Scotland is neither a microstate nor a super power. But it belongs squarely to the family of rich, educated, technological societies found in the OECD and EU.

There is no doubt then that an independent Scotland would have some consequence in the world, on a par with the likes of Norway, Denmark or Sweden. The SNP is also committed to joining the EU and NATO, giving the new state leverage in the main Western alliances. However, this does not exhaust the debate. It is plausible to argue that big nations such as the UK – with their large populations, superior capital endowment and economies of industrial scale – have more clout in the world than smaller ones, especially in times of crisis. This can be seen in the lead taken by the UK in securing a global commitment to fiscal reflation in the aftermath of the 2008 Credit Crunch. It is also possible to argue that the demand of Scotland, Catalonia, the Basque Country and the Flemish part of Belgium to form independent states inherently weakens the ability of the EU and Eurozone to act collectively in the face of economic crisis. From this perspective, Scottish society gains more from being part of the collective UK, where the constitution is flexible enough to let Scotland use the diplomatic weight of the British state to express its own interests on a European and global stage.

To sum up, sovereignty would certainly give Scotland increased diplomatic and economic manoeuvrability, but with this would come new risks and a necessary loss of British leverage. Can we quantity these gains and the losses? To coin a phrase, what unique 'sovereignty capital' would the creation of its own state afford Scotland to further its own interests, particularly in the current global situation?

A New Model: Small State Globalisation

Outside of danger zones such as the Middle East, it is fair to say that global economic pressures rather than security issues dominate when evaluating the effective sovereignty of small nations. The international downturn triggered by the banking crisis of 2008, followed by events in the Eurozone, clearly indicates the vulnerability of all nations – large and small – to unforeseen events in a highly integrated world economy. But are small nations any more at risk than, say, the United States or the UK where the Credit Crunch originated? In fact, there is an emerging view that small industrial economies such as Scotland possess a unique set of advantages when it comes to navigating the globalised economy, as compared to very large nations. The United Nations Industrial Development Organisation (UNIDO, 2009) concludes: 'Small highly dynamic economies are displacing mature, developed countries as global industrial competitors.'

Small economies of the European industrial kind tend to be more export-focused than larger ones. This follows from the smaller size of their domestic market relative to GDP. But small countries are not just 'structurally open', they are also 'functionally open' in the sense that they pursue trade openness as a conscious policy choice; e.g. the tax-cutting fiscal competition exhibited by Ireland and Sweden. Economic efficiency demands that small industrial economies concentrate on only a few product or service lines, so they specialise in niches that are too small for large nations to fill comfortably. This ability of small nations to exploit niche export markets has been increased by the emergence of global supply chains and the ease with which technology is transferred – meaning that small countries can build competitive advantage in manufacturing high value components. Call this the 'small state globalisation' model.

The two undoubted success stories of small state globalisation are the Netherlands and Switzerland. They have parlayed their export success into the creation of powerful global companies, e.g. Shell, Phillips, Heineken, and Unilever in Holland, and Nestle, Zurich, Credit Suisse, Roche, Novartis, UBS, and ABB in Switzerland. Thus lack of political clout is compensated for by commercial clout. It is a model that can be replicated; viz. the success of the Gorenje company in Slovenia, which now has a five per cent of Europe's kitchen appliance market.

Small industrial economies are also big foreign investors. Surprising as it may be, Denmark's overseas direct investment is on the same scale as China's – suggesting that the 21st Century may not necessarily be dominated by Washington and Beijing. And the financial markets of Luxembourg and Switzerland control a larger proportion of US sovereign debt than does China. Beijing may have a huge sovereign wealth fund which it can use for diplomatic leverage, but the China Investment Corporation had assets at the start of 2013 of only $482bn compared with $667bn in Norway's equivalent.

The small state globalisation model means more than being efficient manufacturers or big foreign investors. It is also about education and innovation, the sine qua non of the contemporary global economy. Small industrial economies with a commitment to cultural pluralism and immigration can provide a sympathetic context for fostering divergent thinking and creativity. As Peter Katzenstein (1985) puts it: 'Small size favours debate and learning and economic openness and international vulnerability mean control over fewer resources and the probability of greater loss. Hence the environmental conditions in which small states operate are particularly conducive for high learning.'

The final component of the small state globalisation model has to do with adaptability. Small nations are certainly vulnerable to exogenous shocks but they are therefore much better at adapting to change and implementing structural reform. Finland lost 15 per cent of its GDP in three years, after the collapse of the Soviet Union destroyed its main export market. But Finnish growth soon bounced back and by 2000 was a phenomenal six per cent as the Finns went into the mobile phone business. Iceland's banks failed in 2008 sending unemployment up to ten per cent. But by

2012 Iceland had recovered and unemployment was below five per cent. Swedish economic growth hit a record low in 2008 but was back at an all-time high by 2010. In 2008, Switzerland had to bail out its banks, which had liabilities several times larger than the country's GDP. Within a few years the Swiss authorities were desperately trying to stop hot money flows from the stricken Eurozone pouring into their country's restored banking system. Overall, the majority of small nations in Western Europe made a faster and stronger recovery from the 2008 Credit Shock than did the UK. How?

First, these countries were able to tailor fiscal policy to their own local needs. A bigger nation may have superior borrowing powers but its fiscal policy ends up a compromise that may not suit specific regions (e.g. Scotland) when it comes to promoting recovery. Ireland's export-led recovery was predicated on its low corporation tax. Sweden returned to growth by slashing income tax, especially for low-income families. Iceland refused to bail out its banks with taxpayers' money and banned the export of capital to ensure bank funds were invested in the local economy. Second, in a small democracy solidarity makes it easier for a government to ask for the necessary economic sacrifices during an emergency – provided everyone contributes equally. That said, it is only fair to point out that there is a downside to being a small nation – the frequent emergence of cronyism, as seen in Ireland for instance.

There is a final interesting twist to the small nation globalisation idea: the so-called 'flotilla effect' of small nations working together to offset the power of larger nations (Price and Levinger, 2012). The increase in the number of new nations since the Second World War is a commonplace observation. But more nations means the global power wielded by larger states is to a degree defused by competition from the new. Particularly if these new nations are rich economically, technologically and culturally, as is Scotland. One extra polity like Scotland has a limited competitive impact. But the arrival of the Baltic States, Slovenia, Scotland, Catalonia, and the Basque Country does have a potential impact, especially on Europe. This may explain the enthusiasm of the Dutch entrepreneur Freddie Heineken for 'Eurotopia', his vision of a network of 75 small, historic European nations and regions, as the economic future.

Scotland and Small State Globalisation

Would an independent Scotland be able to exploit small state globalisation with its accent on trade, innovation, and adaptability?

Scotland clearly fits in the category of a small, open economy that would pursue an export-led strategy. Scotland's external trade as a proportion of GDP (including with the rest of the UK) was 49 per cent in 2010, and 60 per cent if North Sea oil is included. That puts us in the same league as Sweden (50), Denmark (53), Switzerland (51) and Norway (42) in export-to-GDP ratio. Scotland can also count a world-class education sector. Three Scottish universities – Edinburgh (21), Glasgow (54) and St Andrews (93) – make it into the prestigious QS global university rankings for 2012; on a par with the Netherlands and Canada and more than from Sweden, Denmark or Finland. Participation in higher education in 2010–11 was an all-time high of 55.6 per cent (of 16–30 year-olds) compared to 47 per cent in England. Some 30 per cent of Scottish students study business-related degrees, the most popular subject specialism. But Scottish student numbers in medical subjects were up 16 per cent in the period 2001–11, and in science and engineering up 20 per cent. As to the argument that Scotland could not have coped on its own with the failure of RBS and HBOS, it was the absence of local regulatory institutions not their weakness that was the bigger cause of the excess risks run by those banks.

However, there are features of the present Scottish economy that would limit the ability to exploit global markets, at least initially. Unlike the Netherlands and other small European industrial nations, Scotland has very few indigenous multinational manufacturing firms. Companies owned firth of Scotland (i.e. in the rest of the UK or abroad) represent provide 35 per cent of employment and nearly 55 per cent of turnover. Indeed, the number of large firms owned by Scots has declined markedly in recent decades. This is important in the independence debate because it means the bulk of the (registered) corporate tax base is foreign owned and controlled.

None of these structural problems are insurmountable. Indeed it can be argued that Scotland's skewed industrial ownership and organisational deficiencies derive precisely from its inability to pursue microeconomic and competition policies appropriate to its needs within the UK. The small nation globalisation model would facilitate adaptation and reform, though the necessary structural changes would take time. This is more than an academic point. The SNP has argued that an independent Scotland would remain in a sterling bloc with the rest of the UK, leaving fiscal policy as the only major economic lever available to a Scottish government. But Keynesian-style fiscal policy in Scotland is unlikely to be effective in influencing aggregate demand because any stimulus would simply suck in imports. It could, however, be effective when directed at supply-side policies to boost competitiveness. Any attempt to use fiscal policy simply to expand domestic demand would, on the contrary, leave Scotland vulnerable to the financial markets.

Small State Sovereignty and Geopolitics

The foregoing assumes a relatively benign political environment in which a small industrial nation can pursue its economic interests intelligently. But political environments are not always benign. How would geopolitics impinge on an independent Scotland? Even the European neighbourhood has experienced turbulence in recent years, e.g. the Russian incursion into Georgia in 2008, the mysterious cyber-attack on Latvia in 2007 (which probably originated from a section of the Russian intelligence apparatus), and the friction between Russian and Ukraine over gas supplies. It cannot be forgotten that Scotland was at the receiving end of a terrorist attack at Glasgow Airport in 2007 or that in 2010 it was revealed that RAF Tornados from Leuchars were being scrambled on average twice a month to intercept Russian Tu-160 bombers and escort them away from Scottish airspace. While a major physical threat to an independent Scotland seems unlikely, small nations are certainly subject to bullying by bigger ones, even in Europe. Witness the use by the UK of anti-terror laws to freeze Icelandic bank funds during the financial crisis.

The geopolitical situation facing an independent Scotland would be affected uniquely by its North Atlantic location. This raises such issues as the security of the West of Shetland and North Sea oil and gas fields, competition over maritime resources and navigation rights, and Scotland's role on NATO's northern flanks – an agenda which is probably more taxing than that faced by many other small nations. As the 21st Century progresses, the melting of the Greenland and Arctic ice caps will add to this complex picture. Climate change has the potential to open up the Northeast Passage to shipping between Europe and Asia, and allow the exploitation of minerals and fossil fuels previously trapped under the ice. Within a generation the focus of global maritime transport could switch to the seas just north of Scotland, with associated economic and security issues.

The United States Geological Survey estimates that the Arctic seabed contains 20 per cent of the world's oil and gas reserves. Unlike Antarctica, which since 1959 has been internationalised under a UN treaty, ownership of the Arctic and its resources remains unresolved. Moscow claims that the underwater Lomonosov and Mendeleyev ridges, which stretch towards the North Pole, are a continuation of its continental shelf. Recognition of this claim would increase Russia's exclusive economic zone by 1.2 million square kilometres. In 2006, an American oil company announced it intended to explore for oil in this area, arguing it was legally a common zone. Moscow retaliated by sending a submarine to the seabed beneath the North Pole and planting a Russian flag. A mini Cold War broke out in the area, which suddenly acquired a new name suitable for an Alistair MacLean novel – the High North. Russia sent Bear bombers to probe Scottish airspace. NATO replied by holding a major exercise in northern Norway that involved troops from technically neutral Sweden and Finland. They played out a scenario in which a hostile power called 'Northland' seized offshore oilfields.

The emergence of this new strategic theatre presents Scotland with opportunities and threats. Given proximity and the Atlantic oil industry, Scotland's interest may lie in the Arctic becoming a common economic zone – Scottish independent oil firms are already prospecting in Greenland waters. The opening of the Northwest Passage could also revive the old 1970s Oceanspan concept, with Scottish ports serving as the European end of a new global maritime trading system. However, there are also increased security risks. There is practically no conventional naval warfare presence left in Scotland, which accounts for half of Britain's seacoast. The 2010 Coalition Government defence review closed RAF Leuchars and all Nimrod maritime reconnaissance planes were scrapped. The UK now has less ability to patrol the Atlantic than at any time since the Second World War. An independent Scotland would be faced with the cost of providing a replacement maritime security presence.

Foreign Policy in an Independent Scotland

What would Scotland's likely foreign policy look like after independence? In a speech in China, in December 2011, Alex Salmond came his closest to defining the SNP's foreign policy philosophy. Citing as his inspiration Adam Smith's *Theory of Moral Sentiments* (reputedly a favourite of China's then Premier, Wen Jiabao), the First Minister said his watchwords were 'sympathy, empathy and solidarity'.

Salmond claims a 'moral' approach to international relationships. Moral not in the sense of 'good' but of understanding that being part of a global free trade economy brings responsibilities as well as rights. He believes that lasting trade partnerships can only achieved if rich Scotland appreciates the problems, needs and aspirations of other nation states – Smith's 'sympathy, empathy and solidarity'. For instance, Scotland helped pioneer the carbon-fuelled industrial economy, so it has a moral duty to help fix climate change. Only then can Scotland expect to sell renewables to Beijing. In a neat phrase, Salmond calls this approach 'sharing ambitions' rather than hypocritical finger-pointing by Western ex-colonialists.

How plausible is this philosophy as the basis for a foreign policy? It is certainly a different starting point from the traditional naked self-interest model of the Foreign Office, and less nebulous than Robin Cook's 'ethical foreign policy' of 1997 (which became a justification for Tony Blair's wars of intervention). Yet Salmond's 'sympathy, empathy and solidarity' remain to be tested in the real world, especially if other states do not reciprocate. It is also the case that the SNP, despite its recent return to supporting NATO membership, remains highly suspicious of US foreign policy. The SNP's commitment to UN peace-keeping activities is longstanding, but it is a moot point whether the party's membership would have been in favour of joining International Security Assistance Force (ISAF) in Afghanistan or committing combat aircraft in Libya in 2011, as did both Norway and Sweden.

Scotland would doubtless enter the international arena with a lot of diplomatic goodwill – which it could use to good effect. But Salmond's Smithian approach to foreign policy is as much transactional as it is moral. The political maturity of an independent Scotland will be tested when it is asked to make the commitments necessary to be effective in world affairs. Norway is only taken seriously as an international peace broker because it is also willing to play at the NATO top table and send tanks to Afghanistan. Would Scotland follow suit? If not, her standing in the world (and effective sovereignty) would diminish.

Culture and Small Nation Sovereignty

The dominant sovereignty model suggests that big nations (e.g. America) can exert cultural hegemony through their larger resources and control over new technology. Thus Hollywood, Facebook and Google set the cultural global agenda which small nations are powerless to influence, except on the margins. For an independent Scotland, which is part of the Anglophone world, there would be few barriers to US and British cultural penetration, if not domination.

However, there is an alternative viewpoint. Sovereignty confers the right to experiment, especially in cultural matters. It is hard, for instance, to defend the proposition that Ireland has been culturally assimilated. In fact, Ireland proves that being part of the Anglophone community can be a strategic asset that Scotland would share. And like Ireland, Scotland has access to a large Diaspora as a means of reinforcing its global image and position following independence. Scotland is among the major migrant nations of modern times. Currently around 20 per cent of the Scottish-born population live outside the homeland while some estimates put Scotland's entire Diaspora at 40 million (Scottish Government, 2009). Much of this Diaspora is concentrated in North America. This is a rich source of business contacts, political influence and inward investment capital that could allow Scotland to exert more influence than is suggested by her modest domestic population.

However, unlike the case of Ireland, there is still a lot of doubt has to how successful Scotland has been at exploiting its Diaspora (Sim and McIntosh, 2007). This may be due to structural issues. The Scottish Diaspora retains a distinctly romantic view of the Home Land, more Walter Scott than Irvine Welsh. At the same time, contemporary indigenous Scottish culture is ill at ease with tartanry. This makes effective engagement with the Diaspora, particularly in North America, difficult to achieve. It is also the case that the recent Scottish Diaspora has become well integrated in its new overseas home, making reverse immigration – bringing skills and capital back to Scotland – difficult to secure. Nevertheless, the Scottish Diaspora remains a valuable resource that could add to Scotland's 'sovereignty capital' in the event of independence.

On another tack, the information revolution has transformed the potential for small cultures to influence the new global commons. True, the digital divide – or lack of Internet access – in poor countries excludes them from modern trade and intellectual exchange. But small rich nations such as Scotland are well positioned to exploit the Internet and social networking on a global scale. Unfortunately, household access to broadband in Scotland continues to lag behind the other UK nations. In 2012 broadband penetration reached 68 per cent of households while the UK average is 76 per cent (second only to France). The problem lies specifically in the low access among poor families in Glasgow. On the other hand, half of Scots now use social networking sites.

Conclusion

The foregoing discussion assumes that national sovereignty confers economic and political power. But is that still true? Is sovereignty itself a diminishing asset in the 21st Century? Is the power that sovereignty is supposed to confer being constrained by new social, cultural and technological forces at work in the world? Viewed in terms of our concept of 'sovereignty capital', is that capital losing its value?

This is the controversial argument put forward recently by Moises Naim, former editor-in-chief of 'Foreign Policy' and now an associate at the Carnegie Endowment for International Peace. Naim's thesis (2013) is that power – political, corporate and ethnic – is not merely shifting from the major powers, it is also decaying. Start-ups trump corporations, asymmetric warfare stymies super powers, and Facebook thwarts dictators. Naim claims a threefold revolution is taking place – characterised by 'More, Mobility and Mentality' – which is challenging the existing model of power. 'More' is his shorthand for more people, more independent countries and more wealth undermining existing monopolies of power. 'Mobility' involves both physical mass migration between and within countries, and includes the communications revolution. 'Mentality' refers to the increasing openness of people to reject cultural and political conditioning, as typified by the Arab Spring.

Even if one rejects Naim's broader conclusions – and he does exaggerate trends – it is clear that the nature and limits of 19th Century national sovereignty are being altered radically by economic and cultural globalism, mass migration and person-to-person communication through social networking. While that process reduces the theoretical power an independent Scottish Government might wield, it also gives that Scotland as a whole more political and economic 'space' in which to operate *vis-a-vis* larger states.

We began by asking if size matters? It does. But small size confers manoeuvrability, which is a precious asset in an increasingly complex and interdependent world.

References

Katzenstein, P. (2003), 'Small States and Small States Revisited', *New Political Economy*, Vol. 8, no.1.

Naim, M. (2013), *The End of Power*, New York: Basic Books.

Price, A. and Levinger, B. (2012). *The Flotilla Effect: Europe's small economies through the eye of the storm*, Cardiff: Plaid Cymru.

Scottish Government. (2009), *Scotland's Diaspora and Overseas-Born Population*, Edinburgh: Scottish Government.

Scottish Government. (2010), *Global Connections Survey*, Edinburgh: Scottish Government.

Scottish Government. (2012), *Business in Scotland 2012*, Edinburgh: Scottish Government.

Sim, D and McIntosh, I. (2007), 'Connecting with the Scottish Diaspora', *Scottish* Affairs, No. 58.

United Nations Industrial Development Organisation (UNIDO) (2009), *Industrial Development Report: Breaking In and Moving Up: New Industrial Challenges for the Bottom Billion and the Middle Income Countries*, http://www.unido.org/fileadmin/user_media/Publications/IDR_2009_print.PDF

Trident's Insecure anchorage

WILLIAM WALKER

THE POLITICAL DIFFICULTIES arising from Trident's location in a Scotland gaining independence are widely acknowledged. The UK government wishes to maintain a nuclear deterrent, 'assigned to NATO', in the form of submarines carrying Trident missiles and their warheads. The Trident force is operated, and can probably only operate, out of two long established bases in Scotland (Faslane and Coulport). The Scottish government has promised to use its sovereign powers after independence is won to remove Trident from Scottish territory. Delivering on its promise would probably entail the rest of the UK's nuclear disarmament, provoking resistance and creating a possible impasse in the negotiation of settled relations between Scotland and the rest of the UK after 2014.

A common assumption is that London and Edinburgh's pro- and anti-Trident policies are firmly anchored, frustrating compromise. Is this the case? Might the anchors in either place be less secure, and policies more mutable, than is usually supposed? With or without a Yes vote in the Scottish referendum, can any safe predictions be made about the Trident replacement project's future given uncertainties over economic conditions, international circumstances and the composition of governments after the 2015 UK and 2016 Scottish elections? No, yes and no will be my answers to these questions.

An Unbending Scottish Stance on Trident?

Nuclear weapons have been deployed from bases in Scotland since the early 1960s. American invention of the nuclear-powered submarine in the 1950s was followed by the search for a suitable base for US Polaris submarines in Western Europe, placing missiles within easy reach of the Soviet Union. After the UK government had volunteered to play host, the search for a suitable site around the UK's perimeter was whittled down to a choice between Fort William and the Holy Loch, the latter being selected on American insistence due to its proximity to Glasgow (a source of skills and of entertainment for bored servicemen) and to Prestwick airport (Chalmers and Walker, 2001). Selection of nearby Faslane and Coulport for the UK's own Polaris and then Trident fleets, carrying missiles purchased or leased from the US, followed naturally.

These basing decisions, taken in secret as was the custom of the time, contributed to the emergence of a vigorous Scottish nationalist movement. Although opposition to the government's nuclear policies was experienced across the UK, a distinctive Scottish attitude towards the deterrent did develop, finding strongest expression within the Scottish National Party. In addition to moral objection to a military strategy based on the threat of annihilation, opposition in Scotland rested on claims of illegitimate, uncaring imposition. A dangerous capability was being foisted on Scotland, close to its most populous city, thereby avoiding its location in England and anywhere near the metropolis. For the nationalist, this was symptomatic of London's imperiousness and insensitivity to the well-being of the Scottish people. It became an obvious focus of the SNP's effort to garner support across the country.

The perception of imposition was reinforced during the Trident replacement debate in 2006–07 that was played out in Whitehall and the UK Parliament without any reference to Scottish interests, and without acknowledgement that Scotland had special reasons for being consulted and heard. Despite the presence of Scottish MPs in Tony Blair's cabinet, notably Gordon Brown, Des Browne, Alistair Darling and John Reid, and on the Select Committees that held inquiries on the proposal, no effort was made to justify Trident's replacement – which entailed basing the nuclear force at Faslane and Coulport for several more decades – in Scotland itself. No Minister ventured north of the border to argue the case. The sense of slight was accentuated when, after the UK Parliament's pronounced vote in favour of Trident's replacement, the Scottish Parliament's equally pronounced vote against it was treated as irrelevant.

Over the half century that nuclear weapons have been deployed out of Scotland, over which period London (and Washington) have retained their exclusive hold on decisions, bringing an end to this situation has therefore been a central goal of the nationalist movement. It has aspired both to restore the safety and security of an endangered populous and to recover the political authority whose lack has prevented Scotland from defining its own relations with the outside world. Trident came to symbolise the loss and potential recovery of control over the national destiny. The attainment of sovereignty and Trident's removal therefore became bound together.

Attitudes to Trident in Scotland are therefore strongly political and dosed in symbolism and high principle. Although not entirely absent, military logic and international interests have not shaped the debate. This said, the SNP's leaders and strategists have become increasingly aware of the constraints on political action that they face now and will face after the referendum. Despite the principled objections, loudly expressed, the Scottish government has done nothing to disturb Trident's operation out of the Clyde since assuming office in 2007, despite the Scotland Act's devolution of authority over policing, emergency services and other activities without which the nuclear force could not function. It has shown no appetite for picking fights with the Ministry of Defence, honouring strictly the 1998 devolution settlement and cooperating where cooperation has been required by London. Its behaviour has stemmed partly from the desire to build a reputation for competence in government, which confrontation with London would have jeopardised, and partly from fears of economic and other forms of punishment. Wishing to extend its sway across Glasgow, it has also been reluctant to take actions raising fears of job losses and economic decline in localities benefitting from the Navy's presence in the Clyde.

At the same time, the SNP's leadership has become sensitive to international reactions to its policies, eager as it is to establish the respect and trust that would ease Scotland's way into recognition as a sovereign state and membership of international organisations. The change of policy on NATO membership, from longstanding rejection to aspiring membership, was an important sign of this sensitivity and the vulnerability attending it. The outcry against the about turn within the Party and narrowness of the vote endorsing the new policy at the SNP's annual conference in November 2012 demonstrated, if there were any doubts, the political dangers of taking a step too far. Delegates were reminded that opposition to NATO was rooted in opposition to nuclear deterrence and the presence of nuclear weapons in Scotland, and that nato remained a nuclear alliance that would not look kindly on a Scottish application for membership tied to insistence that Trident should go. In response, the conference was assured by Party leaders that Trident's removal was non-negotiable. The anti-Trident policy was therefore reiterated amidst acknowledgement that removal could not be carried out overnight. The SNP's defence policy, as it was emerging, also envisaged Faslane becoming independent Scotland's main naval base. The policy's credibility hinged on the removal of all nuclear submarines from Faslane, allowing its conversion to a base for conventional forces alone. This proposal again had the effect of tying a future Scottish government to Trident's eviction.

The Scottish government therefore seems likely to take a hard line on Trident in the White Paper setting out its case for independence that will be published in November 2013. It will give some room for negotiation on the timing of departure, and on Faslane and Coulport's operation under lease in the interim, without conceding that the submarines' stay could be lengthy even if the rewards offered by London were substantial.

It is open to question whether and for how long a Scottish government, possibly of another party political complexion, could hold this line after a referendum had delivered independence. It may be sorely tempted to use Trident as a bargaining tool in negotiations, trading a long stay for concessions on issues more immediately vital to Scottish interests. An immediate shift must however be unlikely, since it would be regarded as betrayal of fundamental principles and policies inside and outside the SNP. After so many promises made over so many years, with Trident's removal being presented as a great prize of Scottish sovereignty, the damage to political trust would be great. A policy of phase-out is probably all that an SNP-led government could get away with, the phase-out's duration still being a combustible issue but probably longer than is currently conceded. Whether a Labour-led government gaining office after the 2016 Scottish election could give more concessions to London on this matter is an open question.

Over time, however, the Scottish government – and people – might become more accommodating. Even today, the breadth and depth of public opposition in Scotland to Trident is not clear. Social attitude surveys are only beginning to ask the appropriate questions. Even if they indicate widespread opposition, most Scots have lived for decades with the nuclear force's presence in their back yard without taking to the streets. It is conceivable that, after the great prize of independence had been gained, Trident's symbolism – its association with external imposition – would lose its edge. The opposite might nevertheless happen if the rest of the UK and allies abroad tried to coerce Edinburgh into accepting Trident's permanent operation out of the Clyde.

An unbending UK *stance on Trident?*

The UK has possessed nuclear weapons, and practiced nuclear deterrence, since the early 1950s. Indeed, it could lay claim to the dubious honour of being the nuclear weapon's inventor. Without the Maud Committee's secret research project in 1940–41, the Manhattan Project would not have been launched in 1942, the bombs would not have been unavailable for use by the United States in 1945, and the East-West conflict would have evolved differently. Furthermore, the Maud Committee's Report of October 1941 provided the justification for possession that still resonates in Whitehall. 'Even if the war should end before the bombs are ready the effort would not be wasted, except in the unlikely event of complete disarmament, since no nation would care to risk being caught without a weapon of such decisive possibilities.'

Over the seven subsequent decades, nuclear weapons and their production systems have become part of the UK's national furniture, the political and strategic ideas associated with them infusing the attitudes of generations of officials, politicians and military personnel, including Scots working within the UK's institutions. They have also been bound up with the 'special relationship' with the United States. The trade in knowledge, materials and equipment between the US and UK – unique among nuclear weapon states – has been regarded, along with intelligence sharing, as a 'pillar' of that relationship. In elite circles, abandonment of nuclear weapons therefore arouses fears of Washington's downgrading of the UK in its foreign relations. Tony Blair's decision to support the US invasion of Iraq in 2003 and his strong advocacy of Trident's replacement were connected. Each reflected the extraordinarily high value that he and others within London's political elite attached to the transatlantic relationship.

The British state's engagement with nuclear weapons has therefore been deep and longstanding. But the UK also stands out internationally for the intensity of public opposition to their possession and the practice of nuclear deterrence. Although ebbing and flowing, public protest has been persistent, expressed in statements issued by many prominent individuals and groups in civil society, including churches and trades unions, and through acts of civil disobedience by CND, the women's peace camp at Greenham Common and Trident Ploughshares among other organisations.

Such civic opposition would have posed little threat to the nuclear weapon programme had it not spilled into party politics. Only the Conservative Party, a few mavericks apart, has been solid throughout in its backing of the nuclear deterrent. The Labour Party has a long history of division on the issue, its leaders struggling to maintain support from the 1950s to the 1970s, pressing for the UK's unilateral disarmament in the 1980s, and reverting in the 1990s to a pro-nuclear stance after its unilateralism was held partly responsible for party splits and defeats in the 1983 and 1987 general elections, and after New Labour had bought into Mrs Thatcher's expansionist, pro-American foreign policy. Tony Blair was confident in 2006 that his campaign to renew Trident would be successful only because he could count on the Conservative Party's unanimous backing when Parliament voted. He won over sceptics in his Cabinet, including the Foreign Secretary, Margaret Beckett and the Defence Secretary, Des Browne by giving them free rein to proselytise on global, multilateral disarmament.

When the UK Parliament endorsed the government's proposals on Trident's replacement in March 2007, the decision was not portrayed as being final. The project was depicted as happening in two stages. During 'Initial Gate' lasting up to a decade, design work would be carried out on the submarines, reactors, warheads and associated communication systems (the same US missiles will be used as previously). During 'Main Gate', lasting 15 to 20 years, these systems would be manufactured and brought into service. Before initiation of heavy spending during 'Main Gate', the decision could be reopened for review with the possibility of a fresh vote in Parliament. Whilst affirming its support for the project, the present coalition government announced early in this parliament that the decision to move into 'Main Gate' would not be taken until after the 2015 general election.

The point here is that the Trident replacement project is not yet fully secure at the UK level, whatever happens in Scotland. Despite the considerable momentum built around it, circumstances can be imagined in which the policy would be re-examined, especially if the UK's public finances worsened and the defence budget came under further strain. Although a previous Labour government was the policy's architect, a Labour Party returned to power in 2015 would have a hard time keeping a lid on the issue, especially if it could only form a government through coalition with the Liberal Democratic Party which has no love of Trident. Given that its predecessor pushed Trident's replacement, and given the lasting fear of tabloid accusations of being 'weak on defence', an incoming Labour government's political instinct would be to persevere. However, Trident would loom large in any review of forward spending, creating opportunity for opponents in the Party to challenge the policy.

Even the Conservative Party's support might weaken if public spending were heavily constrained. The historian Hugh Trevor-Roper, who belonged on the political right, once wrote that 'there is far more humbug in England on the Right than on the Left. For instance, on the Right one must not tilt at *any* sacred cows, even if they are unorthodox sacred cows, for the sanctity of such cows is more important than the truth of any doctrine or idea' (letter to Nicky Mariano, 7 November 1957 in Davenport-Hines, 2006). The nuclear deterrent remains one of those sacred cows. Nevertheless, Trident has its sceptics within the Party and among communities that traditionally vote conservative, including senior figures within the Army, Air Force and indeed parts of the Navy that no longer have interests in nuclear deterrence and would prefer scarce resources to be spent on conventional weaponry relevant to them. George Osborne, the Chancellor of the Exchequer and reputedly a sceptic himself, ensured that the costs of Trident's replacement would impinge on the armed services' interests when requiring that nuclear deterrence would have to be funded out of the defence budget in future, placing it in competition with other military needs. Previously, spending on nuclear weapons had been financed out of special, often secret, budgets.

Trident and the Referendum's Early Aftermath

If the referendum results in a No vote to independence, especially by a large margin, the Ministry of Defence will assume that 'the Scottish question' has ceased to exist, probably for a generation. It can forge ahead with Trident's replacement, keeping Faslane and Coulport as the UK's principal nuclear bases. Were another referendum conceivable within a decade or two, the replacement project would be so far advanced and embedded by that stage that threats of removal within the system's lifetime would no longer be meaningful. Whitehall could relax.

There would remain the possibility of UK government elected in 2015, whether Labour, Conservative or another coalition, deciding that Trident's replacement with an equivalent system could no longer be justified, given high opportunity costs and changing military needs. In response, either the UK could abandon nuclear deterrence, or retain it but adopt a cheaper system, perhaps using cruise missiles launched from aircraft or attack submarines. Studies carried out recently within the Cabinet Office, hitherto a sop to restive Liberal Democrats within the coalition, might then acquire significance. The most likely outcome is still that the Trident replacement project would survive, especially if the international security environment became more precarious. An unfriendly Russia, assertive China and nuclearised Iran would make it more difficult for any government to abandon Trident, whatever the relevance or irrelevance of a British nuclear deterrent to balancing their power and countering their threats.

If the referendum delivered a Yes vote, the situation would immediately be different. It is likely that negotiation of a framework treaty, setting out the two governments' broad understandings and objectives across the main policy fields, would be an early priority. The Scottish government seems to expect the treaty's conclusion before the Scottish parliamentary election in May 2016, 18 months after the referendum. This may be fanciful in light of the intervening UK general election (probably May 2015), the possible change of party or parties in government in London, the predominately English preoccupation with Europe, and the political shock and confusion that would probably follow a Scottish vote for independence. Come what may, a framework agreement would be required sooner rather than later to settle internal affairs and begin addressing external relations, including UN recognition and EU membership.

The important point is that, de facto before de jure, Trident's future would become the subject of negotiation between two states and would no longer be London's sole prerogative. The bases' legal and operational status, and the terms under which the nuclear submarines functioned and navigated the Clyde (which would become Scottish territorial waters down past Arran) in any interim period, would have to be determined in what would essentially be an international negotiation. The various obligations attending Scotland's necessary membership of the Nuclear Non-Proliferation Treaty would also have to be taken into account. The basing of a nuclear weapon state's entire nuclear force on the territory of a non-nuclear weapon state would be unprecedented, although not illegal under NPT rules provided that the nuclear weapon state retained total control over the weapons. NPT member states would expect Scotland and the rest of the UK to establish clearly the political terms under which the latter's nuclear force would be based in Scotland, and to determine the precise boundaries beyond which the international safeguarding of nuclear materials and facilities (a requirement of NPT non-nuclear weapon states) would not extend in Scotland. All told, it is unimaginable that the UK/rUK government and Parliament could approve the replacement project's entry to 'Main Gate' without agreement with Edinburgh on a raft of issues.

How long this would take, and whether agreement satisfying both sides could be reached, is anyone's guess. It seems unlikely that this issue would alone be allowed to frustrate conclusion of the required framework treaty. But it could still be very problematic. The Scottish government could not be seen reaching an agreement keeping the door ajar to Trident's permanent stay in Scotland, whatever the rewards on offer. The phasing of Trident's removal would be up for negotiation, not the fact of its removal. However, the cost of holding to a tough line could be very high if it soured the atmosphere in other negotiations and invited retaliation. Yet faced with a reasonably conciliatory Scottish government, the government in London would still be in difficulty since any departure from the Scottish nuclear base in less than 40 years (Trident's expected lifetime) would entail opening new bases in England or Wales. Besides an extra cost running to many billions of pounds, no government could be sure from the vantage point of 2015 or 2016 that its best efforts could deliver the required bases. Indeed, the current mood music emanating from Whitehall is that alternatives, especially to Coulport, do not exist outside Scotland.

Even if Trident's lengthy stay in Scotland could be negotiated, would the UK government and Nuclear Navy be comfortable operating the nuclear force out of another independent state? Probably not. The extent of cooperation required from the Scottish government, and the demands that London would inevitably face for consultation on safety and other matters, including operational matters, would be much greater than under devolution.

The Ministry of Defence has been tight lipped on how its nuclear policies would be affected by a yes vote in the referendum. Its response in January 2013 to the Scottish Affairs Committee's report on Trident emphasised the costs to Scotland, in terms of lost employment and charges for relocation, whilst saying little about the prospects for opening new bases in England or Wales (French and American options were ruled out), including the processes by which sites would be selected and approved. If the Ministry is looking unflinchingly at the political circumstances that could follow independence, it will probably be having a fit of anxiety. It will realise that it risks losing political control over the replacement project, its cost and implementation becoming inherently unpredictable.

Conclusion

The momentum behind large technological projects and the inertia attached to infrastructures developed over decades should never be under-estimated. Add the deep rooted belief in elite circles that the possession of nuclear weapons protects the UK's security and its great power status (belief is the correct word, since neither attainment is open to empirical demonstration), and it would be a courageous UK government that dislodged Trident from its moorings. Equally, it would be courageous, some would say foolhardy, for the government of an independent Scotland to insist on stripping its much more powerful southern neighbour of a cherished capability.

In the debate about Scotland and Trident, most attention has focused on the wisdom and practicality of the Scottish government's proposal to remove the nuclear force from its territory. There are many awkward questions, few of which will receive clear answers before the referendum. Among them, how tolerant would the Scottish people and political parties be of Trident's stay in Scotland, for how long and under what terms? What would be the precise costs and benefits to Scotland associated with Trident's removal? What would be international attitudes towards a Scotland that insisted on Trident's eviction if there is nowhere else for it to go?

However, there are also many awkward questions for the government in London, few of which will again receive clear answers before the referendum. What price would it be prepared to pay for permission to retain the nuclear bases? Is there any other part of the UK that would accept a nuclear base – especially a Coulport-equivalent – in its vicinity without a political fight? Would the Ministry of Defence in London, and its American partner, be happy in any circumstance to deploy the entire nuclear force from a base in another sovereign state?

For the SNP, getting rid of Trident has long been proclaimed as one of the main prizes of sovereignty. For Trident's friends, among them members of a Conservative Party likely to benefit electorally from Scotland's independence, its protection is an important reason for fighting to preserve the Union. Come what may, Trident will remain a potent issue as 2014 approaches, its fate thereafter beyond prediction.

References

Chalmers, M. and Walker, W. (2001), *Uncharted Waters: The UK, Nuclear Weapons and the Scottish Question*, Tuckwell Press.

Davenport-Hines, R. (ed.) (2006), *Letters from Oxford: Hugh Trevor Roper to Bernard Berenson*, Phoenix.

Scotland and the United Kingdom

AILEEN MCHARG

*The Scottish Executive are in hock to new Labour in London ...
London Labour's latest tactic is to bind the Scottish Executive into
Westminster's agenda, through Joint Ministerial Committees.*

(Alex Salmond, quoted in Hazell, 2000: 164)

Intergovernmental Relations: Risks and Opportunities

Whatever independence means in the modern world, it is clear that it does not mean isolation. An independent Scotland would be enmeshed in a web of international relationships, ranging from *ad hoc* bilateral or multilateral treaties to membership of a host of regional and global organisations, with differing functions and formal decision-making competences, impinging on national sovereignty to greater or lesser degrees. These would probably include the European Union (EU), the United Nations, the World Trade Organisation, NATO, the Council of Europe, the Organisation for Economic Co-operation and Development, and the Commonwealth, amongst others.

Nevertheless, as our nearest neighbour and major trading partner, Scotland would be likely to retain a particularly close relationship with the rest of the United Kingdom (rUK). This would arise for a number of reasons. First, it is likely that there would be a number of transitional issues requiring ongoing negotiation, and perhaps joint administration, for some time after independence. The more quickly independence takes place – and it has been suggested that negotiations could be concluded in time for the next Scottish Parliament elections in May 2016 (Scottish Government, 2012: para. 4.5) – the longer the transitional period is likely to last. Secondly, there would be potential policy 'spillovers' or 'externalities' suggesting a need for continuing co-operation and co-ordination. Spillovers occur where policies adopted in one country impact upon another, for example, by creating new problems to be addressed, or by constrain-

173

ing the options practically available to it, and could arise, for instance, in relation to environmental pollution, public health, economic or social policy, immigration, national security, or the criminal law. Such potential spillovers would no doubt be of greater significance for Scotland than for the rUK, given its much smaller size, and therefore weaker ability to absorb external costs. But they would not be negligible for the rUK either, for instance, in relation to cross-border pollution or public health threats and, perhaps most significantly, border control and national security.

Thirdly, more extensive intergovernmental relations (IGR) would be required if, as the SNP proposes, some elements of union with the rUK were to be retained after independence. These might include: a single energy market; a common currency; the monarchy; defence co-operation; a single financial regulator; a common travel area (and therefore joint border controls); joint citizenship and reciprocal voting rights; a 'social union'; co-ordinated transport networks; and a variety of shared services and scientific, technical and research programmes. Again, Scotland might have more to gain from on-going co-operation in these areas than the rUK. However, there are many examples worldwide of co-operation between neighbouring countries, and particularly close co-operation can be expected between countries which were formerly united. For instance, since their so-called 'velvet divorce' in 1993, the Czech Republic and Slovakia have enjoyed dense and regular interactions, and remain entangled on a variety of technical and practical issues, such as sharing some foreign embassies. Nearer to home, and despite a much messier break up, the UK and the Irish Republic have retained close links ever since the latter became independent in 1922, including a common travel area and labour market, citizenship and voting rights, and rights for Irish citizens to hold public office and join the armed forces in the UK. Moreover, since the 1998 Good Friday Agreement, there has been extensive and formalised intergovernmental co-operation both between the Irish and Northern Irish governments, in the form of the North-South Ministerial Council (NSMC), which supervises a number of joint implementation bodies, and with the UK more generally, via the British-Irish Council (BIC) and British-Irish Intergovernmental Conference (BIIC).

Finally, and irrespective of any formal linkages, co-operation is likely to arise between an independent Scotland and the rUK because of common interests and shared outlooks. Their geographical proximity, common language, and the legacy of union in the form of similar laws, institutions, political and cultural attitudes, and common interest groups, are likely to make the two countries natural allies on many issues, as well as to produce pressures for policy convergence.

Of course, many aspects of the future relationship between Scotland and the rUK will be dealt with through one-off negotiations, without any need for on-going co-operation (citizenship and voting rights, for example). In many other instances EU rules and decision-making procedures (assuming that Scotland becomes, and the rUK remains, a member) will be sufficient to deal with policy overspills and ensure necessary harmonisation, although this will both facilitate and constrain the degree of integration between them, since EU non-discrimination rules require any special treatment for nationals of one Member State to be extended to those of all others. Even so, EU membership is unlikely to remove the need for more specific IGR between Scotland and the rUK. For instance, the Czech Republic and Slovakia co-operate *within* the EU, along with Poland and Hungary, in the so-called Visegrád group. This group is in fact one of several more or less formal regional groupings within Europe, each with their own intergovernmental machinery – the Benelux Union, the Franco-German Alliance, the Nordic Co-operation and the Baltic Co-operation.

Effective management of the relationship with the rUK is therefore likely to be crucial to the success of independence; to the ability of Scotland to exercise meaningful control over her destiny, rather than simply operating in the shadow of her larger and more powerful neighbour. At the same time, though, IGR poses a threat to the coherence of the independence project in two senses. First, IGR is an area in which it is notoriously difficult to exert democratic control. As we know from the EU context, as well as from experience of IGR under devolution and in federal systems, intergovernmental decision-making tends to strengthen the hand of governments at the expense of parliaments. Paradoxically, therefore, insofar as Scottish independence is justified in terms of popular sovereignty, there is a risk that extensive IGR might simply produce a new form of democratic deficit. Secondly, there is also a risk that IGR becomes a vehicle for re-integration. Again, as we know from experience in the EU and other regional groupings such as the Nordic Council, there is a tendency towards 'competence creep', as spillovers from one policy area to another create pressures for additional harmonisation. In fact, IGR is the point at which the boundaries between independence and other potential constitutional futures for Scotland, such as sovereignty-association or confederation, become blurred. Hence, depending upon the nature and extent of IGR, we might end up with what looks more like a recasting of the union than independence in any meaningful sense.

In the event of independence, IGR arrangements would therefore need to be developed which would maximise Scottish influence in areas of common interest, but minimise the potential democratic deficit and the risk of unwanted assimilation. There are already mechanisms in place to handle *intra*-governmental relations within the UK between devolved and central governments, in the form of Joint Ministerial Councils (JMC) alongside, as mentioned above, more genuinely *inter*-governmental arrangements encompassing Ireland. Although the issues to be dealt with under devolution are not the same as those which would arise after independence, and IGR would proceed upon a different legal basis, these existing mechanisms could nevertheless form the basis of post-independence IGR. They have, however, been extensively criticised. Accordingly, drawing upon experience under devolution, as well as lessons from other regional groupings, the remainder of this chapter outlines the choices which would have to be made in relation to the handling of IGR, and seeks to identify the approaches which are likely to be most successful.

Developing Machinery for Intergovernmental Relations

A number of decisions would have to be made when deciding how best to conduct IGR with the rUK:

- Should relations take place on an ad hoc basis as issues arise, or should there be provision for routine interaction and co-operation between the two governments?

- Should IGR be conducted informally, or be placed on a formal footing? What would formal IGR machinery look like, and on what principles would it operate? Should it be legally binding or not? Should there be separate bodies for specific areas of co-operation or general institutions, or both?

- What functions should IGR arrangements perform: information exchange; consultation; negotiation; dispute resolution; executive functions?

- Who should be involved in IGR? Should it involve parliaments as well as governments? Should relations be conducted bilaterally between Scotland and rUK, or on a multi-lateral basis for the whole of the British Isles?
- When should arrangements be established (pre- or post-independence), and by what process?
- What arrangements should there be for publicity and scrutiny?

Maximising Scottish Influence

Three factors seem likely to be particularly relevant in ensuring that an independent Scotland is able to make its voice heard in matters of common interest. The first and most important is the establishment of formal mechanisms for intergovernmental co-operation. This is suggested by experience under devolution, where a highly informal approach to IGR is widely believed to have strengthened the hand of the UK government at the expense of the devolved administrations. There is, in fact, a double element of informality in the current arrangements. To begin with, they are based purely on a Memorandum of Understanding (MOU) between the four administrations, supplemented by a series of overarching and bilateral 'concordats'. According to the MOU, it is merely 'a statement of political intent, and should not be interpreted as a binding agreement. It does not create legal obligations between the parties.' (Cabinet Office, 2012: para 2) In addition, IGR in practice are considerably more informal: the principles and procedures laid down by the concordats are rarely referred to, and the formal decision-making forum established by the MOU – the JMC – meets infrequently. Indeed, the JMC plenary did not meet at all between 2002 and 2008. Although formality has increased somewhat since the SNP came to power, IGR are still conducted largely on an *ad hoc* and bilateral basis, enabling the UK government to determine the extent to which and the terms on which discussion takes place. The devolved administrations have no means of ensuring that they are consulted or their views taken into account and it is clear that, on some occasions at least, their interests are simply overlooked by UK policy-makers.

In any case it seems inevitable that IGR will be more formal after independence. There is an instructive contrast between the informality of *intra*-governmental relations within the UK, and the much greater formality of the *inter*-governmental institutions involving the Irish government, which have a statutory underpinning in the Northern Ireland Act 1998, and indeed have constitutional recognition in the Irish Republic. The factors which have supported informal relations under devolution – in particular civil service links and party affiliation – are likely to be weakened, albeit not entirely destroyed by independence. At the same time, the tendency for the rUK government to ignore Scottish interests is likely to be become more pronounced. It would therefore seem to be desirable to establish well-defined and legally binding expectations as to how IGR will be conducted, including rights to receive information and call meetings, clear decision-making processes and criteria, a standing secretariat and a regular programme of business. While resort to judicial or other third party enforcement is unlikely to be necessary, a legal underpinning will be important in signalling the seriousness of each party's commitment to intergovernmental co-operation (and will in any event be necessary to the extent that cross-border institutions have specific executive, and not merely consultative, functions).

A second factor which seems likely to increase Scottish influence is the existence of general forum for intergovernmental co-operation, and not merely functionally-specific bodies, although these will probably be required as well. Since the two governments are likely to have different priorities and concerns, a general forum increases the scope for mutually advantageous trade-offs, as well as increasing flexibility to deal with unexpected issues, and facilitating political oversight of any cross-border implementation bodies or joint services. It is, however, important that any such body has genuine business to transact. Gallagher argues that, with the exception of the JMC (Europe) which has met regularly because of the need to agree a common UK line on EU matters where these impinge upon devolved competences, the JMC machinery simply 'ran out of steam [because] no one knew what they were for' (Gallagher, 2012: 201). Nevertheless, despite initial doubts that there was a real role for the BIC to perform, it has grown in significance and influence, acquiring a permanent secretariat in 2007 and expanding its areas of work.

One reason for this appears to be that the devolved governments see it as a more equitable forum than the JMC. It operates by consensus amongst all its members (the British and Irish governments, the three devolved governments, plus representatives from the Channel Islands and the Isle of Man), with a rotating chair, and unlike the JMC is not therefore dominated by the UK government. This suggests that a final way of increasing Scotland's influence (or, perhaps more accurately, diluting the rUK's influence) would be to conduct IGR on a multilateral rather than a purely bilateral basis. On the other hand, it seems unlikely that a multilateral approach would be feasible in all circumstances. Even under devolution, it seems that there are a limited number of issues on which the devolved administrations have common interests. Moreover, the degree of continuing integration with the rUK that the SNP appears to envisage may be far greater than the Irish government is prepared to contemplate.

Securing Effective Accountability

A major criticism of the current IGR arrangements concerns their lack of democratic oversight. A number of issues arise here. The first relates to the way in which the MOU and concordats were developed, which occurred late in the devolution process and entirely behind closed doors. There was a formal vote in the Scottish Parliament to endorse the arrangements, but no detailed scrutiny, and no Parliamentary involvement at all at Westminster. It is clear that the lack of political attention to IGR helped to perpetuate UK dominance because it meant that the MOU and concordats largely simply codified pre-devolution arrangements for liaison between the Scottish, Welsh and Northern Ireland Offices and other UK government departments.

No doubt there will be a similar temptation – and pressure from the rUK government – to continue with pre-existing IGR arrangements as far as possible, especially in areas of transitional co-operation, but this should be resisted. Independence provides the opportunity for a clean break and to put IGR on a footing more appropriate to relationships between sovereign governments. This suggests both that IGR arrangements ought to be treated as a key part of the post-referendum negotiations over the terms of separation, and that they should be subject to the approval of both the Scottish and UK Parliaments. It might be objected that this would involve committing a government which does not yet exist. However, as argued above, the terms of post-independence engagement with the rUK are a central determinant of the nature of the constitutional change which independence will involve and therefore they should not be regarded as purely a matter for the executive. Nevertheless, it might be appropriate for IGR arrangements to be subject to early review by the new Scottish Parliament. Indeed, the House of Lords Constitution Committee recommended that the MOU and concordats should be made for a fixed-term only (House of Lords, 2002: para 43), and arguably the same should apply to post-independence arrangements.

The second issue in relation to democratic oversight concerns the ability of the Scottish Government to make binding commitments in inter-governmental fora without Parliamentary involvement. The drafting of a new post-independence constitution for Scotland provides an opportunity to place foreign affairs – currently an aspect of the royal prerogative – on a more satisfactory legal footing. For instance, it may be appropriate to constitutionally entrench and to strengthen the principle currently contained in the Constitutional Reform and Governance Act 2010 that treaties are not normally to be ratified if the House of Commons objects. In addition, the Scottish Parliament may wish to adopt, and legally codify, a version of the so-called 'scrutiny reserve' which prevents the UK government agreeing to proposals in the EU Council of Ministers before the relevant UK parliamentary committees have scrutinised them.

A more radical proposal would be to develop inter-parliamentary institutions alongside intergovernmental ones. For instance, the Nordic Council began in 1952 as a forum for inter-parliamentary co-operation, with delegates drawn from the domestic parliaments of each of the member states or territories (Denmark, Finland, Iceland, and Norway, plus the Faroe Islands Greenland, and Åland). It was not until 1971 that the Nordic Council of Ministers was established, and the parliamentary body still remains the source of most co-operative initiatives. By comparison, inter-parliamentary links within the British Isles are currently very under-developed. A British-Irish Parliamentary Body was established in 1990, which was renamed the British-Irish Parliamentary Assembly and its membership expanded to mirror that of the BIC in the wake of the Good Friday Agreement. However, it is a very low profile body – it does not, for instance, have its own website – which has failed to make a significant impact. It is, moreover, disconnected from the intergovernmental machinery. Proposals have been made that it should develop a closer relationship with the BIC and exercise political oversight over it. However, it seems unlikely that it will ever come to resemble the Nordic Council, given the different political traditions in the Nordic countries, where executives are much less dominant than they are in the UK and Ireland.

The final issue, then, is the ability of national parliaments to scrutinise effectively the conduct of IGR, and particularly to oversee the work of any joint implementation bodies. Current IGR arrangements are seriously deficient in this respect. One significant problem is access to information. One of the principles on which the MOU is based is confidentiality, stating that '[e]ach administration can only expect to receive information if it treats such information with appropriate discretion.' (Cabinet Office, 2012: para 12). In addition, information is exempt from disclosure under both the UK and Scottish freedom of information legislation if it would prejudice (or substantially prejudice, in the case of the Scottish Act) relations between administrations within the UK (Freedom of Information Act 2000 (FOIA), s.28; Freedom of Information (Scotland) Act 2002 (FOISA), s.28). Although communiqués have been issued after each JMC meeting since 2010, as well as an annual report, these are so brief as to be virtually useless. The annual report for 2011–12, for instance, was only three pages long. In addition, there has been a lack of parliamentary interest in IGR. There is no committee in the Scottish Parliament with responsibility for scrutinising IGR, and arrangements for UK wide bodies to be held to account by the Parliament for their activities in Scotland are limited and haphazard. The Calman Commission concluded that '[t]he near complete absence of scrutiny of intergovernmental relations at present is indefensible.' (Commission on Scottish Devolution, 2009: para 4.190)

Access to information is likely to remain an issue after independence: international relations is also an exempt category under current freedom of information legislation (FOIA, s.27; FOISA, s.32) and likely to remain so, since some degree of confidentiality in intergovernmental negotiations is no doubt necessary. Nevertheless, any blanket requirement of confidentiality should be rejected, and greater efforts should be made to ensure appropriate publicity and oversight. More formal IGR by itself is likely to help in this regard, since it will make it easier to ensure that intergovernmental contacts are properly logged and minuted. The NSMC and the BIC also provide a model for parliamentary involvement which could usefully be emulated. Under the Northern Ireland Act 1998 (ss.52A and 52C), the First Minister and Deputy First Minister are required to provide advance notification to the Northern Ireland Assembly of the date and agenda of each NSMC or BIC meeting, as well as the names of those attending, and participating ministers are required as soon as reasonably practicable afterwards to report (usually orally) to the Assembly, thereby ensuring a routine opportunity for debate.

Keeping Integration in Check

The last consideration to bear in mind when developing IGR arrangements is to ensure that they do not take on a life of their own, becoming a vehicle for unwanted reintegration with the rUK, and thereby threatening Scotland's newly reacquired sovereignty. The risk is likely to be greater the more formal the institutions that are established, the stronger their decision-making powers, and the greater the extent to which they enjoy their own democratic legitimacy. The obvious example is the EU, but the NSMC and the BIC have also been described as 'confederal' institutions (O'Leary, 1999: 23–27), and explicitly compared to the EU. Indeed, suspicious that the NSMC would be a means of centralising governing authority within the island of Ireland, Unionist politicians initially boycotted its meetings, and insisted on the establishment of the BIC as a counter-balancing force to strengthen ties with the UK.

The issue here, though, is perhaps not so much the extent of continued co-operation with the rUK as the spirit in which it is conducted. If Scotland does become independent, many of those who voted for it are likely to have done so on pragmatic rather than ideological grounds, and so may support extensive continuing ties with rUK. Tierney usefully distinguishes between 'partnership co-operation' and 'assimilationist co-operation' (Tierney, 2007: 745), and it is the latter rather than the former which is to be avoided. Thus, the Nordic countries have engaged in extensive co-operation, which has increased far beyond that initially envisaged, yet without impinging on national sovereignty. Similarly, the NSMC joint implementation bodies have not engaged in the sort of 'technocratic entrepreneurship' (Tannam, 2006: 420) that might have been expected, because the expansion of north-south co-operation into new policy areas has been effectively held in political check.

A variety of factors might be relevant in preventing unwanted assimilation, including:

- the decision rules adopted by intergovernmental bodies – i.e., a requirement for decisions to be made unanimously
- the topics chosen for intergovernmental co-operation: confining co-operation to low profile and non-contentious issues in the Nordic region helps to maintain consensus

- multilateral rather than bilateral IGR: in the EU, widening member-ship is often seen as an antidote to deepening integration
- the attitudes of the parties: a clean break with IGR under devolu-tion may help to deter casual assimilationism, especially on the part of the rUK government

In fact it is the attitude of the rUK which is likely to be the major obstacle to the development of equitable IGR post-independence. Unlike the Nordic Council or the NSMC, where the participants are roughly equal in size, there is an inescapable power disparity between Scotland and the rUK. This has always been a fundamental problem for Scotland, and independ-ence cannot alter this basic geo-political fact.

Conclusion

Keating argues Scotland has long faced a strategic dilemma within the Union: a trade-off between self-government or influence at the centre (Keating, 2009: 171). To its supporters, independence offers a more sat-isfactory solution to that dilemma than the *status quo*, promising a new era of effective co-operation with the rUK on the basis of equality and mutual respect. Opponents sometimes focus on the worst-case scenario, in which the rUK simply refuses to engage in IGR and Scotland is forced to cope with the consequences of decisions taken without reference to its interests. In reality, this seems an unlikely prospect. However, as has been argued in this chapter, IGR do pose a double risk: of creating a force for re-integration which is subject to limited democratic control. If independ-ence means dissolving the parliamentary union in order to replace it with a governmental union, it is not clear that it will represent a constitutional advance.

References

Cabinet Office (2012), *Devolution: Memorandum of Understanding and Supplementary Agreements*.

Commission on Scottish Devolution (2009), *Serving Scotland Better: Scotland and the United Kingdom in the 21st Century*.

Gallagher, J. (2012), 'Intergovernmental Relations in the UK: Co-operation, Competition and Constitutional Change', *British Journal of Politics and International Relations*.

Hazell, R. (2000), 'Intergovernmental Relations: Whitehall Rules OK?, in Hazell, R. (ed.), *The State and the Nations: The First Year of Devolution in the UK*, Imprint Academic.

House of Lords Select Committee on the Constitution (2002), *Devolution: Inter-Institutional Relations in the United Kingdom*, Second Report 2002–03, HL Paper 28.

Keating, M. (2009), *The Independence of Scotland: Self-Government and the Shifting Politics of Union*, Oxford University Press.

O'Leary, B. (1999), 'The 1998 British-Irish Agreement: Power Sharing Plus', *Scottish Affairs*.

Scottish Government (2012), *Your Referendum: Your Choice*.

Tannam, E. (2006), 'The EU 'Model' and Administrative Co-operation: the Case of Northern Ireland and the Republic of Ireland', *Public Administration*.

Tierney, S. (2007), 'Giving With One Hand: Scottish Devolution Within a Unitary State', *International Journal of Constitutional Law*.

Scotland and the EU

NOREEN BURROWS

THE THEME/SLOGAN of 'Scotland in Europe' has been part and parcel of the SNP independence project since the late 1980s. It is synonymous with the leadership of Alex Salmond and the modernisation of the SNP. It is an approach which seeks to reassure Scottish voters that a split from the UK will not result in an isolated and inward looking independent country and seeks to ensure the international community that Scotland will remain firmly linked with our major trading parties and political allies. It is based on economic arguments about where Scotland's interests lie in terms of its markets and philosophical arguments about the place of Scotland in the world. The current SNP position is that, following a vote for independence, Scotland would seek to open negotiations for a continuity of membership of the EU, including a continuity of current UK opt-outs on the Euro, the Schengen agreement and the UK budget rebate (Sturgeon, 2013).

To date the discussion has been dominated by legal and constitutional issues rather than by questions of substance. First was the issue of whether any legal advice had been sought or given in relation to the legal status of an independent Scotland. The admission that the Scottish Government had not in fact sought or received such legal advice only came to light after threats of legal action had been made to obtain sight of any advice that had been given. Then came a number of statements, including that from the President of the European Commission, that an independent Scotland would have to apply for membership as a new state although he did not specify if this would be before or after actual independence had been attained. The European Commission has also stated that it would not provide detailed legal advice unless asked for by an existing member state of the European Union and the UK has taken the view that it will not ask for such advice from the Commission until such time as advice is needed, that is, should there be a vote for independence in the referendum.

The UK government has published a report as part of its Scotland analysis programme on the legal and constitutional implications of Scotland's independence (UK Government, 2013). This report concludes that Scotland, on leaving the UK, 'would become an entirely new state' and the rUK would continue retaining its existing rights and obligations in international law. The report analyses the position from principles of public international law and draws a distinction between a continuing state which remains in the same legal position as the original state, in our case the UK, and the new state, in our case Scotland. A continuing state would continue its membership of the EU but the new state would need to negotiate its position and seek agreement from other states on its continued membership of the EU.

An alternative view has been proposed by Judge David Edward, formerly judge in the European Court of Justice. He argues that principles of public international law would not necessarily apply to questions of membership of the EU although they would apply to membership of other international organisations (Edward, 2012). Arguing from the perspective of EU law itself, he takes the view that EU law is a new legal order of international law and any question in relation to Scotland's continued membership should be found in the sprit and scheme of the EU treaties rather than in general principles of international law.

Pointing to the obligation to negotiate an orderly withdrawal where a Member State decides to withdraw from the EU in accordance with Article 50 TEU, he suggests that an orderly transition would be required when a part of a state exercises the right of self-determination and secedes from the state that is a member of the EU. He bases his argument on the principles of EU law of good faith, sincere cooperation and solidarity. From a practical perspective he also points to the existence of multiple existing reciprocal rights and duties which would automatically end should Scotland cease to be considered a member of the EU. His conclusion is that the EU institutions, EU Member States, including the UK, as well as Scotland are obliged under EU law to enter into negotiations prior to independence taking effect. He further suggests that an accession treaty would not be required, rather an amendment to the existing treaty regime.

So the lawyers are not agreed on the constitutional issue and the question is not settled by reference to the existing treaties which are silent on the specific point of what happens when part of an existing Member State seeks independence from that state. In truth the matter of how the whole issue will be taken forward will be decided by the European Council and it will be a political and not a legal decision. The European Council, composed of all the Heads of State or Government of all the EU members, together with its President and the President of the European Commission, is the body responsible for providing the general political direction and policy of the EU (Art 15 TEU). It is also the body to which applications for membership are addressed (Art 49 TEU) and the body which would set out the guidelines governing the withdrawal of a Member State who expressed a wish to withdraw from the Union (Art 50 TEU). It would be for the Council therefore to determine the guidelines to be followed in the event of a part of a Member State seceding and at the same time expressing a desire to remain within the EU. In order to avoid the negative practical consequences outlined by David Edward, it would be in the interests of all parties to deal with the issue at an early stage and it would be for the UK government to request that the matter be placed on the Council's agenda.

How the Council will deal with the request cannot be predicted in advance. There will be some states in the Council with a particular interest, such as Spain or Belgium who face similar demands from within for independence, Catalonia and Flanders. These states may seek to require that Scotland applies afresh for membership arguing that a dangerous precedent might be set if Scotland is permitted to continue its membership without following what they would perceive as due process. Other states, who have themselves become recently independent, may take a more relaxed view. The position of the UK government will be crucial. The UK Government has agreed to work in good faith with the Scottish Government and has indicated it will respect the outcome of the vote. In light of a vote for independence the UK should therefore present the Council with an argument for minimal change and a smooth transition as a result of Scotland exercising the right of self-determination, a principle of international law accepted by all the Member states of the EU. The Council traditionally works by consensus so the UK would not be outvoted in the Council but may have to accept compromises. The outcome will be guidelines setting out the process and the criteria for Scottish membership, whether by a new application or by negotiations for continuity of membership.

Where a state applies to become a member of the EU, negotiations are based on the Copenhagen criteria which are guidelines drawn up by the Council. A new member of the EU requires to demonstrate that it has democratic institutions which support human rights; it has a functioning market economy and that it accepts the obligations of membership of the EU. It also has to show that it has incorporated the existing body of EU law, often known as the *acquis communautaire*, into its own domestic legislation. These will presumably be the kind of guidelines applicable to Scotland. There is no reason to suppose that any additional level of obligations would be required to be met. However, as noted, the Scottish government has indicated that it wishes to retain the existing UK opt-outs on the Euro, the Schengen area and the rebate.

Until Scotland achieves an independent status it will not be a Member State of the EU. Negotiations in the Council and elsewhere will therefore be led by UK government ministers and UK officials. Presumably the Scottish government will seek a strengthened memorandum of understanding with the UK government on how negotiations will be conducted and who would be involved at all levels. Scotland would not have an independent right to negotiate or a vote in any proceedings on the negotiations. Relations with the UK government would therefore be crucial in this negotiation period.

All of this seems to be relatively straightforward. However, the referendum on Scottish independence is taking place in turbulent times in Europe and, although it is impossible to predict the future, we can at least spell out the known unknowns. Assuming that Scotland votes in favour of independence in the 2014 referendum with a view to attaining independent status in 2016 and continued membership of the EU, what will have happened in the intervening years elsewhere? European and domestic politics will not have stood still to wait the outcome of the Scottish vote.

In the UK, there will have been a general election in May 2015. This would be the last occasion when Scottish voters would vote in a UK general election and therefore influence the outcome of the election. It is not inconceivable that the Conservative party will be re-elected or form some kind of coalition with other right wing parties such as UKIP providing a more generally Eurosceptic approach to European politics. David Cameron is on record that he would view an election victory as a mandate for renegotiation of UK membership terms with a view to a referendum on UK membership sometime in 2017. During negotiations on Scotland's membership of the EU, therefore, the UK would also be seeking a very different set of negotiations on the relationship with the rUK and the EU making for a very difficult and potentially conflicting set of negotiations. The Scottish Government would have to take a view on the extent to which it would wish to be part of negotiations which potentially repatriate some powers from the EU to rUK. Nicola Sturgeon is on record that Scotland would be a good European which might suggest a scenario where Scotland would not wish to repatriate powers leading to a two-tier approach to the EU within the current UK. The negotiations in the Council might become bogged down and it will be important to separate out the key issues. Nicola Sturgeon has certainly tried to put some clear tartan water between the UK and Scottish government positions on the EU indicating that the SNP at least is not seeking renegotiation of terms.

However Scottish voters might be influenced by developments in the rUK. In the past there has been little evidence to show that Scottish voters are more pro-European than their English or Welsh neighbours although given the recent rise in Euroscepticism amongst English voters this may change. In the situation where negotiations result in repatriation of powers or further opt-outs for the UK, Scottish voters may also demand a referendum on EU membership or for renegotiated terms. Scottish voters will not have a say in the 2017 referendum if Scotland is by then independent. It is not clear whether the enthusiasm of the Scottish government for EU membership reflects the views of the Scottish electorate now and how the Scottish electorate would react to rUK events.

Elsewhere in Europe there are also signs of possible impending changes. Mr De Wever, the elected Mayor of Antwerp, is on record as saying that his centre right New Flemish Alliance will use the 2014 general election in Belgium as a test for a mandate for his party seeking to create a confederation in Belgium composed of two separate parts. Such a constitutional challenge would form an additional layer of complications for the EU and it is likely that some form of common approach would have to be taken to Scotland and Flanders in how negotiations are conducted for continuing membership although the agenda for negotiations would be different in both cases, for example in respect of the Euro. In Spain, Catalonia is still seeking an independence referendum and it may be that such a referendum takes place some time between 2014 and 2016 creating a further layer of complexity. One of these three scenarios will be the precedent for any further EU approach, irrespective of their very different constitutional histories, but having three possible secessionist scenarios will require the EU Member States to come to a common view on how to approach this new political reality.

Within the EU itself there may well be changes as a result of the Euro crisis. If the answer to the crisis is more Europe then Treaty reform is back on the agenda with possible future consequences in terms of further differential rates of integration. At the moment there is reluctance for Treaty reform in light of possible rejection of reforms by European voters. The proposals for a European Constitutional Treaty had been stopped in their tracks by French and Dutch voters in referenda leading to the compromise of the Lisbon Treaty, itself subject to keen scrutiny by the German constitutional court. Any revised treaties might be subject to further rejection by European voters, including UK voters, since the European Union Act 2011 requires a UK wide referendum if new powers are to be transferred to the EU. Changes at the EU level are therefore likely to be potentially hugely significant.

These political factors form the background to negotiations within the Council. They create uncertainty as to the likely outcome of negotiations. However, whether Scotland has to apply afresh or whether continuity of membership is agreed it is almost certain that Scotland will have to demonstrate how it meets the Copenhagen criteria outlined above.

If Scotland decides on independence there are a range of issues to be settled which indirectly or directly impact on questions of EU membership. The Scottish government has indicated that it would foresee a written constitution for Scotland and, assuming that the constitution follows the examples of constitutions from other democratic countries, we can assume that it will set out the democratic institutions that will replace or complement existing institutions. We have a Scottish Parliament now but we may wish to reform the current parliamentary structures in a new Scotland, for example with the introduction of a revising chamber. We have a court structure, but with a written constitution we might introduce a constitutional court. What it will be necessary to demonstrate to our potential EU partners is that the new structures will continue to ensure democratic government in Scotland.

These new structures will also need to ensure that human rights are observed in the new Scotland. Human rights in the UK are supported by a complex web of legislation and institutions. Scotland would need to accede to the European Convention on Human Rights. In the constitution or elsewhere there would need to be provision to ensure that human rights were applied by public authorities and by the courts. The UK Human Rights Act currently performs this function for Scotland so a new Scottish Act would be needed to incorporate the European Convention provisions or a Bill of Rights provided for as part of the Scottish constitution. Equality legislation will be needed to ensure that there is no discrimination on grounds of nationality, race, sex, sexual orientation, age, belief or disability. Once again, an equality clause or clauses in the Scottish constitution might be the way forward in this respect.

Scotland will also need to demonstrate how it will give effect to EU law in its territory. This might be an issue for the constitution with a provision stating that directly effective provisions of EU law are to be given effect by the courts. Alternatively, it might be an issue for the Scottish Parliament to incorporate the EU treaties and secondary legislation into Scots law. At the moment this is affected by a UK Act of Parliament which will cease to apply in Scotland if Scotland becomes independent. The approach to be taken will depend on the constitutional theory underpinning the new Scotland. One approach would be to vest sovereignty in the people rather than in Parliament in which case a constitutional provision is required. If the new Scottish parliamentary institutions inherit parliamentary sovereignty then an Act of the Scottish parliament along the lines of the 1972 European Communities Act would be required.

Scotland would also need to demonstrate that it has fully incorporated EU law at the date of independence if membership is to be effected smoothly and without the need for transitional provisions. At the moment EU law is incorporated into the law of Scotland either by an Act of the Scottish Parliament or Scottish secondary legislation or by UK legislation which has effect in Scotland. The bulk of this legislation is UK legislation. Decisions will have to be made about whether Scotland requires separate legislation, which would mean a deluge of legislation needed in very short order, or whether there could be some umbrella piece of legislation which borrowed the relevant UK law incorporating EU law until such time as there was a need for Scottish legislation for example when amendment was required. Over time therefore, there would be a separate body of law implementing EU provisions in Scotland but in the short term what is currently UK legislation would continue to apply. Where common institutional structures exist as a result of EU requirements, negotiations between the Scottish and rUK governments would be required either to separate out these institutions into component parts or else to establish new Scottish institutions. The Equality and Human Rights Commission would be one such example but there are many more.

On the question of the Euro there has been some debate about whether Scotland would be obliged to adopt the Euro as its currency. The decision to move to a single currency was taken during the negotiations for the Maastricht Treaty which came into force in 1992. That Treaty created an economic and monetary union and laid down criteria to be followed by all Member States in their economic policies. In particular the criteria related to the need for price and exchange rate stability and sound and sustainable public finances. All Member States are members of the economic and monetary union but, at Maastricht, Denmark and the UK opted out of the decision to adopt the Euro as their currency. Since then, Denmark organised a referendum in 2000 on whether to abrogate the opt-out but the government was defeated and so Denmark has retained, like the UK, its opt-out. Sweden, meanwhile, met the convergence criteria by 2003 but in a referendum voted against adopting the Euro. During accession negotiations with new Member States those that met the convergence criteria have joined 17 of the current 27 members use the Euro as their currency. Others are working towards convergence with a view to membership. These states are known as Member States with derogation and Sweden is (nominally) included in that group. At the moment therefore there are four categories of states in regard to the Euro: those who use the Euro; those who have opted out; Sweden which does not have an opt-out but which has not decided to join for domestic political reasons and those countries working towards membership of the Euro but do not yet meet the criteria. A fifth group may yet emerge: those states who may exit the Eurozone for economic or political reasons but who remain as members of the EU.

Those who claim that an independent Scotland would be obliged to adopt the Euro base their arguments on two premises. The first that Scotland would likely to be seen as a new Member State and the second that all new Member States must, by definition, commit to adopting the Euro as their currency. This latter argument is based on the existence of an article in the TEU which states that 'The Union shall establish an economic and monetary union whose currency is the Euro.' (Art 3(4)). All Member States must sign up to this treaty. The argument therefore goes that Scotland as a new state must accept the Euro as its currency.

In fact most new accession states have wished to join the Euro and part of the negotiations with them has been around meeting the conditions necessary for membership and there has certainly been an assumption that new Member States would want to cooperate fully within the EU to the extent envisaged in the Treaties. Where they have been unable to meet the criteria the position of such states is covered by transitional provisions in the TFEU (arts 139–144 TFEU) and this group of States is known in legal terms as Member States with a derogation. They have obligations to adjust their economic and monetary policies so as to position themselves at some time to be able to participate fully in all the arrangements regarding the Euro.

As discussed above, it is not clear if, in the negotiations, Scotland would be treated as a new Member State or as a state having continuing obligations and rights within the EU.

If it were to be treated as a new Member State Scotland would want to argue that there could be a different reading to Art 3(4). It could argue that a new Member State must accept the discipline of being a member of the economic and monetary union without accepting the Euro as its currency. Scotland could point to that fact that new members are required to sign up to the values set out in the Treaty and must respect them (Art 49 TEU) but the principle of an economic and monetary union is not one of the values set out. The values underpinning the Union are respect for human dignity, freedom, democracy and respect for human rights (Art 2). Thus, Scotland could argue, there is no treaty base for forcing new Member States to join the Eurozone. Scotland could point to Sweden as a country without a formal opt-out and perhaps Poland, whose declared aim of joining the Euro in 2012 was diluted given the crisis in the Eurozone. State practice therefore could suggest a more nuanced reading of the Treaty provisions than the hard-liners suggest.

If Scotland were to be treated in the negotiations as a state with continuing obligations and rights, it would of course argue that the Maastricht opt-out of the Euro applies equally to it as to the rest of the UK.

The second major opt-out that the Scottish government has indicated it wishes to retain is the opt-out from the Schengen agreement. The Schengen area is essentially an area without internal border controls and where there is a substantial body of legislation on criminal procedures, immigration and other security matters. Initially developed outside of the EU framework, Shengen is now very much part of EU law. The UK and Ireland opted out of the Schengen area retaining, with the Channel Islands, a common travel area between themselves, maintaining border controls towards individuals coming from other Member States of the EU and all non-EU nationals. In addition, the UK has negotiated that where new legislation is proposed in the area of freedom, security and justice, it may opt-in to such legislation.

Those who argue that Scotland would be a new Member State argue that the retention of this opt-out is untenable. The Lisbon Treaty brought all these aspects into the Treaty framework and a new Member State would be obliged to accept in full the provisions on freedom, security and justice. The logic of this approach is that Scotland would require to dismantle border controls for EU nationals. However, for rUK and Ireland new border controls would be required. From the perspective of the current UK and Ireland this would be a recipe for chaos and either they would be forced to accept Schengen together with the newly independent Scotland or erect costly border controls. It would therefore be in the rUK interest to support a negotiating point whereby a newly independent Scotland could retain that opt-out.

As well as these questions of substance, how Scottish membership of the EU would be effected would be a key point in negotiations. David Edward has suggested that an accession treaty would not be required and an amendment to the Lisbon treaty is all that would be necessary. His argument is based on the assumption that Scotland would be some form of continuing state. Treaty amendments would be required, for example, in the rules governing the institutions, the votes in Council, the number of MEPs and so on. An alternative to this approach would be that a Protocol on Scotland could be attached to the Lisbon Treaty setting out the agreements reached in the European Council which could stay in place until the next revision of the treaties. The third option is that an accession treaty is required. Such a treaty would certainly be required should it be decided that Scotland is to be treated as a new applicant state. Whatever process is agreed, all the Member States will need to ratify treaty amendments, a Scotland Protocol or an accession treaty in line with their own particular constitutional requirements which prove difficult for countries such as Spain or Belgium. In some cases, this might mean a referendum on the issue.

To sum up. If Scotland votes for independence and wishes to continue as a member of the EU it is likely to be the precedent for the way in which the EU approaches such issues providing Catalonia or Flanders have not beaten Scotland to it. As a precedent, the EU Member States will need to decide what would be the framework for negotiations. Does Scotland need to apply afresh or can some continuity of membership be negotiated? If the former is the case, would there need to be interim arrangements maintaining in force all the current complex relationships in force, legal and political and what form would those interim arrangements take? If continuity of membership is the approach taken, what are the guidelines to be followed in terms of procedure and substance? This chapter argues that these are political and not legal questions in the first instance. Agreement will need to be reached in the European Council. This will not be easy given the political context in which negotiations will take place. However there is no alternative to such a political approach. This level of decision-making is and must be political and cannot be dominated or solved by lawyers and legal arguments.

References

Edward, D. (2012), *Scotland and the European Union* posted on Scottish Constitutional Futures Forum, 17 December.

Sturgeon, N. (2013), Speech to the European Policy Centre, 26 February.

UK Government (2013), *Scotland Analysis: devolution and the implications of Scottish independence*, Cm 8554.

Have Scottish dreams diverged from English ideals?

DANNY DORLING

Pity Scotland, so near to England and so far from God.

(Diaz, 2012)

SCOTLAND IS FAR from a model society. Occasionally Scottish social statistics shine, as when comparisons are made with educational inequalities in England, but England is hardly a great comparator in most of these cases. For example, the English have the most iniquitous secondary education system among countries of the rich world. Scotland looks good when compared to England as regards education, but that is no great achievement.

In deciding their future, people in Scotland need to look beyond comparisons with England and towards what Scotland could be, but they should also worry about what it might become. An independent Scotland could be even further from utopia than is Scotland as a subservient partner in the union. At the same time current selfish trends rising within England may spur many on within Scotland to promote independence to insulate themselves from the cold winds of libertarian neo-liberalism blowing up from London.

The world is changing. Recently I booked my place at the 2013 Edinburgh Book Festival. Asked to click a nationality, I had to make a choice, for the first time in my life, between English and Scottish. I have never been English before, but there is nothing at all Scottish about me. Reluctantly I ticked English. Maybe those were the only options in earlier years on that website, but it feels different today. It feels as if there is now a real choice being made.

Education – Is Scotland Aiming Higher than England in Aspiration for all its Children?

Currently 23 per cent of British school educational spending goes on the seven per cent of pupils who are privately educated.

(Reay, 2012)

In Britain as a whole, almost a quarter of spending on secondary school children is spent on just seven per cent of children. This is not the seven per cent who are most disadvantaged, but the seven per cent who almost all start off in life with some of the greatest advantages. Their families tend to be rich or very rich. They tend to be healthy. They also tend to be well ahead at school when they are young, usually attending a state primary school.

In many affluent OECD countries, policy-makers have chosen to concentrate education spending on the children who need the most help to lift them up towards the average. In Britain policy-makers have chosen to create an educational environment which encourages the most affluent seven per cent to opt out of the state education system and hence be far less concerned about what happens within it.

Many, if not most people in England are unaware that the elite of Germany and France send their children to state schools, albeit often still a little more elitist state schools. This is the picture in Scotland overall but there are significant exceptions and pockets of opting-out (such as Edinburgh and parts of rural Perthshire). Across all of Lothian some 12 per cent of children are privately educated. Most of these children are concentrated in Edinburgh, where the proportion is higher, although for some children privately educated there their home address may be outside of that city, and some are boarding. In contrast, in most other parts of Scotland, the proportions being privately educated are practicably zero, especially in large areas where there simply are no private schools (Dorling, 2012a: 40).

The affluent in Southern England are very often not aware that in much of the rest of England, let along the UK, very few people send their children to private schools, even amongst the most affluent elsewhere. The map below shows the proportions of children who went to private school up to two decades ago. Today's map would be very similar. The pattern changes only very slowly over time.

In Scotland, even in the poorest areas, children do better at school, on average, than do their counterparts in England. Why schools do better in Scotland is not a question this chapter tries to answer. The reasons would range from the more widespread belief, centuries ago, that all people needed to be able to read the bible, to having a less affluent elite who might like to opt out of universal provision, especially in Edinburgh, but who mostly cannot afford to.

Figure 1

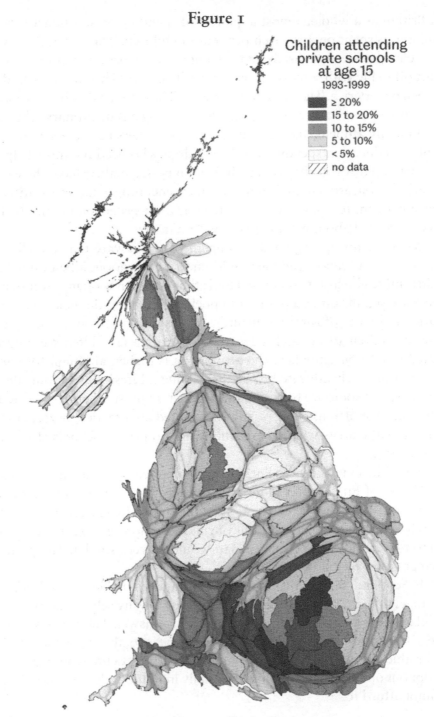

Children attending
private schools
at age 15
1993-1999

- ≥ 20%
- 15 to 20%
- 10 to 15%
- 5 to 10%
- < 5%
- no data

Source: Analysis of national school league tables for Britain 1993–99

Figure 2

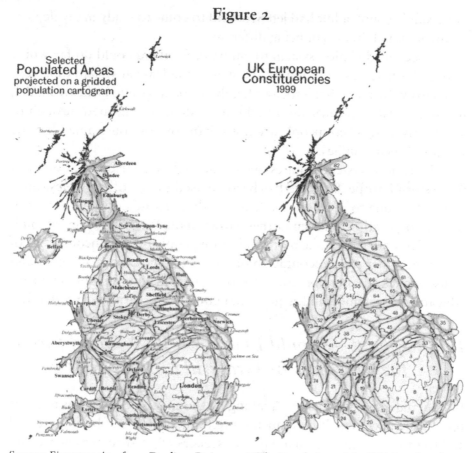

Source: Figures 1 & 2 from Dorling, D. (2012a) 'The Population of the UK', London: Sage.

One often unanticipated result of Scotland's educational successes is that out of the poorest areas a few young men every year gain good qualifications and often leave the neighbourhood; often forever. In England, in areas that are almost as poor, far more of the young men stay – including the most able – because their schools let them down. In a perverse way this has benefited Sheffield Brightside and harmed Glasgow Shettleston, even if it has helped a few of the young men (Garner, 2012).

Scotland's policy on higher education shows an aspiration to be better than England. Last year for the first time in my life I asked my first year students to identify where they were born and not one was born in Scotland. This is from the first cohort to be charged £9,000 a year. Of course not a single young adult had left Scotland to come to study in my depart-ment. Scotland dreams of being different.

To see an education system to emulate, Scotland could do far worse than to look across to Denmark. However, the Danish system took cen-turies to evolve into what is today a highly cooperative and inclusive model, where the state educates almost all that wish to be educated through to their early 20s, where people are not reliant on (or constrained by) the wealth of their families.

The Danish system requires one of the highest general taxation rates in Western Europe. Scotland has become used to one of the lowest rates of taxation due to decisions made in London. Those decisions are set to reduce corporation tax even further – toward the Western European mini-mum. They are set to take more and more people on low incomes out of taxation, rather than encourage more firms to pay average incomes and to use that as a better tax base. To move towards an even more inclusive educational system would require changing much else about Scotland.

Employment – Should Every Job Be A Good Job or the Workless Be Grateful for Any Job?

In England unemployment was falling by the end of 2012. It was not that there were new jobs. It was much more that benefits had been increased so little for so long that £9 a day 'job seekers allowance' was not a sum many adults could imagine surviving on. People would do almost any work available. Others would work part time rather than not work at all and people would undertake work that, in other countries, a better educated work force would shun.

Often the English media presents the English as work-shy, claiming that immigrants come in to do the jobs that the English don't do. Younger, fitter, and very often better educated immigrants from Eastern Europe are often preferred for work such as caring for the elderly, but it is not lack of enthu-siasm that leads to high, if often falling, unemployment in many parts of England, it is lack of money to pay wages. The same may well be true of Scotland. What is more, it is not lack of money overall; in aggregate we have never paid ourselves as much as we do now, in both Scotland and England. It is lack of money for the bottom 90 per cent of people in employment.

The total salary bill in England and Scotland has never been as high as it is now. However, a small number of people receive a disproportionate amount of that bill. If the share of the top ten per cent were reduced back to what they received in the 1970s, still far more than the other 90 per cent but not as much more as today, then there would be enough money to pay for full employment (Dorling, 2012b). This is not full-employment on the minimum or even living wage, it is full employment on a far more decent wage for many.

Furthermore, if the share of GDP that was taken up by wages rose, and that that was taken by profiteering fell, and even more equitable distributions of incomes could be achieved with salaries at the top remaining static and those at the bottom rising over time. This is what occurred in much of the 1920s, 1930s, 1940s, 1960s and almost all of the 1970s across the UK. But it may not be what the English idea now is. The question here is not about suddenly becoming more equal. It is about long-term aspiration.

Britain had full employment when income inequality was lowest (see Figure 2). England may no longer desire that. If Scotland wants to go a different way, then it may need to go its own way and the lines in Figure 2 above will all split in two, the Scots lines falling in an independent and progressively more equal Scotland year on year after 2014, while the line in England continues to rises ever upwards back up to Downton Abbey style 1920s servant keeping levels of inequality.

Housing – Is Social Housing Part of the Mix or a Safety Net for the Poorest of the Poor?

How we are housed shows how we have come to value one another. We built public housing because we were no longer willing to tolerate slums. We tax large properties a higher amount because that is fair and because it is inefficient to have only one or two people living in a large property. What matters is that we want everyone to be decently housed. However, attitudes to housing are changing.

A Scottish consensus on what is decent and right might be about to collide with a new English idealism that you only 'deserve' to be well housed if you have worked hard enough for it, and that people who have more children than 'they can afford' should not complain when they have to live in low-quality, damp, inadequate housing. It is all they deserve, whereas – in England at least – if someone has property worth a great deal

Figure 3

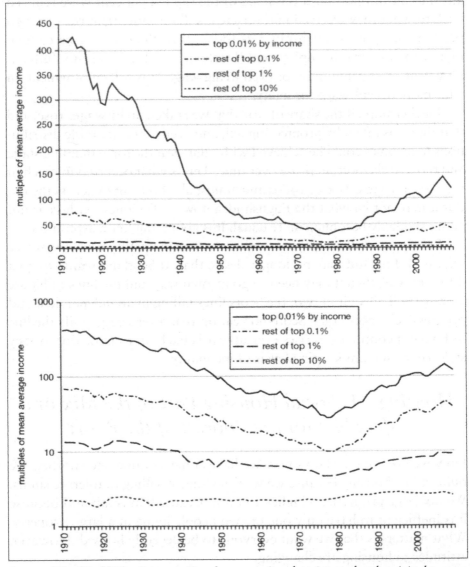

Source: The World Top Incomes Database, missing data interpolated, original source: Atkinson, 2007.

Figure 4:
The Number of People Wealthy Enough to Pay Inheritance Tax who Died by Area in 2007/8

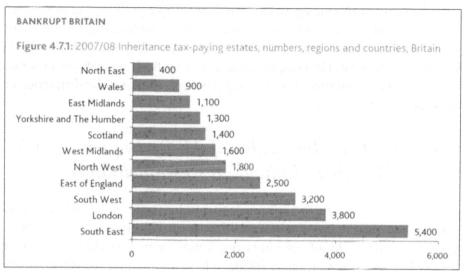

BANKRUPT BRITAIN

Figure 4.7.1: 2007/08 Inheritance tax-paying estates, numbers, regions and countries, Britain

Area	Number
North East	400
Wales	900
East Midlands	1,100
Yorkshire and The Humber	1,300
Scotland	1,400
West Midlands	1,600
North West	1,800
East of England	2,500
South West	3,200
London	3,800
South East	5,400

Source: Dorling, D. and Thomas, B. (2011) Bankrupt Britain: An atlas of social change,
Bristol: Policy Press

of money, increasingly that is presented as the just reward for honest toil or special ability.

The graph above, of the number of estates paying inheritance tax, shows how, in Scotland, housing is much less an issue of wealth than in England. Only three English regions have fewer households wealthy enough to pay inheritance tax and all three of these are far less populous than Scotland. Most of the wealth that is taxed when people die, for the tiny seven per cent rich enough to pay inheritance tax in the UK, is wealth held in bricks and mortar. Almost all of that wealth is held by a minority of households living in South East England.

In the South of England many people now think of their home as their future financial insurance against the threat of poverty in old age. This is the case despite only a minority of households even there having a mortgage that is mostly paid off, or owning outright. In Scotland (and much of the north of England and in Wales) thinking is different because homes are not worth so much, even for the minority who own outright. Far more people rent from housing associations, other registered social landlords the council away from the South East of England.

In Scotland the government is 'committed to ensuring that by 2012 every unintentionally homeless person will be entitled to settled accommodation' (Scottish Government, 2012). And the Scottish housing regulator has said that 'During 2012 we will develop equalities outcomes and we publish these as part of our overall strategy setting out how we will meet our equalities duties. These will be published by the end of December 2012.' (Scottish Housing Regulator, 2012). Both aspirations may not be met in full or on time, but in comparison to England the difference in attitude is stark.

Health – Can the Health of All Be Improved or is Health an Individual Responsibility?

The Scottish health record is known throughout the rich world for how poor it has been in comparison to other countries. Recently it has been discovered that a decade ago life expectancy for men in the very poorest areas of Glasgow was actually falling. These are the first recorded falls in life expectancy in Britain for any group to be reported since the depression of the 1930s:

> We found that male premature mortality rates rose by over 14 per cent in Scotland over the ten-year period between the early 1990s and 2000s in persistently deprived areas. We found no significant rise in mortality elsewhere in the UK and that the rise among men in Scotland was driven by results for Glasgow where mortality rates rose by over 15 per cent during the decade.
>
> (Norman *et al*, 2011)

Even more recently life expectancy across Scotland rose by more than six months in just one year for both men and women. It is too early to tell, but the tide may finally be turning. What happens to trends in health in Scotland depends as much on what happens to education, employment and housing in the grey areas of the City of Glasgow, outlined above, as on anything else.

Blame people living in these places for their misfortune – as if it were their fault that the housing here was poor and the job prospects still often dire – and we should expect life expectancy to continue to fall in a global economic recession/depression. See the people of these areas as victims of

Figure 5:
Persistently Deprived Areas of Glasgow Which Have Seen Absolute Mortality Rises in Men

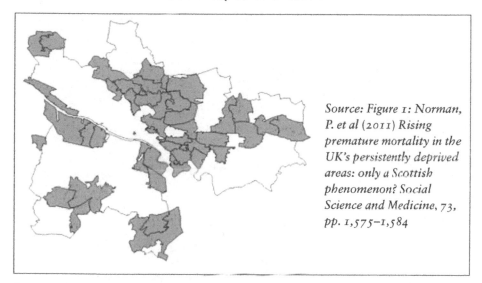

Source: Figure 1: Norman, P. et al (2011) Rising premature mortality in the UK's persistently deprived areas: only a Scottish phenomenon? Social Science and Medicine, 73, pp. 1,575–1,584

forces outside of their control, and act accordingly and just as the tide was turned in the 1930s, so too it could be turned again, but there is a problem.

The problem with introducing a more and more progressive health policy in Scotland is that it runs counter to what is becoming the new common sense in much of southern England. The government in London increasingly blames those who are ill for their illnesses. It does not want to look for the reasons behind the reasons that people smoke and drink, why some get fatter than others or why the British are more likely to be obese than almost any other set of people in Europe. The government in England preaches the gospel of individual responsibility. In doing so it glances up at the health record of Scotland with disdain.

In England health care is being privatised. In Scotland it remains nationalised. The English privatisation may only have been possible because opposition from the other countries of the UK was muted as, at first, it looks as if English 'health reforms' would only affect England. That was a mistake.

The American private health care companies moving into England will already be looking enviously north of the border for the huge profits that could be made introducing 'competitive' out-patients schemes, general

Figure 6:
Life Expectancy in 1997–99 and per cent change to 2007–9
by Scottish Council areas

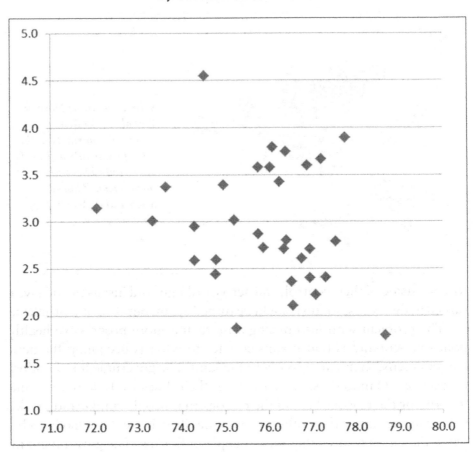

Source: (GRO Scotland, 2013).

practitioner provision, and other 'services'. The members of the House of Lords who voted the health privatisation bill through so enthusiastically in 2012, many in the pay of private health care 'providers' as company directors or advisors, are unlikely to ignore their financial masters' need to expand into Scotland.

To be truly safe from English privatisation and profiteering, Scotland may come to believe that it requires the ultimate legal safeguard – independence. If not now, then soon. If and when that comes about then perhaps it would be best to: *Pity England, so near to Europe and so far from fair.*

Inequality and Exclusion within Scotland

Being the second largest nation in the union, a 'region' of the UK until only recent rhetorical change has had the effect of obscuring inequalities within Scotland. Scotland contains areas with the lowest life expectancies in the United Kingdom, but it is also (although far less famously) known for its enclaves of areas where people enjoy far better health than most people in the UK. If it were not for such good health in some parts of Scotland the national average life expectancy would be far lower.

Since 1997 there has been a slight equalisation of health inequalities within Scotland. Life expectancy in Glasgow rose by 3.1 per cent to stand at 74.3 for men and women combined by 2007–09. In contrast, the improvement in East Renfrewshire over the same period was of just 1.8 per cent although people there still live almost six years longer than in Glasgow today (GRO Scotland, 2013). This is what a decline in health inequalities looks like, and it has occurred while Scotland was still part of the union, but with a devolved administration and a party in control in Westminster that contained a great many Scottish MPs. There is no guarantee that this trend will continue either with a different set of parties in power in Westminster since 2009, or if Scotland were to leave the union.

Although there is a great deal of variation in Figure 6, in general the further you look to the right, where life expectancy was higher in the late 1990s, the lower each diamond is. Each diamond represents one of Scotland's council areas. The highest is West Lothian, which has experienced the greatest advantage and improvement in its relative position over the course of the last decade. The lowest diamonds, East Dunbartonshire and East Renfrewshire, are the two areas which saw the least improvement. It is possible that this is because these areas in earlier decades benefitted from people leaving Glasgow to move to them and that such migration has reduced a little as conditions within Glasgow improved.

An independent Scotland could well become a country in which the issues of redistribution within the land rise to the fore. Would people in the areas to the right of the scatter shown in Figure 6 begin to resent the continued higher public spending that tends to be the case in areas to the left of Figure 6. The areas are deliberately not labelled on the Figure to keep this question hypothetical, but as soon as you see where we are talking about, and if you know Scotland well, you might begin to see how this issue could become important.

As things stand within the union Scotland as a whole receives more funding per head than do people in England. Much of that extra funding is used, in effect, to improve living conditions in some of the poorest parts of Scotland. The transfer of monies is, in effect, from wealthier tax-payers in England to poorer parts of Scotland, especially Glasgow. Even if Scotland could secure rights to all the oil fields that lie off its coast, and could resist English attempts to draw a diagonal line out to sea as some continuation of the land boarder up towards Norway, higher funding per head in places like Glasgow could become seen as a transfer from wealthier parts of Scotland in future. A very imaginative government could present it as funding from wealthier parts of the North Sea, but for only as long as profits from there continued.

Now extend the argument from health to education, housing, jobs and the environment. Add the costs of supporting populations in very low dense mountainous areas and islands, the costs of ferries and train lines, the costs of protecting the natural environment, preserving some of the oldest Universities in Europe and weigh those costs against the needs of people in 'middle Scotland' (a term which will not mean the central belt). For decades when too little has been spent on the poor, on benefits, or on hospitals or schools in Scotland it has been because the national arrangement with England has been to blame, or at least it could be presented in that way. The Barnett formula has not been fair compensation for the oil. Take that argument away and the question then becomes: which old fault lines will re-emerge and which new ones will form?

All the arguments made here are only a great problem if a large component to Scottish identity has been identity formed as a counter to English domination. That part of Scottish identity that builds on solidarity, mutual understanding and the sense that you do well when everyone around you does well could be used to mobilise action to prevent economic and ideological divides growing were Scotland ever to become independent again.

One area the urgently requires more work is an assessment of change in Scotland since devolution in comparison to say change in the North East of England or across all of Yorkshire. The improvement of the housing stock, changes in health, gains in education since the trend before and after devolution may all appear, I suspect, to generally suggest that devolution can be linked to an era of falling inequality in contrast to rising inequalities in nearby parts of England. The health trends shown above in Figure 5 suggest that is the case. It is harder to compare educational trends because of such different systems and now differing university funding. Comparison of the changes found between the 2001 and 2011 census north and south of the border might well suggest that when more decisions are made more locally more has been achieved.

The implications of findings from analyses of the 2011 census on the possible benefits of the devolution period could well be used to suggest that under independence even greater progress could be achieved. However, it may be just as valid to claim that as significant achievements have been made without independence then independence is neither necessary nor sufficient for greater social progress, solidarity and the future reductions of inequalities. In the short term, the implications of the tsunami of budget cuts to services in both Scotland and the north of England are likely to dominate the debate, and many people living far from London in both England and Scotland may well blame Westminster and the bankers of London. In the long term, there will still be bankers in Edinburgh and it is not hard to imagine them, and the government there, increasingly be blamed for the woes of the West and North of Scotland.

Conclusion

This chapter has contrasted trends in the four areas of education, employment, housing and health, at times using geographical data, to suggest that a widening of the gap in ideals and aspirations may be occurring between Scotland and England, including perhaps in how people are viewed as possibly all part of a society (Scotland), or needing to know their place better in a social order that will always separate out winners and losers (England). Such a summary may stereotype too much, but hopefully illustrates where we may be currently heading and how we may be becoming much more 'us' and 'them' than we used to be.

What may matter most for Scotland is not whether to vote for or against independence, but what direction an independent Scotland might take. An independent Scotland which was not genuinely a Scotland dedicating to returning to a system of values that saw everyone as valuable may not be a Scotland worth fighting for independence for. Finally, while independence might make Scotland far more legally separate from England it would not alter the basic geography. Mexico still suffers from neighbouring the United States despite not being subject to its direct laws and diktat.

References

Diaz, P. (2012), According to Wikipedia but with Apologies to General Profirio Diaz, as apparently he did not actually say: "Pobre México! ¡Tan lejos de Dios y tan cerca de los Estados Unidos!" (Poor Mexico, so far from God and so close to the United States!), see http://en.wikipedia.org/wiki/Porfirio_D%C3%ADaz

Dorling, D. (2012a), *The Population of the UK*, London: Sage.

Dorling, D. (2012b), *The case for austerity among the rich, IPPR Discussion Paper on Promoting Growth and Shared Prosperity in the UK*, London: Institute for Public Policy Research: http://www.dannydorling.org/?page_id=3008

Dorling, D. and Thomas, B. (2011), *Bankrupt Britain: An atlas of social change*, Bristol: Policy Press.

Garner, R. (2012), '£9,000 fees putting a generation of boys off university', *The Independent*, 13th December, http://www.independent.co.uk/news/education/education-news/9000-fees-putting-a-generation-of-boys-off-university-8411859.html

GRO Scotland (2013), 'Table 1: Life expectancy at birth in Scotland 2007–2009 by administrative area, and comparisons with 1997–1999 (Persons)', http://www.gro-scotland.gov.uk/statistics/theme/life-expectancy/scottish-areas/archive/admin-area/2007-2009/tables.html

Norman, P. *et al* (2011), 'Rising premature mortality in the UK's persistently deprived areas: only a Scottish phenomenon?', *Social Science and Medicine*, 73, 1575–1584.

Reay, D. (2012), *What would a socially just education system look like?*, London: The Centre for Labour and Social Studies (Class) http://classonline.org.uk/docs/2012_Diane_Reay_-_a_socially_just_education_system.pdf

Scottish Government (2012), *Housing Strategy*, http://www.scotland.gov.uk/Topics/Built-Environment/Housing

Scottish Housing Regulator (2012), *Our Approach to Equalities*, http://www.scottishhousingregulator.gov.uk/our-approach-equalities

Beyond 'the Global Kingdom': England after Scottish Self-Government

ANTHONY BARNETT

THE POTENTIAL INDEPENDENCE of Scotland means above all a new relationship with England. Even after independence we would be joined at the hip. I am writing as an Englishman who would like to see a Yes vote. Were Scotland to vote for independence in its coming referendum moves would immediately be set afoot to create some sort of confederal arrangement to resolve common matters.

An assertion of formal sovereignty, therefore, means reasserting relations with England, not severance. Scotland will take responsibility for governing itself internally (in accordance, of course, with the international agreements it is bound by) while acting in its own interests within the external fields of international affairs and economic resources in the global market place. But at the same time both its internal affairs and its external interests will be shaped in the first place by the magnetic force of its relationships with its historic and geographic neighbour with ten times its economic weight and with whom it has shared sovereignty in a unique bi-national arrangement for over 300 years.

To repeat, independence for Scotland would make a new relationship with England. What England thinks and does, therefore, has a considerable impact on the prospects of Scottish independence.

To get at this fundamental point in a different way, suppose we English were to seek and obtain *as the English* the limited degree of self-determination that the Scots now enjoy, with our own domestic parliament. We would surely proceed to invite Wales, Scotland and Northern Ireland, to join a federal association in which we all enjoyed our domestic self-government as nations, including over our separate domestic economies and tax regimes, while reshaping the shared union of the UK for mutually-agreed external policies and co-operation.

Such a new constitutional arrangement would deliver domestic self-determination while sharing sovereignty in a non-arbitrary framework. To be part of a union state within which Scotland would have political and moral equality and domestic self-government (while granting England a fair degree of larger influence that accords with its size) would obtain a definite form of independence for Scotland. It seems to me from admittedly partial, unscientific, personal soundings, that such an arrangement would end effective demand in Scotland for 'full independence'. There would be more than enough self-government for all the countries to look to themselves for their creative energy.

I would still prefer to see a confederal outcome with full juridical independence and the end of Britain as a formal state. I think this would release a more positive decentralising politics here, south of the border. The point I wish to make in a book of essays on Scottish independence and self-government, is that the English could propose a federal relationship that would: a) satisfy a clear majority of Scots who want to govern themselves when it comes to their own domestic concerns; b) emancipate the English; and c) articulate Britain in a modern, constitutional form.

So why isn't this on the table? Why don't the English propose this? Especially when it is probable that we, the English, too would embrace such a federal arrangement. For example, the Houses of Parliament could be retained as, or rather returned to being, the parliament of England while a British federal union assembly of the UK could be created in, say, York.

The authorities and their media in London will do everything they can to prevent the emergence of any alliance that could call for such a choice. Much the most important fact, however, is that there is hardly any discernible movement calling for it. The Campaign for an English Parliament is honourable but not influential. Without representative English institutions, we English are unable to politically reconsider our relationship to Scotland. If only the English would 'wake up', so the argument goes, there would not be a problem about reforming Scotland's relationship. Instead, the British state is a cataleptic entombment of healthy democratic impulses.

This argument has its origins in the Scottish movement that began with devolution. Those who have come to consider the national question in the UK through the eye of Scotland, as I have, share the frustration. What is the matter with the English? Why can't my fellow countrymen see that our pride, humanity and democracy are being fettered by the British state? The Westminster/Whitehall regime is deploying its familiar weapons of intimidation to crush a Scottish referendum Yes vote with all the usual tactics – such as trading on economic uncertainty and fear-mongering.

Isn't it obvious that the real objective is to crush the hopes of us regular English folk?

If the Scots choose freedom, the English might be next! It is *our* own dangerous and lively English imagination that must be deterred and is the real target of the brutal bullying of Scottish dreams now underway. We English will also be very much the losers should Scotland bend in subordination to the British political class.

This is my view, but I want to argue against myself and the presumptions of Scottish nationalism, to consider two questions. First, the vitality of England's Britishness needs to be understood if it is to be confronted. For Scots to win a majority of their fellow-countrymen to the new relationship with England means those who favour a Yes vote must saying something positive to the English about what this relationship should become.

This means acknowledging a lack of reciprocity. Here in England the independence of Scotland does not in the first place mean a new relationship with Scotland, about which most English think and care little. A Scottish Yes vote for independence is going to be a challenge alright, but of a different kind: odd as it may seem, it will force the English to work through a new relationship *with Britain* with which we identify with internally, as I show below.

Second, in order to situate this issue we also need to ask briefly whether the European process is not in fact the shaping force. We may like to discuss the internal arrangements of government across the UK as if we are masters of our fate. But perhaps the whole set of debates is a function of the transformation of Europe. This angle is given new relevance and credibility with the rise of UKIP in English politics and its demand for independence from Europe.

England-Britain

In 1982 I wrote an instant book on why Parliament went to war over the Falklands, *Iron Britannia* now recently re-issued. Although Welsh and Scottish regiments were deployed it struck me as an English adventure (Barnett, 2012). Material on nationhood within Britain was limited at the time and for my chapter on 'Falklands Pastorialism' I questioned people about their national identities. Those who were Scottish or Welsh had no problem saying if they felt Welsh first and British second, or Scottish second and British first. They experienced two distinct over-lapping national allegiances and were able to compare and contrast their importance quite naturally. But when I asked English people the same question – 'Which comes first for you, being English or being British?' – many simply *could not understand* the question. They felt equally they were both, at one and the same time, in a way that was inseparable. To ask them to compare their allegiance to Englishness and Britain as if these were distinct identities did not make sense.

As awareness of Englishness has grown this phenomenon has diminished. But this must not lead us to deny the authenticity of the experience, the fusion of Britishness and English into a particular nationalism of its own. It goes back to May 1940. Britain entered the Second World War as an empire but emerged as a *country*. It was a keystone in a victorious alliance but while the US and the USSR both became forms of empire the United Kingdom found itself stripped of its world primacy while retaining the institutions and loyalties that had created and led the Empire intact in Westminster and Whitehall. A singular form of nationalism resulted.

In 1982 I reached for a simple metaphor to communicate the hard reality of the resulting experience. Imagine a coin, the outer face is British – the British navy – while the inner is English – the English countryside. When I asked the English to rank their feeling of being British against their Englishness, it was like asking a currency, were it to be conscious, whether it felt itself to be more obverse or reverse. It is indeed a question that is senseless: there have to be *two sides* to a coin but it is one coin nonetheless. The currency of English-Britishness was similarly double-edged but singular after 1945.

For the Scots and Welsh this means that English can be infuriatingly oblivious of the domineering consequence of what appears to be a presumption that they 'speak for Britain'. The fused nature of their nationalism elides Englishness and Britishness. This appears to be a claim over Scotland and Wales, which are also British. Thoughtlessness, however, means overlooking something you know and can be reminded of. Instead, for the English being British is an authentic, private description of themselves that has little if anything to do with the Scots and the Welsh (until they are reminded of them).

I state this at some length because viewed from Scotland it appears to be an arrogant, misconceived and unsustainable presumption of mastery, not indifference. It is therefore often mistaken as no more than a perfidious form of a claim to rule as if the object of desire was Scotland and Wales. But what if it *is* indifferent to them? What if it is not a claim over bordering nations but an inner resolution? More important, what if this illogical and obtuse irrationality is a strength?

When it comes to England and its Anglo-British nationalism there is a deep vein of energy and confidence for it to draw upon. As Liah Greenfeld has shown in an analysis Tom Nairn has developed, English presumption is rooted in its being the 'first born' nation in the 16th Century and then the pioneer of the industrial revolution. England did not need to react to others to initiate its own nationalistic modernisation: others they had to respond to it, most notably across the Atlantic (Greenfeld, 1992; Nairn 1997). The result is a nationalism that does not 'need' to be defiantly self-conscious and therefore can 'get away' with shape-shifting far more than most.

Moreover, the state that oversaw the country that enjoyed pole position was created in 1688 not as a restoration, as Burkean mythology pretends, but rather, as Steve Pincus demonstrates, after the 'first modern revolution'. This was the outcome of a conflict between two alternative modernising projects, that of absolutism and commercialism, with the second becoming ascendant.

So that from its beginning, the constitutional culture that emerged in England has been a modernising one, seeking to preserve its first-born presumption with its open, commercial cult of flexibility (Pincus, 2009).

Notoriously uncodified, therefore, with at the height of Empire in the later 19th Century a political culture that sneered at the paper constitutions of others, it was nonetheless self-consciously constitutional, with the forms, norms and protocols of government very much written-about and, indeed, prided in.

To skip forward, when Margaret Thatcher drove through her inglorious embrace of neoliberalism she funded it with the gushing oil of Scotland's North Sea. At the same time she also generated self-belief amongst her followers by tapping into the energy of the vigorous legal-constitutional culture of the 19th Century, trapped below the sediments of the 20th.

This led to a crisis for Labour as its industrial base was dismantled by a Prime Minister who used the sovereignty vested in the executive to undo the parliamentary-welfare consensus Labour had relied upon. The modernisation of Labour that eventually resulted included an unprecedented programme of constitutional reforms to redress parliamentary authoritarianism, first set out by John Smith in his 'Charter 88' lecture calling for a 'new constitutional settlement' with a Bill of Rights (Smith, 1993).

Tony Blair inherited this programme and his team felt obliged to deliver its headline reforms in what was to prove an unprecedented, shattering transformation of the old constitution – sweeping away its checks and balances as the civil service was disciplined and hereditary peers defenestrated. A long-resisted Human Rights Act incorporated the European Convention into British law, Freedom of Information was watered down and delayed but even then was sufficient to blow open the Commons expenses system. Above all there were new Parliaments in Scotland and Wales, and a Mayor for London all legitimised by referendums. It can be seen as the start of the inner Europeanisation of Britain, exemplified by the Good Friday Agreement over Northern Ireland.

This movement towards democratising Whitehall-Westminster as a system was blocked by Blair, who refused even to give a speech drafted for him about how the reforms introduced a programme of change. Blair and Brown embraced 'globalisation' rather than constitutional democracy. They sought legitimacy through releasing personal economic energy promised by the wealth and growth of the North Atlantic financial machinery rather than releasing democratic energy through opening up government with a new constitutional settlement.

The result – a continuation of Thatcherism but by other means. In some ways it was better, with significant domestic investment in health, welfare and education. In other ways it was worse as it reproduced Thatcher's hyper-centralised version of Britishness now unrestrained by her belief in parliamentary protocol and tradition - while casting aside the decrepit but still real elements of checks and balances in the old constitutional order.

Instead of Scotland's new Parliament being launched, therefore, as part of the democratisation of Britain it was isolated from the other far-reaching reforms rather than integrated with them. Looking back, Derry Irving, who as Lord Chancellor played a key role in fast-tracking through the legislation, lauded the 'piecemeal' character of his achievement as a British tradition. But piecemeal change comes slowly, bit by bit. After 1997 huge pieces were broken up and replaced at the same time. The result was a disaggregation of the British constitution and a loss of legitimacy for the entire political order – not its piecemeal renewal thanks to the digestible assimilation and absorption of step-by-step reform.

Challenged before the election about his willingness to allow the Scottish Parliament some minimal tax-raising powers, Blair replied that it would be like a 'parish council'. You could say that the road to next year's referendum started then. Had New Labour accepted the intrinsic importance of this key reform it would have necessarily sought a way of integrating it. Instead, Blair and those close to him convinced themselves of the unimportance of their constitutional reforms. Who really cares about rights? What does it matter if the Welsh have an Assembly? Putting the superficialities of psephology before the consequences of principle, they agreed with each other in their scabrous language they used to convince themselves of they were men, that voters cared as little as they did about 'rights' and 'assemblies'.

The result was a Parliament in Scotland that was born an orphan. A new centre of sovereignty was created by a mother Parliament that pretended its offspring did not matter. This political philistinism ensured that in Scotland and Wales (and even in London with its Mayor) politicians had to find their own way forward – and an autonomous political process was born. Orphaned at birth they had to grow up fast.

Blair could well have been perceived as the agent of directionless, incoherent and disintegrative change (that he in fact was). But he wanted to project an image of purpose. Wrong-headed, bellicose support of American hegemony and military recklessness provided the solution. Incapable of making even the shortest speech about the Human Rights Act that his own government had passed, for fear of making himself accountable to his own people, Blair bid instead for planetary leadership and set out in his 'Chicago Doctrine' to demand the right to intervene anywhere in the world to free *other* people from arbitrary tyranny. The displacement worked in the way that a bubble distributes surface tension into the appearance of a fantastical object. Under Blair, Britain stretched out to become the pretentious *global kingdom* whose aftermath we now inhabit (Hassan and Barnett, 2009). Here indeed the imperial sentiment of Britishness and its ghosts was summoned to keep the body politic at the 'high table' of the security council.

The disasters of New Labour are too easy to scorn. Any assessment of this extraordinary period deserves another kind of measure in terms of the energy that it released and displayed. In different ways both the British political class and the unwashed of the islands emerged with new laurels.

The Upturning of the British Axiom

Not only was an astonishingly wide-ranging sequence of reforms driven through by a state that was supposedly sclerotic; voters who were supposed to be passive and indifferent also vigorously embraced them. The depth and significance of this double-change is hard to register as we are within it. But it is essential to do so to combat a lazy perception of the British system as merely one of decline. The best way to measure what was achieved and where we are now is perhaps by looking back to the 1970s.

In the mid-70s, as the post-war settlement came to its calamitous end, Labour's Prime Minister Harold Wilson told his press secretary 'I have nothing new to offer.' (Wheen, 2009: 218). They had gained office only thanks to the profound incompetence of the preceding Heath government, whose Cabinet Secretary was famously removed from Downing Street in a straight-jacket (safe, rapidly-acting tranquilisers had yet to be developed). The exhaustion and irredeemable complacency of the post-war ruling order whose greatest ambition was to manage decline culminated in Wilson's replacement 'Uncle Jim' Callaghan.

At the same time, the main popular organisations, the trade unions, churches, clubs, associations and parties, were stubbornly defensive, corporatist and self-interested. A benighted and blocked 'welfare' society was preserved by an upper class that had long encouraged the brutalisation and dependency of regular citizens, which conveniently confirmed the need for its own relative civilising role. Their controlling influence had been transformed from its pre-war openly imperial order into a more discreet 'establishment' mapped in all its unaccountable sloth, low-level greed and narcissism by Anthony Sampson (Sampson,1962).

The result a decade later was disintegration and immobilism, along with double-digit inflation, defiance and helplessness. Both the ruling order and the public order were blocked in regressive narrow-mindedness. It culminated in 1979 when Scotland voted narrowly and unenthusiastically for its own Assembly in a referendum.

Out if it emerged Thatcher and Thatcherism, funded by the immense windfall of North Sea Oil that turned the UK into a beneficiary of OPEC oil prices. As the consensus politics of 1945 fell about itself, her polarising, leader-centric alternative was legitimised by the drama of the Falklands War. Permitted by Thatcher's own short-sighted dogmatism the conflict was won despite the odds ensuring her subsequent supremacy. This she used to destroy, rather than renew, most of Britain's own manufacturing and engineering base. Nonetheless, Thatcherism addressed the crisis of the seventies with a sense of, if not real purpose, then an all-important sense of conviction and responsibility for one's life.

The end of traditional labour collectivism does not leave market individualism as the only alternative. The tragedy of 20th Century socialism was that it was unable to articulate an attractive and effective concept of the social that protected liberty, enhanced democracy and regarded the use of a state power as a necessary but inherently dangerous aspect of common government. But another aspect of the modern, the multiple growth of the international: as experience (with travel and migration), as a problem (climate and the environment), as knowledge (the internet) was not dependent on control from above. Toleration, multiculturalism and especially the greater equality of women, reshaped social attitudes through the period of New Labour, masking its instinctive restrictiveness. Perhaps a key here is the growing appeal of human rights. The battle will be to ensure they are held and developed in common rather than reduced to being an essentialist entitlement: rights that are emancipating, fought for and gained by joint humanitarian action rather than being regarded as static fundamentals awaiting legal definition.

The moment that defined the twin growth of a hyper-active, market-driven political class and a wiser, self-confident public, was the Iraq war. Were human rights something that Washington imposed by Cruise missile or was our common humanity best protected by only using war as a last resort?

Why is it important to revisit this moment in a discussion of the future of the UK as a whole, faced with a Scottish independence referendum? Because a different Britain emerged from the confrontation over Iraq. And it is this Britain that Scotland will need to leave if a Yes vote is to succeed.

A referendum is quite different from an election that tries out one government as the replacement of another. The Yes campaign will seek to present independence as 'normal', bringing Scotland back to a situation of health, for good reasons. But the implication is that the state of Britain has become abnormal and unhealthy. Again, there are good reasons for such a claim. But how unhealthy is it? How irrecoverable is Britain's disability? A Yes vote is an irreversible decision to leave the Union. So the question – 'What kind of country is England/Britain now that so shapes the Union?' – is going to decide the 2014 referendum.

The answer is that England/Britain is in a very bad way but with very positive human resources and self-belief seeking a way forward. The combination is hard to describe. The Iraq war was and remains a formative moment in its emergence. The superficial view of the great opposition to the Iraq war is that it showed the public is powerless and protest is pointless. For the political class a similar lesson is that it is always possible to 'tough it out' when there is opposition on the streets and outside the structures. However great the pressure, the 'realists' say, it will go away and you will not. For the classic politico especially but not only on the left, the lesson is that the people are powerless.

There is another more consequential understanding. The fundamental terms of trade of British politics were reversed. The basic axiom of Britain's uncodified constitution, the unquestioned first premise on which its legitimacy is based, is – or until 2003 *was* – that the elite knows better, sees further, is wiser, than the greedy and gullible unwashed. Yes, the generals can be donkeys and the elite headed by appeasers. But in the end a Churchill will arise to save the day. It is not that British rulers are without fault, not at all, but that relative to the 'masses' they are the better guardians of the interests of all.

This was changed by Iraq. The first premise of British rule was upturned by the largest demonstration in British history. Since then a generation has grown up with an articulate, justified contempt for the Whitehall and Westminster regime and its main political parties quite distinct from previous generations in its self-confidence. Their distrust of the stupidity, greed, love of power and lack of democratic legitimacy of the dominant order seems to be confirmed and reinforced by the financial crash and the bailing out of the bankers. An inner confidence comes with being right and knowing you are right, even if you are sad and angry about what you know. Ed Miliband, who at least is aware of the outgoing tide, says he wants to restore trust in British politics. But why? The distrust is based on good judgment. Surely it would be far better and more original if he sent his party the task of trusting the citizens, especially younger ones.

If you look at what happened to British politics in terms of Iraq from the optic of the political system, which is what almost all comment does, then you seen far reaching damage. But if you look at it from the perspective of popular politics you see a positive demystification, a sense that the public can reach its own better and more honest view. Whereas the political class is struggling to get the public to believe in it, the public is learning to believe in itself.

Today, viewed from Whitehall the Scottish Parliament is deemed a 'problem'. Why? Because it has indeed taken on a life of its own and even elected a majority SNP government that it was supposed to prevent. Political life in Wales also is being transformed thanks to its Assembly, whose extremely narrow referendum endorsement was the starting point for a now irreversible autonomy. In London the creation of a Mayor with the second largest direct electoral mandate in Europe after the French Presidency provided a way for two politicians who were suffocated in the routines of the House of Commons to prove their skills and appeal. The Human Rights Act has been a triumph, as the judiciary becomes a far more self-conscious player while people across the UK have a new-found belief in their rights. The hatred that is being stirred up against it is a measure of its importance. Finally, freedom of information could hardly have had a greater impact in shaking the entitlement of the political class. None of this was in the script.

Once people in Britain, who are often understandably sceptical of reform, experience a genuine change and actual 'empowerment' they put it to use. Reform works! The classic, conservative, establishment voice warning that there is no point in advocated democracy as people won't change, or know how to use it if they have it, has been demonstrably proved wrong.

The uncomfortable paradox for those supporting a Yes vote in Scotland is that this positive energy works both ways. True, it is providing the steam behind the Scottish Parliament itself. But it is also feeding energy into a positive sense that people can do things together rather than separately, into the sense that the UK is providing human rights and freedom of information and is reforming – and is even by encouraging Wales to devolve ensuring that Scotland is not 'alone'.

Even the hyper-activity of the elite and the bluster of Boris Johnson feed into the remaking of British self-confidence and creativity in the South East especially. The two active forces combined in the contemporary British moment of the Olympics. While the weather rained on the ridiculous parade of boats supposed to popularise the monarch's golden anniversary earlier in 2012, the Queen emerged as a 'genuinely fictional' character in the opening ceremony of a profoundly parochial, self-indulgent but domestically brilliant display that celebrated the transformation of pastoralism into multiculturalism. It also demonstrated that the two-sided coin of England's Britishness could be reminted for this century.

Scotland's reply can still endorse independence. If the First Minister offers his people £500 per head to welcome their freedom as a rich country, polling suggests that the Scots will think it well worth it. And England's response will be a tolerant, Olympic 'good luck!'. But the dialogue between the two will not be the fervent demand for separation from a broken country. The positive attractions of British tolerance and transformation need to be recognised and drawn upon, and how access to them will be retained explained by those backing a Yes vote. Otherwise the threat of the loss of a renewed, tolerant Britain will hold Scots to English cousins.

The ideological superiority of independence as the route to a more plural, tolerant and contemporary worldview once seemed obvious when the alternative was the benighted nostalgia of British backwardness. But this no longer holds in the simple way it seemed in the 1990s. England/ Britain too is trying to shake off the melancholy of an archaic past. Scots who prefer to stick with this are not simply being reactionary. Any appeal for a Yes has to acknowledge the positivity that is south of the border and seek the adventure of going further in an open collaboration.

The European Dimension

But what if the English reject this nascent, tolerant future and embrace UKIP? It was striking how after UKIP beat the Tories into second place in the Eastleigh by-election at the end of February that none of the London commentators spotted what all Scottish analysis was immediately aware of: that the party that has the UK in its actual name is an English phenomenon.

Ben Wellings argues that the rise of an English consciousness is linked to hostility to Europe, that nationalism in England has embraced from the start a prejudice against Brussels, 'opposition to Europe became characteristic of politics in England although it was often still couched in terms of a defence of the UK or British sovereignty' (2012: 219).

Indeed, for most English readers this would seem so natural and obvious as to be barely worth observing, *of course* a nationalism will pitch itself against the larger force of the EU. In fact this is peculiar and exceptional. From the start the European process has been about saving the European nations, 'rescuing' their nation states in Alan Milward's phrase. But for Britain, while its elite may have sought to join for similar reasons of 'national' there was a unique risk that followed from it not in fact being one nation. An uncodified, multinational entity is bound to be threatened by membership of a larger codified multinational entity pledged to 'ever-closer' union.

Now the crisis of the Euro and the political weakness of the European Union in the face of German insistence on austerity makes the British look wise – even if the UK's banking and debt crisis is arguably worse. In another twist of the serpent's tail, UKIP's call to leave Europe looks less bizarre and more attractive. Could its influence be especially rebarbarative for Scotland? If, instead of seeing a positive, generous Olympic England arise with whom Scots could collaborate, a Boris Johnson-Nigel Farage alliance brokered by Murdoch arises to instigate right-wing populism south of the border then all my argument against myself about the potential renovation of English-Britishness can be put aside. I would not bet on it.

References

Ames, C. (2011), 'Memo reveals intelligence chief's bid to fuel fears of Iraqi WMDs, *The Observer*, 26 June.

Barnett, A. (2012), *Iron Britannia: Time to take the 'Great' out of Britain*, Faber Finds.

Cook, R. (2004), *The Point of Departure*, Simon and Schuster.

Greenfeld, L. (1992), *Nationalism: Five Roads to Modernity*, Harvard University Press.

Hassan, G. and Barnett, A. (2009), *Breaking Out of Britain's Neo-Liberal State*, Compass.

Nairn, T. (1997), *Faces of Nationalism: Janus Revisited*, Verso Books.

Pincus, S. (2009), *1688: The First Modern Revolution*, Yale University Press.

Sampson, A. (1962), *Anatomy of Britain*, Hodder and Stoughton.

Smith, J. (1993), *Charter 88 Sovereignty Lecture*, Charter 88.

Wellings, B. (2012), *English Nationalism and Euroscepticism: Losing the Piece*, Peter Lang.

Wheen, F. (2009), *Strange Days Indeed: The Golden Age of Paranoia*, Fourth Estate.

Faraway, so close: Scotland from Northern Ireland

ARTHUR AUGHEY

I WAS ONCE asked to describe the relationship between Northern Ireland and Scotland. The expression which came to mind was the title of a film by Wim Wenders, *In der Naehe, so Fern*, the English translation of which is *Faraway, so Close*. It seemed to capture both the sense of commonality so often assumed between the two as well as the gulf in their respective experiences. Similarly, Graham Walker called his history of that relationship *Intimate Strangers* (1995), a title suggesting that feelings of proximity need not necessarily mean comprehension of, or sympathy with, the main currents of political life in either place.

That remains true today. To misunderstand the relationship has often been attributed exclusively to a distinctive parochialism on the part of Northern Ireland's politicians and commentators. For example, one journalist (Leask 2012) pointed out that the present constitutional debate in Scotland had provoked unusually little public response in Northern Ireland and put this down to the fact that politicians there had become used to the world looking in at them. Rarely did they bother to look out at the world. While there is some truth in that proposition, it would be unfair to push it too far. In the past, politicians as well as commentators in Northern Ireland did look out to other conflicts – South Africa, Israel-Palestine, even Algeria – to find analogies for the local conflict. Today, they look to other conflicts – Colombia, East Timor, even Iraq – as suitable cases for the Northern Ireland peace treatment.

The common factor in both cases is preoccupation with the particular. This is perfectly understandable and it is not confined to only one side of the North Channel. For, as Walker observed of Scotland's interest in Northern Ireland, despite all the historical and cultural links most Scots like to keep Northern Ireland at a safe distance and their intellectual engagement with it has been undistinguished. Leask's own article was a good example of that rule of thumb. So it is not unusual that the independence debate in Scotland has been interpreted in distinctly local terms. And it is not unjustified, since whatever Scotland decides in 2014 is bound to have an impact on the debate about Northern Ireland's future.

It is interesting to contrast the current form of political discourse in both places. Until quite recently, the concern of those discussing Northern Ireland was with the question of constitutional options. Scholarly texts and conferences would examine alternatives such as a united Ireland, British-Irish joint sovereignty, power-sharing or full integration with the United Kingdom. After the Belfast/Good Friday Agreement, the emphasis changed. There developed a broad consensus (however tentative) on the shape of political structures and this made the older debate appear redundant. To use a phrase popularised by Peter Mandelson when he was Secretary of State for Northern Ireland, there was now only one show in town. Albeit hesitantly, the main focus of interest from the late 1990s shifted to questions of institutional procedures. What are the conditions that best secure stability in the Assembly? How can power-sharing devolution be made to work more efficiently? What are the appropriate strategies to promote trust between political parties?

The transition, at least at the level of official discourse, has been from an unsettled to a settled state. One could argue that in the last five years the debate in Scotland has moved in the opposite direction, from procedures to options. The notion of a settled will for devolution implied a stable relationship, a process not an event certainly, but a process of minor procedural modification. The focus recently has been on options – independence, devo-max, devo-plus, devo-more – and the impression is of an unsettled popular will. In short, whatever one's view of the matter, the prospect of an independent Scotland is not inconceivable. It is this political counter-current which sets the scene for reflections on the manner in which the Scottish debate impacts upon Northern Ireland politics.

This chapter considers how events in Scotland have been interpreted through the very different prisms of unionism and nationalism and republicanism, concluding with some reflections on their unspoken but pragmatic common ground.

Unionism

Speaking at the Grand Orange Lodge of Scotland commemoration of the signing of the 1912 Ulster Covenant, Dr David Hume (BBC 2012a) claimed

that Ulster-Scots are 'stakeholders' in the future of Scotland and he questioned the justice of holding a referendum on independence that would
ignore their input. A Union without Scotland, he argued, would be a
poorer place and Ulster looked anxiously at the prospect. In language
familiar at Orange demonstrations every 12 July, Hume proclaimed: 'We
will not forsake you as your forefathers did not forsake us'. This speech
was received with a mixture of incredulity and disdain not only in
Scotland (it was the occasion which provoked Leask's remarks) but also
in Northern Ireland. The principle of what touches all should be approved
by all – despite Dicey's advocacy of it in the case of Irish Home Rule – has
never been persuasive in the territorial politics of the United Kingdom.
Rather, James Mitchell's term 'a state of unions' better captures the rule
of British plebiscitary democracy.

The Northern Ireland border poll of 1973 set the precedent that what
touches a part should be approved only by that part, a precedent confirmed in the referenda in Scotland and Wales in 1979 and 1997 and to
be repeated in the Scottish referendum in 2014. No wonder Hume's naive
unionism invited ridicule. Though he chose to express it clumsily, in an
indefensible manner and in the language of 1912 not 2012, he did intimate nevertheless a concept of the United Kingdom which informs not
only the instinctive response of Ulster unionism but also the platform of
those in Scotland who oppose independence.

That concept is the paradoxical, Weberian, one of *elective affinity* or
kindred by choice. It does not presume that everyone and everywhere in
the Union are the same. It proposes that different nationalities elect to
stay in constitutional relation with one another and that this relationship
constitutes an affinity giving meaning to the term British (though it is
interesting that the word British was not used at all in the Ulster Covenant
the anniversary of which Hume was celebrating). To put that in language,
familiar now in Northern Ireland but of relevance to Scotland: multinational affinities are sustained on the basis of consent and people can
only be convinced by those constitutional arguments which they themselves are already prepared to accept. In sum, the Union comprises a
principle and an ideal. The principle is free association (elective) and the
ideal is multi-nationalism (affinity). This means that the shape of the
Union at any time is always open to negotiation. The United Kingdom, in
other words, exhibits the dual aspect of contract – instrumental bargaining for resources between nations, regions and central government – and

solidarity – mutual support and risk sharing. What devolution has done is to recalibrate that ambivalent association.

The democratic recalibration since 1997 and the institutionalisation of national difference make explicit what always implicit: that the United Kingdom is a constitutional artifice. What Hume conveys, albeit obscurely, is anxiety that the artifice will come to seem artificial and that free-born Scots will be persuaded that only an independent state can secure authentic expression of their identity. In other words, historical affinities could be lost by an ill-considered choice, manufactured by the seductive propaganda of the SNP. To put that more starkly, it may confuse the truth that Scottish identity is inextricably bound up with British citizenship. That was precisely the meaning of Lord Trimble's observation (Bussey 2012) that Scottish independence would do violence not only to the identity of the Scots but to everyone in the United Kingdom. Though similar things are said regularly in Scotland by those opposed to independence, what is unique to Ulster unionist expressions is their undertone of incredulity, mixed with a hint of perfidy. There are two related responses here.

The first, for want of a better word, is existential. Ulster unionists do find it hard to accept that Scots would seriously consider leaving the United Kingdom. Ulster unionist self-understanding is one of heroic resistance against nationalist and republican attempts to subvert their British citizenship. While they may share with members of the SNP some (contractual) suspicions of policy-making priorities at Westminster they cannot believe that they are of such moment to deny historical affinities or to choose political separation. Hence the existential anxiety: unionists think that the Scots could never vote for independence and yet fear that they may elect to do so.

For example, in January 2012 the former leader of the Ulster Unionist Party (UUP), Tom Elliott (2012), made headlines in Scotland with his remark that 'the constitutional approach' of Alex Salmond seemed to pose a greater threat to the Union than the violence of the IRA. That remark, however, was the conclusion to a passage in which he spoke of how unionists had endured 30 years of the Troubles which were designed to break their will. The willingness to withstand the IRA's campaign only demonstrated 'our judgement on the value of the Union'. The message is that the Scots should value it as well. A very different inflection has been given by others to the same argument, contrasting the Irish republican tradition and that of the SNP. This involves a continued condemnation of the first and a back-handed compliment to the second. Thus the Democratic Unionist Party (DUP) MP Nigel Dodds (2012) noted the irony that Scotland may indeed leave the Union without a single murder or a single bombing, though he was confident that in 2014 the Scots would choose otherwise.

The second response is political. Having once felt that they were on the 'window-ledge of the Union', to use the term coined by Peter Robinson in 1985, devolution across the United Kingdom has ironically helped to make unionists feel more integrated into the constitutional architecture of the state. In a speech to the British-Irish Association in Oxford, Robinson (2012), now leader of the DUP and Northern Ireland's First Minister, announced with some confidence that Northern Ireland was no longer a place apart. Unionists have no 'present fears' about the security of their constitutional position. Indeed, an opinion poll in the *Belfast Telegraph* in June 2012 had shown that only seven per cent of voters would vote to remove the border.

Since 2007, when the Assembly became fully operative, support for Irish unity had been decreasing even though electoral support for Sinn Fein had been rising (Clarke 2012). And if one were pushed to identify some common ground between politics in Northern Ireland and Scotland that would be a tempting comparison. One could also point to the growth in support for the SNP along with only minor fluctuations in popular support for independence. Robinson was even moved to argue (as had Trimble a decade earlier) that a new Northern Ireland was in the process of emerging in which the question of Irish unity was no longer relevant.

To those who claim that the Belfast Agreement of 1998 is only a holding position, others with an acute sense of history can respond by saying that the 1920 Government of Ireland Act was also considered to be a temporary measure, though it delivered 50 years of constitutional stability. Nevertheless, it is interesting to note Robinson's deliberate use of the term *present* fears. The anxiety here is of a different order to the first. It is, in short, that having succeeded in establishing institutions that have managed to settle and to secure Northern Ireland's position, events in Scotland could see the debate shift once again from procedures to options, re-opening questions which unionists had hoped were now settled.

Another former UUP leader, Lord Empey (BBC 2012b), speaking in the debate on the Scotland Bill, suggested that one result of a nationalist victory in the 2014 referendum might be a reigniting of the Troubles. In this dramatically pessimistic vision, he envisaged Northern Ireland ending up 'like West Pakistan', with a foreign power on one side and now on another. When I put that possibility to another unionist politician, he hesitated, smiled and replied: 'We would become the Alaska of the Union'. Though the Alaskan option would be better than the West Pakistan option, neither of them would be very comfortable or secure.

Nationalists and Republicans

It is the prospect of that discomfort and insecurity which appeals to the anti-unionist instinct. It is exactly this potentially indeterminate position of Northern Ireland that has encouraged speculation (informed by a certain *Schadenfreude*) about the consequences of Scottish independence for Ulster unionists. Mary Kenny (2012) thought that without their 'closest kinsmen' unionists would indeed be uncomfortably out on a West Pakistan/ Alaskan limb. The expression she used was 'orphaned, basically'. If anxiety captures the unionist disposition, there are a number of expectations that constitute the nationalist and republican position. The first essays a more sophisticated, geopolitical reading of events than Kenny's, linking together in a web of predicaments the United Kingdom's relationship with the European Union, the referendum on Scottish independence and an emergent English backlash to devolution. These are then read into a scenario about Northern Ireland's future that suggests hitherto unthinkable possibilities.

For example, the respected *Irish Times* journalist Paul Gillespie (2011) recently claimed that there was not only a profound Scottish-English divide in national identity but also in attitudes to European integration. The intersection of these and other political divisions, he believed, had generated a crisis of British identity that made the polity less stable. The coincidence of a Conservative dominated, Eurosceptic England seeking to loosen ties with Brussels and an SNP dominated Europhile Scotland looking to Brussels as a forum for national re-assertion make break-up appear a larger possibility than the opinion polls suggest.

For Scots this argument has a familiar lineage and it can be traced more expansively in the work of Tom Nairn. Of course, it is based on a range of questionable assumptions which have been frequently challenged but the specific references to Northern Ireland are revealing. The reasoning proposes that the real affinity of Ulster unionism is indeed with Scotland and that, if independence occurred, the prospect of remaining part of an England-dominated successor state would not be so attractive. The expectation that this will promote constitutional reflection on the character of the new relationship is well-made for it is something which, from a Welsh perspective, First Minister Carwyn Jones has already mooted. The emphasis in the Irish case is not on a refashioned Union – Gillespie defined the post-independence condition as 'a failed British' state – but an expectation that Scottish independence will compel unionists to look more favourably on either Irish unity or Irish federation. If each step in this speculative sequence is controversial and if its conclusion seems unlikely it is not entirely fantastic. Who, a few years ago, would have predicted a functioning Northern Ireland Executive dominated by arrangements between the DUP and Sinn Fein?

The second is an anticipatory republican strategy that wishes to put Irish unity back on the political agenda. Sinn Fein has committed itself to campaign throughout 2013 for a border poll. Speaking in the Dail the party's president, Gerry Adams (Sinn Fein 2012), claimed that unity remains a live issue which has been given added impetus by the forthcoming Scottish referendum. Responding to his proposal, Taoiseach Enda Kenny ruled out such a poll for the foreseeable future and for very good reasons. Though a border poll is provided for under the terms of the Belfast/Good Friday Agreement it can only be called by the Secretary of State for Northern Ireland when a change in constitutional status seems likely.

Not only does public opinion within Northern Ireland remain clearly opposed to unity but also Irish public attitudes are lukewarm at best. The question is why should Sinn Fein wish to use the Scottish case to justify pushing the issue now? One can suggest a number of reasons. In the Republic of Ireland, Sinn Fein wants to steal the mantle of republican authenticity from its electoral rivals, especially Fianna Fail. In Northern Ireland there is an impulse to prove that Sinn Fein is not only a party of internal administration but also has not abandoned the ultimate goal of a 32 county republic. Furthermore, it serves as a riposte to those dissidents who seek to remove from the party its own mantle of republican authenticity. Moreover, anticipating the prospect of Irish unity and linking it to Scottish politics serves to invert Dodd's references to the IRA campaign. In what Gerry Adams has called 'the big democratic phase of our struggle', the struggle now involves achieving that unity exclusively through the ballot box, thereby drawing a veil over Sinn Fein's violent heritage.

While the active strategy is understandable in traditional ideological terms its central motivations in this instance are mainly tactical.

There is a third disposition which shares the analysis of the first, re-affirms the value of the second but is actually very cautious about returning the debate from procedures to options. This is the position taken by Martin McGuinness who, as Deputy First Minister in the Executive, is most intimately involved with the details of administrative procedure. In an interview with *The Times* (Wade 2012), described there as 'a dramatic intervention', McGuinness thought that there is an air of inevitability about Scottish independence (even if it was not delivered immediately by the referendum vote) and he linked this inexorable end of the Union to the Belfast/Good Friday Agreement. However, he was coy about making any prediction about the future of Northern Ireland and one could only infer that the inevitable departure of Scotland entails also the inevitability of Irish unity. It was expressed thus and elliptically: 'In my view the future will be served by ending the Union and removing partition'. The stress was not on the end but on the means.

Firstly, Sinn Fein had now charted a democratic and peaceful course toward the traditional end. Secondly, there are practical ways in which the institutions already established in Northern Ireland can expand their responsibilities. In particular, McGuinness argued that Northern Ireland representatives should have greater fiscal autonomy. This was quite logical. If you believe that every step in devolution leads to break-up then greater fiscal powers – whether it is called, as in Scotland, devo-more, devo-plus or devo-max – is a useful political investment. In the Northern Ireland case, McGuinness could even point to the consensus among local parties that devolution of corporation tax is a good thing. This has the advantage of keeping faith with the spirit of procedure while enhancing the option of Irish unity. It is a rather clever balancing act but it involves a significant historical fallacy.

Inevitability is not necessarily inevitable. Indeed, predictions about the inevitable demise of Northern Ireland have been made regularly since 1922, normally specifying a timescale of 'in 20 years time'. One is tempted to say of Sinn Fein policy that Northern Ireland is now as it should be because it is on its way to becoming what it ought to be, part of a united Ireland by exclusively political means. In the meantime the 'ought' (Irish unity) takes on the shape of the 'is' (a devolutionary settlement). Here is a narrative that concerns itself immediately with procedures and not with ultimate objectives and where the experience and enjoyment of executive power encourages the suppression of dissent and challenge. Ironically, this may actually be a narrative which appeals to the broader nationalist electorate since they are not without hope that devolution will deliver separation from Great Britain: Irish unity, yes, but not quite yet. And this is a disposition, one can argue, which is not too distant from the centre of gravity in the SNP.

Differences in Common

That unionists, nationalists and republicans should respond to events in Scotland in these very different ways is unsurprising. It would be misleading, however, to suggest that matters in Scotland have encouraged a widespread public debate. Certainly, there is a unionist anxiety that, having secured Northern Ireland's position within the United Kingdom (the claim of both the DUP and the UUP), a Scottish vote for independence has the potential to disorder things again. Certainly, nationalists and republicans expect that a Scottish vote for independence will compel a re-assessment of Northern Ireland's relationship with the rest of the island. Though the anxiety and the expectation have been articulated on a number of occasions what is possibly surprising, given Northern Ireland's political reputation, is that they have not been articulated with the customary communal panache.

The party political contributions mentioned in this chapter have been periodic and are not illustrative of systematic engagement. For the moment at least there is little incentive for political leaders to emphasise the issue. Firstly, the simple calculation is that Scotland's choice will not be influenced by interventions from Northern Ireland and that whatever interventions are made could be counterproductive. For unionists it is legitimate to express sentiments of affinity, for nationalists and republicans to hope for SNP success but the truth is that both these expressions are concerned with the state of local, rather than Scottish, politics. Whatever their personal views on the future of Scotland, there is little incentive for party leaders to talk up the possibility of the United Kingdom's break-up. In public Sinn Fein is happy to accept a self-denying ordinance (despite his 'dramatic intervention' McGuinness advised against getting involved in the Scottish debate) and the leaders of the UUP and DUP publicly state that independence will not happen. There is no wish to disrupt present arrangements or to distract from current policies by indulging in displacement politics. Northern Ireland has enough problems.

Secondly, the principle of consent at the heart of the Belfast/Good Friday Agreement, a principle confirmed in joint referenda on the island of Ireland in May 1998, provides confidence in the durability of the institutions. Whatever happens in Scotland in 2014 one can argue that there is now a solid predictability about political arrangements in Northern Ireland. This comfortable assurance about the continuity of procedures, not options, may be misplaced because events, as Harold Macmillan knew, can disorder even the most carefully laid plans. It may only represent a contingent condition, a sort of democratic neutral, where the old constitutional questions have been put on ice but where the potential for power-sharing to deliver creatively is limited by a lack of trust. Here is a delicate balance between political improvement and the ever-present possibility for deterioration, as the disruptive protests by loyalists over the Union flag at Belfast City Hall in December 2012 demonstrated. How easy it is to release the genie of confrontation and how difficult it is to put it back in the bottle. One journalist described this ambivalent state as one where 'the aspirational co-exists with the precautionary' (McKitterick 2003) and it is understandable if most politicians on all sides would put the Scottish question into the precautionary category.

Conclusion

The role Scotland plays in Northern Ireland's politics is a bit like a sealed container and this explains the apparent paradox which this chapter has identified. On the one hand, it is sufficiently sealed and the referendum sufficiently distant for politicians to address it with relative equanimity, relying on the Agreement of 1998 for security. On the other hand, that seal locks in the passions that for a generation helped destabilise politics and society: unionist anxiety about the future of the Union and nationalist and republican expectation that the future is Irish unity. In this case too, the definition of relations between Scotland and Northern Ireland - faraway, so close – remains appropriate.

References

BBC News Northern Ireland (2012a), 'Scottish independence: Orange Order in Ulster Scots referendum call', 25 September, http://www.bbc.co.uk/news/uk-northern-ireland-19710873 (Accessed 3 November 2012).

BBC News Northern Ireland (2012b), 'Empey fears Scottish independence could reignite NI troubles', 26 January, http://www.bbc.co.uk/news/uk-northern-ireland-16749576 (Accessed June 8th 2012).

Bussey, K. (2012), 'David Trimble warns against Scottish independence', *Belfast Telegraph*, 2 March.

Clarke, L. (2012), 'Border poll: Just seven per cent of voters would say yes to Irish unification tomorrow', *Belfast Telegraph*, 11 June.

Dodds, N. (2012), 'Adams is 'detached from reality' with border poll call', press release, 9 November, http://www.mydup.com/news/article/adams-is-detached-from-reality-with-border-poll-call (Accessed 10 December 2012).

Elliott, T. (2012), 'The implications of Scottish independence', 16 January, *Tory Hoose*, http://www.toryhoose.com/2012/01/the-implications-of-scottish-independence-tom-elliott-mla-leader-ulster-unionist-party/ (Accessed 3 November 2012).

Gillespie, P. (2011), 'Case builds for Scottish independence', *Irish Times*, 24 December.

Kenny, M. (2012), 'Scottish divorce will throw North's identity into chaos', *Irish Independent*, 16 January.

Leask, D. (2012), 'As others see us: the view from Northern Ireland', *The Herald*, 26 September, http://www.heraldscotland.com/politics/viewpoint/as-others-see-us-the-view-from-northern-ireland.2012099521 (Accessed 5 December 2012).

McKitterick, D. (2003) 'How others see us', *Belfast Telegraph*, 25 November.

Robinson, P. (2012), Speech to the British-Irish Association, Oxford, 10 September, http://www.peterrobinson.org/MainNewsArticles.asp?ArticleNewsID=4752 (Accessed 3 November 2012).

Sinn Fein (2012), 'Adams calls for border poll' press release, 16 October, http://www.sinnfein.ie/contents/24737 (Accessed 3 December 2012).

Wade, M. (2012), 'McGuinness: Scottish independence inevitable', *The Times*, 1 May.

Walker, Graham (1995), *Intimate Strangers* Edinburgh: John Donald Publishers.

The Irish Experience

NIAMH HARDIMAN

IT IS PERHAPS not too surprising, given the many historical affinities between the two countries, that the Irish experience is seen to be of particular interest when it comes to thinking about options for Scotland. Given Ireland's current economic woes, drawing inferences for another country might be thought of as somewhat akin to George Bernard Shaw's advice to parents: 'If you must hold yourself up to your children as an object lesson (which is not at all necessary), hold yourself up as a warning and not as an example.' So what follows is not intended either as a template or as a morality tale, but rather as a reflection on some issues that have loomed rather large in Irish public debate over time. Whether or not there are any inferences to be drawn for public debate in Scotland is an open question.

In the first half of 2013, Ireland holds the Presidency of the European Union, for the seventh time since joining the EEC (as it then was) in 1973. This rotating responsibility prompts reflection on various aspects of Ireland's political independence, on how well we have managed our economic affairs and on the quality of our democracy. The global financial crisis that started in 2007 has highlighted in retrospect many things that were not well managed during the period of sustained growth from 1994 onward. It has become clearer that there were problems in the way the economy was managed, and that many of these problems owe their origins to defects in Irish political institutions themselves. Ireland's current experience of deep recession, and the requirement to implement painful spending cuts and tax increases under the EU-IMF loan programme it was obliged to enter in November 2010, have to be understood in the context of the wider European framework of policy-making, and specifically in the context of the rules governing the Eurozone. There is no serious political grouping expressing Eurosceptic views in Ireland, and the great majority of people continue to support Ireland's membership of European Monetary Union and of the European Union itself. However, as the crisis drags on, we also see new tensions emerging between what people expect of their political representatives, and what those politicians are in fact able to do.

Managing Economic Policy for Good or Ill

Ireland's experience illustrates both the advantages and the disadvantages of European economic interdependence in a particularly stark way. During the 1950s, and long before it joined the EU, Ireland had begun to develop and industrial development strategy based on promoting foreign direct investment, supported by preferential tax incentives and generous grant aid. Even though this policy orientation has been debated and challenged several times over the decades, and even though tax incentives had to be modified in the late 1980s to conform with European competition law, the basic policy mix remained largely unchanged. This made it possible for Ireland to build up an export capacity from a low base of domestic economic development, and in a context where there was a limited pool of indigenous entrepreneurs and not much native venture capital. As soon as Ireland joined the EEC (as it was in 1973), it benefited from a surge of inward investment, mostly from the US and Japan, whose firms wanted a production base in a European country from which they could easily access the wider European market. Something similar happened again in the late 1980s and early 1990s, though now based on a rather higher combination of skills, especially in pharmaceuticals and information and computer technology. The completion of the Single European Market in 1992 opened new opportunities for foreign investors, and Ireland was able to draw in a disproportionate volume of the increased US capital then looking for profitable investment opportunities.

Ireland enjoyed a prolonged period of unusually rapid economic growth from 1994 until the crisis erupted fully in 2008 – the period of the 'Celtic Tiger'. This brought about rapidly increasing rates of employment, as previously unemployed people were able to find jobs, more women entered the labour market, and new generations of well-educated young people readily found work. Many Irish people who had previously emigrated, and who had acquired skills and experience abroad, took the opportunity to return home. Indeed, for the first time, Ireland became a magnet for people from other countries, a country to which people wanted to move instead of an emigrant nation forever sending its own people away to look for work. Ireland, along with Britain and Sweden, were the first to open their labour markets to people from the new EU member states of East-Central Europe. Quite suddenly, the arrival of new shops selling Polish and

Latvian goods testified to the presence in our midst of whole new communities and cultures.

But the kind of development path that Ireland had chosen was not unproblematic. Irish industrial policy was heavily focused on attracting foreign direct investment, but it was difficult to see how indigenous productive activity could be fostered. Many of the Irish high-tech start-ups during the years of the economic boom owed their origins to people who had gained experience in multinationals, and an Irish software development industry with significant exporting capacity grew up rapidly. But the pattern of industrial development was quite lopsided. The high-tech sector was mostly foreign-owned, and although it employed relatively few people, it accounted for the great bulk of the value of exports. Meanwhile, the large number of Irish-owned firms tended to be much smaller in size, and to produce mostly for the domestic market. The old challenge of the late-comer to industrial development persisted: Irish firms saturate the domestic market quite quickly and must export if they are to grow further, but this is difficult to do from a small base. Irish-owned firms find it difficult to grow past a certain point in order to become large players. Many of the most promising and profitable firms tend to be bought out by multinationals. The challenge of finding a sustainable mix of economic activity, with a significant domestic growth capacity, is still not resolved.

Relying on multinationals as the engine of growth has worked well for Ireland, for as long as they are willing to invest. But it leaves the Irish economy vulnerable to swings in the international economy, and this helps explain why the Celtic Tiger period should really be understood as falling into two time-periods. From 1994 until about 2000, investment by foreign firms generated a great deal of extra domestic economic activity. Large numbers of new jobs were also created in the domestic economy, very many of them in service-related activities, in high-value-added areas as well as in lower-skill personal service activities. But the collapse of the dot-com bubble in the US in the early 2000s had unfortunate consequences for Ireland, where information and communications technology firms were so important. From 2000 until 2007 or 2008, the emphasis switched away from export-oriented economic activity and toward construction as the main source of growth. The government recognised that a property price bubble was developing, but it was unwilling to intervene too actively. This provided a great many new jobs in construction, and new opportunities in property speculation that benefited developers, the banks that lent the ever-increasing sums of money, and the lawyers and accountants who supported the deals. Employment in construction came to account for some 15 per cent of all jobs, twice what is generally regarded as common in a normal growth context, and the revenues generated by construction-related activities (sales transaction taxes, capital gains taxes and so on) provided a buoyant source of tax buoyancy to government. Once the crisis hit, therefore, Ireland was particularly vulnerable to the sharp collapse of house prices and the sudden cessation of activity in the construction industry. Large numbers of men, mostly with relatively low skills, were suddenly made redundant, and the job losses quickly extended to many areas of service activity such as retail and personal services, many of which were jobs filled by women; over time, ongoing recession destroyed jobs in many other sectors.

In an economic downturn, it might be thought that there may be scope for government to step in to stem the worst effects of the downturn with additional spending. Indeed, a number of other European governments undertook some stimulus measures in 2008 and 2009 to prevent the recession turning into a new Depression. However, the Irish government did not take part in this recovery effort, but turned fairly quickly toward prioritising the need to stabilise the public deficit. The reasons for this are complex, and owe something to the lessons they believed needed to be learned from an earlier period of fiscal consolidation in the late 1980s, when getting the public finances in order, it was argued, helped to create the conditions for making Ireland a credible destination for new investment.

Indeed, the Irish public finances, which had seemed quite stable and buoyant during the 2000s, concealed some problems that were only exposed by the onset of crisis. Tax had become dangerously reliant on revenues from construction, and other sources of revenue had been weakened. Personal income tax rates were cut, and up to 40 per cent of low-income employees had been given complete exemption from income tax. This followed from the preferences of centre-right Fianna Fail-led governments, which were in power from 1997 until 2011, for a low-tax, low-welfare-services policy mix, which they believed was most conducive to job creation. Electorally, this proved popular. People welcomed the increases in disposable income that resulted, and lower taxes helped dampen demands for higher pay. The trade unions, although not very keen on this approach, went along with it, because as long as total tax revenues were buoyant, lower income taxes did not result in any worsening of public service provision. Indeed, total public spending was on an upward curve, as government committed extra funds to more jobs, higher pay, and higher rates of welfare payments and other transfer spending. For a time, it seemed as if Irish people could have it all: we could have both the penny and the bun. But the combination of a narrowing revenue base and increasing spending commitments proved to be a fragile and contingent combination. This is why the deficit gap widened so sharply during 2008 and 2009.

In hindsight, it is easier than it was at the time to recognise the dangers of having a budget mix that was so susceptible to crisis, particularly because Ireland had, since the turn of the millennium, been part of the Eurozone, which greatly altered the scope of domestic policy choice. The logic of European Monetary Union (EMU) meant that no member state could alter interest rates to help its own economy, nor could they devalue or otherwise change their exchange rate to gain competitiveness or boost jobs and exports. This placed all the pressure of managing the domestic economy in a stable manner onto the control of relative costs within each country. If a country let its cost base worsen relative to other Eurozone members, it would pay a price, mostly in the form of higher unemployment. In order to keep governments from spending their way out of trouble, and thereby undercutting the cost-containing efforts made by other countries, the Stability and Growth Pact (SGP) put strict limits on the size of the deficit governments could run (three per cent of GDP), and the scale of debt they could incur (60 per cent of GDP). Because so much decision-making was now run centrally, market lending to Eurozone member states came to be seen as more or less risk-free, and countries like Ireland, Spain, and Greece were able to borrow on international markets at rates that were very close to those of the largest and strongest economy, that of Germany. There was a strong expectation that even though member states of the Eurozone had very different sorts of economy, they would converge in the way these functioned under the rules of EMU.

However, it became clear quite quickly that the Eurozone had a number of unanticipated consequences. Not only were the SGP rules too weak to enforce, but the low cost of borrowing had the paradoxical effect of creating a surge of capital inflows into Ireland and other peripheral countries, where growth potential seemed strong. But the most common outlet for all this lending was in property. This was the source of the uncontrolled property boom, which peaked between 2005 and 2008. Inflationary pressures mounted in the Irish economy, as employees pushed for higher pay to enable them to meet rapidly rising house prices. It was not possible for government to raise interest rates to dampen the rate of borrowing, because interest rates were set centrally, by the European Central Bank, and were most responsive to the needs of the strongest core countries; and as German growth was sluggish, interest rates were kept low to help prevent job losses there.

Ireland was accumulating many problems of sustainable growth by the time the crisis broke. But what proved to be the biggest catastrophe of all centred on the financial sector. Irish governments had followed the British lead in adopting a light-touch regulatory stance toward the banking sector. This followed from its efforts to build up a tax-incentivised centre for internationally traded financial services in Dublin from the late 1980s on. It was also consistent with a more general view, widely held in Irish political circles, that the main banks lending into the Irish economy could be trusted to regulate themselves such that their own profitability would not come at the expense of excessive risk or of damaging their own share-holders' interests. Unfortunately, intensifying competition for business in a runaway property boom meant that the main banks made ever larger and risker loans, and the structure of incentives for the top managers, similar to the experience of the large British banks, placed few restraints on their willingness to gamble recklessly with their own institutions' via-bility. Adverse market assessment of the performance of the main Irish banks had already caused their share prices to slide by the time Northern Bank collapsed in Britain. By the end of September 2008, they faced immi-nent collapse. In an event that is still not fully understood or explained, an emergency all-night meeting between senior bank officials and govern-ment ministers resulted in the Irish government providing guarantees to the main Irish banks, without any full assessment of the scale of the lia-bility they were undertaking.

The total cost to the public purse of bailing out the banks is estimated at almost £63bn. To put this in context, total GDP in 2011 was £159bn. The scale of this public responsibility for private sector bail-out is consid-erably larger than in any other OECD country. The politics of how this is to be managed is the subject of ongoing contention between the Irish govern-ment and the European authorities.

The scale of the banking crisis in Ireland compounds the crisis in the public finances. It is now all too clear that under-regulation of the finan-cial sector has had devastating consequences. Not unlike the Icelandic case, the Irish banks competitively goaded one another into ever-riskier lending practices. In the absence of strong domestic oversight, and with no controls on European lending practices, they exposed their businesses, their shareholders, and ultimately the whole Irish economy and Irish society to devastating losses, and to crushing recovery efforts into the foreseeable future.

Large countries that control their own currencies, or large countries with large internal markets for their goods and services, need not worry so much about vulnerability to international fluctuations: they have a wider range of policy options they can deploy in the bad times. Small countries are much more vulnerable in the international economy. The implications for a small country such as Ireland are much the same as those learned over time by the small Scandinavian countries. Public spending must be solidly underpinned by a solid tax base, and public deficits in small economies are judged harshly by the international markets. Furthermore, regulations of banks must be taken a great deal more seriously than Irish governments believed was necessary. The belated lesson for Ireland is, as US political scientist Herman Schwartz has noted, that 'small states must behave more prudently than large ones, not because it is the right thing to do, but because it is the only thing they can do' (Schwartz 2011).

Institutional Design and Political Accountability

Economic policy decisions are made by a whole range of policy actors, so it is appropriate to reflect on the features of institutional design and political practice that may have generated some of propensity to make the kind of decisions that, as we have seen, have contributed to the origins and management of the crisis.

We might think of this as a problem of how to generate good policy decisions to try to avoid things going wrong; and if things do go wrong, how to find out what happened to the right people can be held to account, with a view to ensuring that similar problems to not arise again. In other words, these are issues to do with the quality of policy formation on the one hand, and ensuring appropriate political accountability on the other.

As in other democratic societies, elected governments set the policy agenda, and the programme for government constitutes much of the work of the public service for the following four or five years. A recurring issue in discussion about Irish politics concerns the quality of debate informing the way government goes about implementing its declared policy priorities.

One such issue has to do with a persistent tendency of economic policy to be pro-cyclical in character. Governments tend to spend heavily during the good times, then when a downturn comes, they have little choice but to engage in harsh retrenchment – the opposite of what prudent fiscal management might suggest. It is perhaps all too easy to blame the voters for letting politicians play too personalised a role in Irish public life, such that they put the need to attend to constituents' requests over the need to be responsible for making sure public policy is coherent and consistent. But it is also true that the incentives in the political system as it is currently constituted have encouraged these tendencies. There is little scope for serious policy debate in parliament, and most politicians therefore see little need to become more expert on policy issues.

The civil service, run on generalist principles, often lacks specialist skills, especially in economic policy analysis. These deficiencies have started to be addressed under the watchful eye of the 'Troika' of lenders (the European Commission, the European Central Bank, and the International Monetary Fund). A new specialist Department of Public Expenditure and Reform has been created, closely linked to the Department of Finance. In line with new Eurozone rules, Ireland has created a Fiscal Council to provide expert commentary on policy. Irish voters endorsed a referendum to give effect to the European Fiscal Pact, constraining the scope of discretionary domestic choice in future. Domestic policy expertise has been strengthened. But this has come about as a result of the extension of the scope of EU oversight, and a consequent narrowing of the scope of domestic policy discretion.

The Irish parliamentary system has provided relatively little effective legislative counter-weight to executive preferences. The Irish system, designed on the Westminster model, affords a relatively weak role to the political opposition and indeed to government party backbenchers. In Britain, many reforms have been undertaken to permit parliament not only to scrutinise and amend new legislative proposals, but also to conduct specialised inquiries. But in Ireland, a constitutional case in 2002 made it impossible for parliamentary committees to undertake many kinds of inquiry. Compared with the British government in Westminster, Irish governments face much weaker institutional constraints that would expose their policy priorities to scrutiny and debate. Indeed, corruption scandals in the 1980s, 1990s and 2000s often centred on cases in which domestic business interests gained preferential treatment or favourable government decisions in exchange for financial support, paid either to the party or in some cases to individual politicians themselves. Yet it proved extremely difficult to hold politicians to account. Similarly, some high-profile cases in which politicians have overseen policy mistakes, or where poor administrative oversight has resulted in damaging outcomes (in managing the costs of care in nursing homes, for example, or in blood contamination scandals), it proved very difficult to establish responsibility or accountability. For a time, Ireland resorted to public Tribunals of Inquiry to investigate such problems. But their extraordinarily high cost and the indeterminate findings they produced led to their falling out of favour, without any clear alternative in sight.

Compared with other European countries, the spectrum of political debate in Irish public life is quite narrow. The main political parties have not been very clearly differentiated in their presentation of the policy choices facing Irish voters. The two historically largest political parties, Fianna Fail and Fine Gael, have been the principal rival contenders to lead government formation, but they have clustered close to each other on the centre-right of the political spectrum. The left or centre-left attracts much weaker support. The Labour Party has found it necessary to compete on policy platforms that would make it possible to form a coalition with one or other of the major parties.

The aftermath of the crisis has challenged much of this, with consequences that are as yet unclear. Fianna Fail bore the brunt of voter anger over the scale of the crisis and the mismanagement that had preceded it: this historically dominant party was reduced to a rump in the 2011 elections. The governing coalition of Fine Gael and Labour has a commanding majority, but has little discretion in policy choice under the terms of the loan agreement. Political opinion is still in flux. It will be some time before it becomes clear whether the lines of political competition re-form on familiar tracks, or whether some more far-reaching realignment may yet be in store.

Economic Government and Democratic Debate in an Interdependent Europe

Among the issues that will decide the future direction of Irish political life is the prospect of economic recovery, not just the resumption of employment opportunities, especially for younger people, but also relief for the many households experiencing severe mortgage pressure in the aftermath of the property crash.

One interpretation of Ireland's current situation is that although it has experienced an economic disaster, it is better placed to deal with this inside the EU, and specifically inside the Eurozone, than if it were obliged to go it alone. After all, the yawning gap between expenditure commitment and revenue flow has to be met somehow: better therefore to manage this through a structured loan agreement. Some economic commentators have pointed to alternative options, for example to the benefits Iceland has gained through bank debt repudiation and a sharp currency devaluation, even if at the expense of the collapse of national living standards. There is virtually no constituency of support in Ireland for either default or devaluation though. Harsh and unpleasant as it is to engage in 'internal devaluation', a departure from the existing policy framework is generally seen as incurring the risk of immense economic dislocation and the probable destruction of recovery prospects.

This is not to say that there is uncritical acceptance of the view that 'there is no alternative', for there is considerable disagreement about the terms of the EU-ECB-IMF loan, about the funding of bank recapitalisation, and indeed about Irish government priorities in implementing the fiscal retrenchment programme. There is therefore widespread support for the view that Ireland should not depart from the European policy framework, but should engage even more actively with it. Irish economic prospects are often seen as primarily dependent on the fortunes of the British and US economies, with a sidelong look at the European economy. But Ireland's economic and political fortunes are now also intimately linked with those of the other countries of the European periphery, and these will be strongly shaped by the terms of debate that hold in the strongest European economies, especially Germany, and in the heart of the European institutions themselves.

And yet this poses one of the most intractable issues not only for Ireland but for the evolving European political system itself. As the late Irish political scientist Peter Mair has noted, there is a growing gap between what he calls the politics of responsiveness on the one hand, and the politics of responsibility on the other (Mair 2009). Politicians are elected at national level to respond to the interests and concerns of the people who vote for them: this is an integral part of what we value in the democratic process. There is little appetite for transferring more political power to European institutions, even if this is said to be a necessary part of crisis management. But increasingly, voters find that they can change their politicians but not the policies at national level, because governments are responsible to actors that are beyond national borders but over whose decisions they have relatively little formative influence. This point holds even for countries that are not part of European Monetary Union, for many new measures to strengthen economic coordination apply to all EU member states, and indeed, Iceland has though it preferable to look for economic security inside the shelter of the EU. Whether or to what degree the emergent system of economic coordination is amenable to real practices of democratic participation and accountability remains to be seen.

References

Mair, P. (2009), 'Representative Versus Responsible Government', Cologne: Max Planck Institute for the Study of Societies, MPIFG Working Paper 09/8, http://www.mpifg.de/pu/workpap/wp09-8.pdf

Schwartz, H. (2011), 'Iceland's Financial Iceberg: Why Leveraging Up is a Titanic Mistake without a Reserve Currency', *European Political Science*, 10(3):292–300.

Nordic Horizons for the Isles?
Instituting regional cooperation

SARA DYBRIS MCQUAID

IN JANUARY 2012 Scotland's First Minister, Alex Salmond, gave the eigth Hugo Young lecture entitled 'Scotland's Place in the World' (Salmond, 2012). The speech addressed how Scotland might move towards and beyond independence, and particularly how the advent of an independent Scotland would reconfigure neighbouring relations. It was no surprise that the speech pursued the idea of some sort of a social union on the far side of the existing political union in the UK, but it was, perhaps, surprising that in doing so, Salmond invoked two institutions that usually fly low under the public radar in domestic as well as international politics: the British-Irish Council and the Nordic Council. These were presented as existing sites and models for cooperation that might both contain and inspire common endeavours in the future.

It has almost become a commonplace to allude to the Nordic countries, when the loosening ties of the UK are debated. From the devolution debates of the 1990s; as part of the peace process in Northern Ireland; and now in the context of the various aspirations for Scotland's constitutional future, the 'Nordic model of neighbourly cooperation' has been frequently proposed as a guiding light if not a final destination for the road ahead. 'Nordic Horizons' are repeatedly used as alternative sources of identification: as examples of small, successful nation-states; as ideal social democracies; as new social, environmental and economic templates; and not least as a source of inspiration when considering the changing constitutional relationships within a 'macro-region'.

However, while Nordic cooperation is regularly invoked in Scotland, the actual institutional framework that formalises this cooperation (the Nordic Councils) remains overlooked, making Salmond's invocation of them worthy of note. These kinds of councils – and there are others, many of them modelled on the Nordic Councils – offer some unique possibilities for smaller states by operating in the space between sovereign states and larger political and economic unions like the EU.

What can the Nordic Council example then offer the Scottish independence debate? A preliminary answer, which resonates with many of the ways Nordic cooperation has been invoked, is that it can illustrate what a new association might look like beyond a political union. The Nordic countries used to be joined together in different constellations but are now established in varying forms of constitutional independence while retaining a voluntary socio-cultural and political interdependence in the Nordic Council. But this answer also underscores the importance of understanding the institutional mechanics of this cooperation – and not merely its idealised goals – if it is to be of use in the Scottish debate.

While there are many similarities between the 'Nordics' and 'the Isles', the two cases are on different trajectories. The current debate in the Nordic countries is about how deeper integration in the spaces between local, national, macro-regional and international can be achieved. Though this is perhaps mirrored in British-Irish relations, which appear to be historically amicable, it is also juxtaposed by the state of internal relations in the UK, in what has been termed a crisis of 'Britishness'. The Scottish independence referendum is arguably also one expression of this state of affairs.

An initial point, then, is that though the Nordic countries can provide useful models for cooperation within the changing Isles, there are also key differences between the trajectories of the two macro-regions that are not easily bridged or glossed over. This is a key point to bear in mind through the following.

The chapter will proceed as follows: after briefly distinguishing the 'Council Model' from other forms of international cooperation, the chapter will introduce and contrast the structures of cooperation in the Nordic Council and in the Isles. It will then go on to introduce some of the new Nordic Council debates before suggesting some problems and possibilities for the Isles in light of the comparison.

Introducing the Idea of a Council Model

The 'Council Model' that arises from the Nordic example could also be called a 'transnational political association' because it traverses the usual confines of sovereignty as well as the boundaries between local, national and international spaces to establish a form of shared macro-regional space. It is different from other international unions and associations (like the EU or the UN) because it rests on a perceived historical and common identity between the members. A high density of linkages, co-mingling and exchanges at the level of civil society is believed to have woven a durable linguistic, social, cultural, economic and political fabric upon which an institutional cooperation is built. This strong vertical integration between civic and political society combines emotional belonging with a more practical focus on common interests. And the ability to glide almost effortlessly between the poles of social and political union makes these councils – unusually – appealing to both unionism and nationalism.

The Council model is used as an important laboratory of confidence-building, updating, exchanging views, developing common policies and thus consolidating a form of transnational identification and democracy. It is operated by consensus and primarily keeps a low-politics focus, which enables it to coexist with other national and international institutions. It has been of particular interest to smaller states worried about being dominated by more powerful neighbours or losing their voice in larger fora.

When the Nordic populations are asked whether they support Nordic cooperation and want to extend it, they are overwhelmingly positive. Still, this masks the fact that the Council model is very much, what is derogatively called, a 'talking shop'. Advances are firmly circumscribed by the principle of consensus and rival binding international obligations. Rapid change rarely pivots on Nordic cooperation and it is a recurring complaint that the inter-parliamentary cooperation has no real capacity for agenda-setting and problem-solving.

Having said this, there are benefits to being 'under the radar', not least in terms of creating and maintaining mutual trust without the regular political grandstanding. While tomorrow might not be different from today following a Nordic Council decision, the politics of small steps taken in unison have produced a range of Nordic policies and laid the groundwork for a number of concrete cooperative initiatives, allowing Nordic countries to punch above their weight in international fora.

While both Isles-wide and Nordic institutional cooperation are examples of 'council models', the respective institutions have very different origins. Nordic cooperation is a form of transnational association, which is often hailed as unique, because the *institutional* model has evolved, not from the top down but from the bottom up: from the grassroots to the tree-tops, from inter-popular civic associations to the institutionalised cooperation between parliamentarians and governments. Political cooperation has endeavoured to create uniform rules and reciprocal rights grounded in a perception of common politico-cultural identities. This endeavour has been undergirded by exchanges and joint ventures at the civic level between schools, universities, media, business, trade unions, NGO's etc. Association has a great deal of historical depth, as the Nordic countries have engaged in various degrees of cooperation, conflict and conquest with each other for centuries.

While Isles-wide cooperation also assumes legitimacy from the density of civic exchanges within 'the Isles', and of course also has profound historical depth, it has primarily developed from the top-down in political elite negotiations. The institutionalisation of this cooperation has largely come with attempts at resolving the conflict in Northern Ireland, in part by recasting the relationships between the peoples of the whole archipelago within a shared narrative and institutional framework. However, this has also opened up possibilities for broader forms of cooperation within the Isles. Indeed, some of the most fervent propagators of isles-wide cooperation have been those representing the new local parliaments and assemblies established by devolution. So while British-Irish cooperation was initiated within the context of conflict resolution, the potential impact of its institutions has a much wider reach not least in a post-devolution UK and presumably even a post-independence Scotland. It is of course this potential Alex Salmond is looking to explore.

Introducing the Institutional Cooperation

Both Nordic and Isles-wide cooperation take place in two tiers – a parliamentary tier and an inter-governmental tier. In both cases an inter-parliamentary tier was established ahead of an inter-governmental tier. However, the infrastructure of the cooperation and particularly the way in which the tiers relate to each other are very different in the two contexts – I will return to this following a brief introduction to the institutions.

Parliamentary Cooperation: The Nordic Council (NC)

In 1952 existing ad hoc parliamentary cooperation between Denmark, Sweden, Norway, and Iceland was institutionalised in a 'Nordic Council'. The impetus was a desire '[...] to promote and strengthen the close ties existing between the Nordic peoples in matters of culture, and of legal and social philosophy, and to extend the scale of co-operation between the

Nordic countries'. After initial resistance from The Soviet Union, Finland joined the Council in 1955.

In practical terms, the sovereign states have the largest delegations while the self-governing territories (Faroe Islands, Greenland and the Aaland islands) have much smaller representations. While the delegations are national, cooperation inside the NC is also organised across national lines in party-based groups and issue-based committees. This ensures a vital national and ideological cross-pressure in parliamentary cooperation. Nordic cooperation has been particularly strong in the areas of culture and education, as well as environmental and climate policy. In recent years overarching themes have included 'a Robust Welfare-state', 'Freedom of Movement', 'a Nordic Voice in the EU' 'Common Arctic Policy' and 'Community, Neighbourhood and Globalisation'.

Parliamentary Cooperation: The British-Irish Inter-Parliamentary Body/The British-Irish Parliamentary Assembly (BIPA)

The British-Irish Inter-Parliamentary Body was established in 1990 on a mandate in the Anglo-Irish Agreement of 1985. The purpose was to provide a link between the Houses of Parliament and the Houses of the Oireachtas, building new relationships in the early stages of what would later become a fully-fledged bilateral peace process. In 2001, following devolution, delegations from the new local administrations in Scotland, Wales, Northern Ireland, as well as Jersey, Guernsey and the Isle of Man joined the body. In 2008 the body was renamed the British-Irish Parliamentary Assembly. Its current mission is 'to promote co-operation between political representatives in Britain and Ireland for the benefit of the people we represent. [And][...] to build on the close relationships established in recent years between politicians throughout Britain and Ireland.' As such, BIPA has been an institutional expression of the changing relationship between Britain and Ireland. The initial role of BIPA was to provide a confidence-building forum for parliamentarians in the context of the Northern Ireland conflict. Beyond conflict its role is yet to be fully formalised. It has been suggested that BIPA could become a unique site of inter-parliamentary exchange where diverging experiences of electoral and parliamentary systems in the intersection between embedded tradition and new journeys can be debated. In terms of outward facing cooperation, and somewhat inspired by new Nordic debates, it has been suggested that BIPA could be a forum for devising common strategies in relation to EU and in regards to international promotion of the Isles, both as macro-regional and regional space. Obviously, this line of thinking is simultaneously curbed by individual nation-branding, radically different levels of EU enthusiasm and various degrees of sovereignty in terms of foreign policy (obstacles not unknown in the Nordic Council).

In both cases the parliamentarians meet in plenary sessions twice a year as well as in their committees and make recommendations to their respective national parliaments.

Intergovernmental cooperation: Nordic Council of Ministers (NCM)

The Nordic Council of Ministers was established in 1971 as the forum for Nordic inter-governmental cooperation. One of the purposes was to maintain Nordic cooperation in the event that one or more countries would become EC members (as Denmark did in 1973 and Sweden and Finland did in 1995). The aim was '[...] to strengthen and expand the institutional foundations for co-operation between the Nordic countries'.

There are currently ten ministerial councils, which meet one to five times a year. One of these meetings takes place in tandem with the annual autumn session of the Nordic Council, bringing inter-parliamentary and inter-governmental cooperation together.

Intergovernmental Cooperation: The British-Irish Council (BIC)

The British-Irish Council was established as part of the 1998 constitutional agreement in Northern Ireland. Its aim was 'to promote the harmonious and mutually beneficial development of the totality of relationships among the peoples of these islands'. It effectively extended the existing bilateral cooperation between the British and Irish governments to include the new administrations in Northern Ireland, Scotland and Wales, relating conflict resolution to overall constitutional reform in the United Kingdom and The Republic of Ireland. Being part of the Belfast Agreement has hampered BIC, as it has been suspended between 2002 and 2007 pending renewed political agreement in Northern Ireland. It has therefore met only 19 times.

BIC does not have standing ministerial councils but instead cooperates through relevant ministers and civil servants in 12 workstreams each led by one of the administrations. The workstream on Energy has perhaps produced the most decisive outcome in the shape of an all-islands approach to an electricity grid and marine renewals.

Relations between the Inter-Parliamentary Level and the Inter-Governmental Level of Cooperation

In both Councils inter-governmental cooperation is by consensus and binding decisions are made unanimously. There are, however, significant differences in the way the inter-governmental and inter-parliamentary levels relate to each other. BIC and BIPA are not formally integrated as complementary tiers of the same cooperation and meet in separate cities as well as on separate occasions.

By contrast, the annual autumn session of the NC brings together the parliamentary and governmental tier, not just at the same venue but in consultation and debate. Following public reports from the respective ministerial councils, parliamentarians can question individual ministers, not exclusively from their own countries but from all the member states. After the end of the Cold War, this procedure has been extended to include policy areas that are not yet formally part of Nordic cooperation, like foreign, defence and security policy. There are no standing ministerial councils for foreign affairs and defence, but the respective ministers for these policy areas meet with their opposite Nordic numbers as part of the annual session. Since 2006 the Nordic prime ministers and presidents have also held their summits in conjunction with the Nordic Council session and importantly, take questions from the parliamentarians across the board.

There is, in other words, a very specific Nordic political culture with a profound degree of integration between Nordic and national politics, which amounts to a form of trans-nationalism that both includes and transcends the individual nation state. Attaching a form of democratic accountability across the Nordic countries arguably aids in developing a trans-national Nordic political community and foregrounds the existence of deep-rooted cooperation. This is further emphasised by the fact that during its three-day session (which is open to the public), the NC takes over the parliament buildings of the host country, allowing for example Finnish politicians to speak from the Danish parliamentary platform. Getting inside each other's political and democratic systems in such a material way is very effective in building politico-cultural relationships.

By contrast, BIPA meet in more neutral conference venues and, despite some effort, have so far failed to become the official parliamentary tier of BIC. In fact BIC has even declined the presence of observers from the BIPA at their summits. The disconnect between the inter-parliamentary and the inter-governmental level means that the fruitful coupling between democratic deliberation and decision-making is lost. While the parliamentary tier arguably provides a permanent structure of transnational democracy, it is divested of power. By the same token the inter-governmental cooperation lacks a broader democratic remit, as well as parliamentary accountability and public transparency.

Maintaining inter-parliamentary links as well as connecting these to the inter-governmental level of cooperation is a pivotal lesson to draw from Nordic cooperation for post-devolution UK. Maintaining the separation of the parliamentary and the governmental tier in the British-Irish context suggests that a top-down attitude persists in the BIC and indicates that government ministers are reluctant to be subjected to trans-national parliamentary scrutiny. This makes the institutions of the Isles decisively different from Nordic cooperation, which is precisely an exercise in compensating the democratic deficit that often prevails in international organisations, in order to maintain a rooted sense of a trans-national political community.

Secretariats

Another crucial difference between the two Councils is the organisation and composition of their secretariats. The NC has a long-standing secretariat that employs 100 people and disposes of a £99 million budget. In comparison BIC has only just opened a permanent secretariat in Edinburgh in January 2012, which is minimally staffed with a budget of only £183,000. Further, recruitment for the secretariats takes place within very different parameters. The people employed by the BIC secretariat are on assignment from their 'parent' administrations, and can be likened to a diplomatic force with clear national loyalties.

In the NC secretariat, people are employed by the NC and not as representatives for narrower national interests. The existence of a permanent secretariat (comprising both tiers of Nordic cooperation) yields many benefits. Firstly, it ensures continuity in a political environment that is by definition characterised by much coming and going, reflecting electoral fortunes in the member-administrations. This 'political tourism' that might otherwise disrupt the flow of cooperation is to some extent tempered by the continuous work of the secretariat. Secondly, precisely because the staff is not bound (officially at least) by national loyalties it can be an institution that 'thinks across': across national interests and across party political interests in order to develop specifically 'Nordic' ideas and policies.

While this kind of strong secretariat yields advantages, it also has drawbacks: it can almost depoliticise cooperation and preempt political debate, as all problems are cleared away by civil servants in between the parliamentary and ministerial meetings. Furthermore, since the secretariat does not always pursue a strictly administrative line, but occasionally actively works to create new Nordic initiatives, it risks robbing the politicians of the policy initiative or pushing agendas that have no political mandate.

The Dynamics of Nordic Cooperation: New Debates

One of the main challenges for trans-national councils is obviously to find suitable common endeavours in an environment that is also characterised by rival national identities, rival international institutions and separate interests. In the Nordic context external dynamics have been pivotal in spurring on cooperation.

While Nordic cooperation rests on a narrative of shared history, norms and identity it is important to remember that the Nordic identity is not only constructed from the inside out but also from the outside in. A number of important contributing external (particularly geo-political) factors have acted as catalysts for Nordic identification and cooperation, and are now increasingly driving changing Nordic objectives.

After the First World War, Scandinavian unity played a crucial role in deflecting outside interference. The same applied during the cold war, where the Scandinavian countries managed to strike a unique balance in a bipolar world assuming an alternative position between east and west (despite the fact that both Denmark and Norway had joined NATO in 1949). In this way external pressures helped foster and nurture the Nordic identity. Today the external impetus for cooperation is particularly found in the enlargement of EU and wider globalisation (accentuating Nordic commonalities); the financial crisis (accentuating the stability of the Nordic welfare-state model); climate change (an area of Nordic expertise); the growing importance of the Arctic (in which the Nordic countries have developed common interests); and the increased competition for seats in international organisations, like the IMF and the World Bank (challenging the inclusion of small states). Arguably, the NC has managed to survive as an institution because it has responded to internal and external dynamics and successfully redefined its purpose and position along the way. Where the period up until the end of the twentieth century was primarily about internal Nordic consolidation, Nordic cooperation is now seen as a launch site for potential global leverage.

New Nordic Debates

The shift from facing inwards to acting outwards is perhaps best illustrated with two examples from recent NC debates. These debates have been said to herald a new 'golden age' of Nordic cooperation, because they unfold bold Nordic visions and horizons, one emerging from the bottom-up and one from the top-down.

In 2009, amidst great media controversy, the historian Gunnar Wetterberg suggested that the Nordic countries should enter into a political union reminiscent of the Kalmar Union of the late middle ages. Adapted to meet the challenges of a globalised world, this would make 'Norden' the world's tenth largest economy and secure a place in G20, according to Wetterberg. The idea was, not surprisingly, immediately denounced by all the Nordic heads of government. However, whilst most politicians rejected the idea of a fully-fledged political union, many nevertheless argued for deeper ad hoc integration and stressed the benefits of a unison Nordic voice in international institutions like the EU, UN, IMF and the World Bank, as well as a unified response to global problems like the financial crisis, and climate change.

Even if the idea of a political union was officially rejected, the Wetterberg proposal has reinvigorated Nordic cooperation. A series of new Nordic imaginings and practical propositions on how to fashion closer links, common and transferable policies for the benefit of all Nordic citizens have since been unleashed – orchestrated in part by the Nordic secretariat – suggesting that 'pie-in-the-sky thinking' can still open new horizons.

Another and related debate began in 2008, when the Nordic foreign ministers requested that the former UN high commissioner, Thorvald Stoltenberg explore geopolitical challenges 20-30 years ahead with a view to drafting proposals for practical cooperation between the Nordic countries on foreign and security policy. His task was to think beyond the electoral horizons of individual governments and to effectively leverage the Nordic dimension to impact on the international community. The subsequent report suggested 13 areas of cooperation, among them an integrated Arctic strategy, joint diplomatic representations abroad, as well as a Nordic musketeer clause akin to Article 5 in the North Atlantic treaty. Again, Stoltenberg's suggestions dramatically broadened the scope and horizon of Nordic cooperation in an international context – and decisively recast the sphere of political community to embrace a bolder, outward-facing perspective. However, the vision remains hampered by the fact that foreign and security policy are not, in fact, part of the formal Nordic cooperation since there are no standing ministerial councils for these policy areas.

An on-going debate in the NC is thus whether common foreign policies and joint forces should become formally included in the Nordic cooperation. These issues are at odds with the traditional 'low-politics' focus of the Council, and obviously strike at the heart of sovereignty sensitivities. The long-term ideology of Nordic cooperation has always been deliberately diffuse, but these new debates are forcing a focus that can strengthen Nordic cooperation.

At the same time hammering out shared foreign policies or political superstructures is also sure to bring out the many existing Nordic ideological differences, complicated further by asymmetrical international obligations. Further, training the focus of Nordic cooperation at the level of a political elite on an international stage, also risks severing the connection to the roots of civil society. And so while new broad horizons might provide the *raison d'etre* for reinvigorated Nordic cooperation in the future, they also hold disruptive potential for the vertical integration of the trans-national Nordic community.

Nordic Horizons for the Isles?

Clearly, these Nordic debates about closer political integration and common foreign policy cannot be easily transferred to the Isles at this time. The two systems of cooperation are on quite different trajectories, reflected not least in Scotland's impending referendum. But a potentially reshaped Council of the Isles might still usefully seek inspiration in earlier iterations of Nordic cooperation and should also draw lessons from its institutional structures.

While it is, as outlined in the introduction, perhaps not difficult to see the attraction of a Nordic style of cooperation for Alex Salmond, it should be clear from this discussion that he faces a number of structural challenges in implementing it. First, BIC has been established through a top-down negotiation by political elites, rather than being the bottom-up result of civic cooperation, which has ramifications for the legitimacy the institution enjoys and so its possibilities to act (which is further circumscribed by the principle of consensus). Second, the lack of stacking of the inter-parliamentary and inter-governmental tiers seriously hampers the development of a viable trans-national political arena, and underscores the fragmentation of the political cultures in the Isles. Third, the lack of a strong secretariat makes the development of new regional visions and strategies more difficult, as the civil service infrastructure that can help spur debates, clear away roadblocks, and produce trans-national policy positions is simply lacking as of yet.

This having been said, the Nordic model for cooperation continues to provide tantalising visions for ways in which small states with strong social and historical linkages can organise themselves in an increasingly globalised world. The extent to which these visions can be materialised in the Scottish future hinges on a number of open questions:

A key motivation for Nordic cooperation is to strengthen and promote the close ties between the Nordic countries based on common values and norms. Is this also the case for the Isles? Can shared norms of governance be identified and developed across the sharp political divides between the countries of the Isles?

The vertical integration of levels (civil society, parliaments and governments) in the Nordic Council both stimulates practical cooperation and nurtures a common Nordic identity. Can the cooperative institutions in the Isles achieve the same kind of integration to become the institutional framework for expressing and developing a common identity? Indeed, is there a common identity to motivate cooperation?

Do the current Isles-wide councils have the institutional muscle to find and cultivate common ground? Or do they risk being used to assert differences and suit more exclusive national interests, rather than expressing and developing commonalities?

The Nordic Council has found a new outward purpose in the face of globalisation, can Isles-wide cooperation explore the same possibilities by identifying common projects on the other side of political union? Or is this avowed interest in increased cooperation between the Isles merely meant to soften the blow of political breakup?

References

Salmond, A. (2012), 'Scotland's Place in the World', Lecture to the London School of Economics, London, 25 January, http://www.snp.org/blog/post/2012/jan/hugo-young-lecture-scotlands-place-world

Women and constitutional debates: engendering visions of a new Scotland

CHRISTINE BELL AND FIONA MACKAY

Introduction

DEBATES LEADING UP to the creation of the Scottish parliament demonstrated the huge potential to galvanise thinking about political change and the promotion of gender equality. However, women's voices and issues of gender equality and gender justice have been curiously absent from the current debates around constitutional futures in Scotland. This relative absence contrasts sharply with their prominence in the run up to devolution in the 1990s. This essay will reflect upon the opportunities and challenges posed for women and gender equality by the constitutional debates in the run up to the 2014 independence referendum.

Women, Devolution and Constitutional Change

Processes of political change and institutional restructuring open up 'windows' or 'moments' of opportunity for reformers – including those promoting women's rights and gender equality. Constitutional change offers those traditionally marginalised a chance to stake their claims in re-envisaging and redrawing political communities. Constitutions, particularly written ones, are characterised by three key aspects: first, they provide a unique space for articulating a state's narrative of inclusion and national identity; second, they set out an institutional power-map for government such as the form of political representation, and the legislative, executive, and electoral rules; and third through provisions such as rights, they capture an aspiration for the future – something that will enable the country to move from the constitution as a political 'deal' whose national narrative and institutions reflect power balances at the time, to a document which sets out broader principles and aspirations of fair treatment and equality.

All three dimensions of constitution-making projects offer possibilities for inclusion and equality or, conversely, exclusion and inequality. These opportunities were well recognised and seized upon by organised women and gender equality advocates in the run up to devolution in Scotland in the 1990s. A coalition of activist women from trade unions, political parties, church groups, autonomous women's groups, and wider civic society mobilised around their feminist and gender identities – sometimes across other significant social and political divisions and identity claims – in order to insert gendered claims for inclusion into the constitutional reform process. Under the umbrella of the Scottish Women's Coordination Group and the rallying banner of the 50/50 campaign, they lobbied for new political institutions, new principles, new provision and new practices that were more responsive to women's concerns, more likely to tackle structural discrimination, and in which women could play a more equal role. The goal was the creation of a fairer and better Scotland for women, men and children.

The subsequent devolution settlement and institutional blueprints attest to their influence. In addition to achieving Nordic levels of women parliamentarians (37.2 per cent of MSPs in 1999), activists also succeeded in building gender equity concerns into the fabric of the new parliamentary and governmental blueprints and structures. Key features included the adoption of equal opportunities as one of the key principles of the parliament, the creation of equality policy machinery in government and an equal opportunities committee in the parliament, a commitment to equality mainstreaming (including gender equality), the adoption of 'family friendly' sitting hours, and the development and participation of women's organisations in a more inclusive and consultative style of policy making. Early and progressive policy gains in tackling domestic violence compared with the rest of the UK demonstrated an apparent equality benefit to devolution, and sustained efforts have been made to consider the gender equality implications of government budgets. As such, the Scottish case bears many of the hallmarks of a successful example of feminist 'constitutional activism'.

In the intervening period, in particular in response to peace and constitution-making projects in the global South, the importance of women's participation in constitutional debates has been recognised and endorsed by the international community. In particular, The United Nations Security Council Resolution 1325 (2000) notes the importance of a gender perspective in peace agreements, in particular with relation to 'Measures that ensure the protection of and respect for human rights of women and girls, particularly as they relate to the constitution, the electoral system, the police and the judiciary' (Para 8). Recently, the UN Human Rights Council established a new working group to examine discrimination against women in law and in practice in political and public life, with a focus on constitutions (UNHRC Resolution 1523). Meanwhile there have been global campaigns to address the chronic minority status of women in political life through the championing of quota mechanisms (implemented through voluntary, statutory or constitutional means). These developments have yielded results: in global terms women's political participation is at an all-time high of 20 per cent, although still a long way from gender parity.

Women and the Independence Referendum debates: Mutual Indifference?

Despite the strong links made between constitution-making processes and the promotion of women's rights and gender equality, the current independence debate does not appear to have caught women's imagination; neither has the prospect of independence. Polls suggest a significant and persistent gender gap of 10 points or more between men and women in terms of support for independence, with women markedly more sceptical about the merits of separation. Over time, women have tended also to comprise a greater proportion of those who are undecided. According to a recent Ipsos MORI poll, overall support for independence increased in February 2013 to 34 per cent. However this was largely as a result of a bounce in male support. Whilst 41 per cent of men reported support for independence, only 28 per cent of woman did so – highlighting a 13-point gap between women and men. Meanwhile a Panelbase survey for the *Sunday Times* in March 2013 reported a gender gap of 22 per cent (47 per cent of men supporting independence to 25 per cent of women polled). The existence of the gender gap cannot be explained by women having a weaker attachment to Scottish identity, as they are no less likely than men to consider themselves 'Scottish, not British'. Scottish Social Attitudes surveys suggest that women, more than men, need to be convinced about the practicalities about, and concrete consequences of, constitutional change.

We suggest that while there are broad reasons why the current process has not yet galvanised civic participation, there may be particular reasons why women remain disengaged that are important to understand because they link to the ambivalent relationship of women to constitution-making practice that has relevance beyond Scotland. These include, the difficulty for women in holding onto earlier constitutional gains with respect to women's participation and the integration of gender equality norms and concerns; the gendered nature of legalistic process arguments in terms of who is enabled and who is disabled to participate; the gendered nature of arguments over sovereignty; and the fact that there is no self-evident 'women's approach' to questions of sovereignty and constitution-making with the question of 'what women want' remaining a complicated one conceptually. These will be considered in turn.

The Difficulty of Holding onto Devolution Gains – Gender Parity is (still) Not the Norm

Organised women and feminist ideas were crucial parts of the broader winning coalition that delivered devolution in the 1990s. The norm of gender parity, for example, was prominent in the devolution debates where it served as shorthand for aspirations of a modern, democratic and inclusive polity, and as emblematic of a progressive civic nationalism. As Tom Nairn noted at the time: 'Nothing, but nothing, will now cause this issue to go away. It has become a small-'N' nationalist banner – an emblem of the kind of country and the style of nationalism people really want' (Nairn 2001: 195). Activists lobbied the Scottish Constitutional Convention to promote women's equal representation, and challenged the political parties to reform their candidate selection and recruitment practices. Campaigners suffered a setback when the Commission of the SCC failed to agree to recommend a statutory quota, preferring instead to recommend a voluntary 40 per cent target and allow parties to regulate themselves. However, the final SCC report, setting out devolution blueprints, included an Electoral Contract signed by the Scottish Labour Party and the Scottish Liberal Democrats, which committed them to field equal numbers of male and female candidates in the first elections to the Scottish parliament. In the end, Scottish Labour was alone in implementing quotas and the only party to achieve gender balance in the first elections although, the SNP as the main electoral rival to Labour, implemented effective but informal measures which resulted in it returning 43 per cent female MSPs in 1999. However, despite the initial gains for women in the Scottish parliament, the trends in political recruitment are stalling or in decline. Gender candidate quotas (both formal or informal) have not 'caught on' across the party system. For example, the SNP has not implemented any measures (formal or informal) since the first elections to the Scottish parliament in 1999. Gender equality measures remain poorly institutionalised within parties and there is little evidence to suggest that political parties have prioritised efforts to reform the norms and practices of political recruitment. Furthermore, despite some policy distinctiveness from the rest of the UK, devolution has not delivered substantially different or better outcomes for women.

More generally, the principle of equality (50/50) or parity (usually understood as 40 per cent) has not been normalised in public life, and women remain relatively excluded. Despite the differential impact of welfare systems on women and men, and the widely documented evidence that current welfare cuts have a disproportionate impact on women, the Scottish Government initially failed to appoint a single female expert to its working group on welfare reform in January 2013. The launch of the referendum campaign in the Summer of 2012 was notable for its all-male platform of speakers; and the routine organisation of all –male or majority-male panels of commentators and 'experts' at public and media events demonstrates the relative indifference of those in power (in media, politics and civic Scotland) to the absence of women's voices and gender equality perspectives in debates. Outspoken critics, such as the journalist Lesley Riddoch and the Scottish Women's Budget Group, have provoked some efforts to redress the balance – and progressive male allies such as political commentator Gerry Hassan have refused to participate in all-male panels – but it is clear that women's equal participation is not central to these processes.

Labour has traditionally had the strongest connections with organised women and gender equality advocates, through its own women's structures and the wider labour movement as well with autonomous women's organisations. Whilst the SNP has a long track record of prominent women, as a party it is male dominated; it also has less developed links with women's organisations and community groups. Activists have had less space to develop feminist agendas within the party, and have been less successful than their counterparts in Scottish Labour and the central British

Labour party at linking party reforms with the issue of women's political under representation, or using gender voting gaps as leverage to prioritise classic 'women's issues' or promote gender analysis. The party's projection of a modern, inclusive and tolerant nationalism has not provided – to date – the conditions for the growth of a feminist-accented nationalism, in contrast with other comparator parties such as Plaid Cymru and Parti Québécois.

Whilst the newly-formed grassroots organisation, Women for Independence, seeks to make those connections and promote a Yes vote, the wider arguments about whether and why independence might be 'good for women' have only just begun to be rehearsed.

The Legalism of the Process Debate – and its Gendered Implications

The second difficulty concerns the nature of the current process. The referendum emerged as a result of the SNP victory in the elections of June 2011. However the debate that ensued for the next year and half concerned whether and how a referendum could be legally achieved and whether the Scottish Parliament had power to hold a referendum, or whether it was *ultra vires* the Scotland Act 1998. This was a debate, which pitted opposing legal interpretations against each other. It has been resolved by the 'Edinburgh Agreement' made between the Scottish and UK governments that the UK would 'devolve' power to hold a referendum to the Scottish government to hold a referendum (through an order made under Section 30 of the Scotland Act 1998). The legalism of the debate over the powers of the Scottish Parliament can be understood as one that also involved substantive issues. In particular, process arguments over the scope of the Scottish government's power disguised underlying substantive questions over what the democratic and constitutional frame for asking the question about Scotland's future should be: one located in Scotland and controlled by the devolved (SNP) government, or a matter for the UK as a whole under the control of the UK government. Conceptually, the process issues revolved around a fundamental question of the extent to which the rules of the default UK constitution were sufficient or appropriate to constraining attempts to change that constitution.

However, the legalism of this first year of discussion was disempowering of wider questions relating to the ambition of independence. It is well noted that legalism carries a price in terms of public participation. This price has been clear in the current Scottish context, postponing and even neutering deeper questions as to what the process was intended to achieve. The 'resolution' of the process in governmental agreement to ask a straightforward binary question relating to independence, means that its initial pathway continues to shape the options available to discuss. The outcome of a 'pact' between two governments has served to narrow the question to an either/or of 'Scottish independence' versus 'continued union to Britain', at the expense of considering whether some sort of more nuanced 'in-between' (so-called devo max, devo plus or devo more) option could have been fashioned. It has done so without requiring any civic process as to *what* is to be asked. While the fine text of the question was not fully resolved (subsequently, the Scottish government has agreed to the recommendations of the Electoral Commission), the critical issue of a binary Yes/No question on independence is now settled. The 'single question' approach in essence frames the issue of change around a change in sovereignty, rather than the question of what powers and what type of Scotland might be on offer.

This process stands in contrast to the more inclusive processes in the run up to devolution, which were characterised by more than a decade of constitutional activism by civil society (in the aftermath of the failed 1979 referendum). Detailed blueprints were drawn up and debated through civil society forums such as the cross party/ non-party Scottish Constitutional Convention, and its working groups, about the shape and form of devolution. Decisions to hold a pre-legislative referendum and its wording (including the-then controversial second question about tax varying powers) were flagged up as part of a manifesto commitment to devolution by the Labour Party in the 1997 General Election. The government's 1997 White Paper *Scotland's Parliament*, was based, in large part, on the framework devised by the scc and its constituent working over long years of deliberation and wider public consultation.

The path taken in the current constitutional debates also makes the impact and content of the independence referendum unclear, again constraining the capacity for full public engagement. Paradoxically, a vote is needed to achieve negotiations, but the actual shape of any resultant independence will rest on the post-election negotiations, within the global political context at the time. Thus the eventual contours of independence remain uncertain. For women, the devil may well be in the post-referendum detail. This process contributes to a dis-empowerment of civic participation as it suggests that the substantive questions as to the shape and content of independence will only be answered post-referendum. In other words, it tends to preclude full attention on constitutional futures – and the envisioning of new social, economic and politics models – issues in which embodied citizens, women and men, and their diverse needs and interests come to the fore.

While these problems apply to civil society as a whole, given women's relative exclusion from the spheres of party politics and legal debates they have a particular gendered impact. Whilst John Curtice (2012) has attempted to explain the gender gap in attitudes to independence in terms of women being less political, more hesitant and less able to take a 'clear view' than their male counterparts, ultimately we have insufficient information to know exactly why the gender gap persists. Nonetheless, we would argue that a 'wait and see' approach would be a rational response to the legalistic and narrow process and the lack of authoritative information and analysis available as to the consequences of constitutional change.

The Gendered Nature of Deal-Making

However, there is another price for women in the 'deal-making' pathway forged to date. The need for an inter-governmental 'pact' to legalise the holding of the referendum, and the pathway of 'vote first, negotiate second', while perhaps unavoidable, also places executive negotiations rather than civil participation centre stage. From a gendered point-of-view the Scottish political landscape is currently striking for the fact that two out of the three major party leaders are women – Johann Lamont for the Labour Party, and Ruth Davidson, for the Conservative Party; while a third woman, Nicola Sturgeon is the Deputy First Minister of the SNP government, with responsibility for promoting a Yes vote. Unusually, women dominate the leadership of the Scottish parliamentary political scene, a consequence, in part of the gender coup delivered by devolution. However, the emphasis on pacting between governments in London and Edinburgh marginalises not just wider Scottish democratic participation but also the women leaders who should be at the forefront of the debate. The Scottish Labour and Scottish Conservative leaders and their strategies stand in a difficult relationship to their political counterparts in London, which play to a different constituency. There is a danger, thus, that their views and those of their electorate are eclipsed. For example, Johann Lamont's tactics on the referendum – a reluctance to propose more powers for the Scottish government– can be undermined overnight by Ed Miliband or even an IPPR report on possible new tax-raising powers. Nicola Sturgeon's position in heading the Yes campaign for the Scottish Government arguably signals female leadership at the heart of the independence debate, but emphasises her role with civil society, rather her role at the heart of government or inter-governmental negotiations, arguably replicating gendered patterns of constitutional negotiations elsewhere. In short, while women hold significant leadership positions, they may still struggle to be visibly central to any deal-making that ensues.

The Gendered Nature of Statehood

At a deeper level, a straight Yes/No question on independence can itself be argued to be gendered. As other contributions to this collection emphasise, sovereignty is increasingly a relative concept. The clear-cut question belies the fact that something other than a clear-cut choice between separation and sharing is on offer. The choice between independence and continued union with the rest of the UK is perhaps a stark one in terms of where 'external' sovereignty – that is, whether Scotland is viewed as a separate state by the rest of the world, as the UK government has sought to emphasise. However, post any successful referendum the actual relationship of Scotland to the rest of the UK is likely to involve a degree of sharing that is virtually unprecedented in terms of most sovereign governments. Already, SNP positions on currency, defence, monarchy and British identity reveal an independence project that intends to retain and share some of the most powerful symbols of the British state, even at the expense of the control that statehood often brings. Issues of particular concern to women, for example day-to-day socio-economic issues, or issues such as violence against women, or protection of part-time workers may be largely unaffected by an affirmation of Scotland's external status as independent and sovereign, with the devil lying in detail of such re-negotiation of the relationship with the rest of the UK as takes place. Moreover, arguably the single most critical dimension of external sovereignty for women – membership of the European Union – which has delivered substantive equality gains for women in the areas of employment legislation, also will need to be negotiated in the wake of any independence referendum.

Evidence from other processes of constitutional or nationalist struggles suggests that women are often less focused on where sovereignty formally lies and are instead more pragmatically focused on how the substance of what sovereignty will offer in terms of women's equality. Women are rightly sceptical that claims to sovereignty as 'big bang' ways to ensure their rights are delivered in one fell swoop. Nationalist causes have a long history of employing women in service of 'national projects' premised on the promise of equality, only to sell out women on achieving statehood, in the face of patriarchal traditional, corporate and religious interests.

Political Contingency and 'Standpoint'

The question of the diversity of women's views also, we suggest, complicates women's commitments to either a UK or Scottish state. In the run up to devolution, a substantial majority of the Scottish population, including women, were in favour of devolution and the establishment of a Scottish parliament. Women activists were clear that devolution would deliver a better deal for women and could coalesce, as part of the wider pro-Home Rule movement, around the relatively simple demands of devolution and women's equal political representation.

The present context is much less straightforward: both 'Yes Scotland' and 'Better Together' campaigns have activist women involved but neither campaign seems to be making the case as to why women as women might have a reason to support either option. Rather the key choice is being presented as abstract: a change of state, or a choice between 'change' versus 'no change'. Yet just as the content of independence appears uncertain for women, so too does the content of the unionist status quo of 'no change': key UK-wide provisions affecting women – welfare reform, the continued existence of the NHS, the Human Rights Act, and of course European Union membership, appear to involve uncertain commitment on the UK government side into the future.

While something as fundamental as a change of state would seem to be about a long-term national project that is in some sense transcendent of the immediate policies of current government, we live in a wider moment of crisis in which political arguments about the necessity of austerity measures enable the implementation of economic and social policies with long-lasting structural consequences for women and their families, and for gender relations. It is indisputable, for example, that women as workers and as service users (in their traditional roles as parents and carers), rely heavily on a social democratic style welfare state. It is also the case that maternity provision, part-time worker's provision and flexible working time developments of benefit to women have been have been propelled primarily from Europe. The approach of the Coalition government to taxation, welfare cuts, family benefits, public sector employment and public spending, all of which have been documented to have a gendered impact against women, arguably amount to a re-working of the social contract. The UK Women's Budget Group calculates that women have shouldered 75 per cent of the austerity cuts to date. Taken together, the Coalition government policies remove incentives for second earners and parent workers; returning us to an outmoded model of male breadwinner-female home-maker. There is also an apparent assumption that shortfalls in crucial social services caused by deep cuts in public spending will be absorbed by families and communities; in practice, this means by women. The move towards private provision in education and healthcare, also have gender impacts and appear nearly as irreversible as nationalisation of railways and utilities in the time of Thatcher. While European law remains a key source of protection of women's rights, particularly in the realm of employment, a move by the Coalition government, or any subsequent conservative government, to withdraw from the European Union or at least key elements of its regulatory regimes, would have a negative impact on women's equality without the equivalent rights being reinstated into UK law, a structural change of magnitude that could outlast any current government (just as the decision to enter the EEC in 1972 did).

For women, we may therefore be in a time where questions of which state to belong to must be evaluated in terms of the policy choice on offer in social democratic terms, precisely because the current choices at the UK level appear to be structural in consequence because they involve partial dismantling and significant retrenchment of the welfare state and public sector. Rather than the transient policies of a time-limited government, such changes are difficult to reverse. In other words, the 'no change' option belies fast moving change and the unraveling of the social contract.

Such an analysis does not automatically lead to support for independence. For the 'change' model obscures ongoing interdependencies and, arguably, subordinate relations between Scotland and the rest of the UK. It also involves a commitment to an open constitutional process more than concrete outcomes, that while holding out opportunities for the inclusion of women, means that pre-commitments to outcome are difficult to make.

It is therefore far from clear what constitutional option would provide the greatest capacity to deliver a 'women-friendly' social and economic model – or even the maximum leverage to resist further erosion of social democracy.

Is It Worth It?

A final issue for women, is whether the debate is worth the time and energy of engaging. After all the majority support for the status quo – or, more accurately, for the devo max/more option not currently on offer – is seemingly solid. Furthermore the outcome is uncertain, its results requiring further negotiation in any case, and the ways in which women's rights are likely to affected are difficult to calibrate. As such, women's relative disengagement can be understood less as indifference, and more as a strategic choice over when and how it is useful to engage. Those engaged in advocacy work might understandably view their time as better used in pushing for core demands, challenging inequalities and injustices, and tackling the immediate consequences of austerity, than in engaging in the possible constitutional framework in which reforms may or may not be delivered. In fact, engaging with the independence debate may have a price for community groups and advocacy coalitions, because however 'neutral' in terms of outcome, it risks alienating funders from either camp. The choice may be a difficult one as to whether to spend precious energies on engaging with an intangible and uncertain process of possible change, or to concentrate on day-to-day demands and risk losing an opportunity to shape the wider political and legal context in a structural way.

Conclusion: How Could the Process be Engendered?

As long as debates are dominated by high politics, abstract legalism and macro-economics most people will be excluded from the process. In particular, women will be excluded because they are already under represented in public and political life. It is also the case that whilst debates are conducted at this level of abstraction, then the connection of constitutional change with issues of central concern to the practical politics of everyday life, and issues of social justice, equality and well-being is obscured. In such circumstances, women are likely to remain on the sidelines as the disengaged, the undecided, and the sceptical.

Women have often sought change by trying to envision and promote the type of society they want to see. Both in the independence debate, and indeed in discussions of what the 'plus', 'max' or 'more' of devolution plus might be, lurk a series of critical questions that are not being discussed as such, but which are self-evidently central to women's lives.

The first is, how Scotland will articulate the distinctiveness of its national project (whether devolution or independence) in terms of questions of inclusion.

The second concerns how it will institutionalise questions of equality and social justice at the level of political and legal institutions, and rights protections.

The third concerns what type of social-democratic model Scotland will follow and whether equality between men and women will be seen as a core value and building block.

Finally, critical to all these questions is: what type of process of engagement will be on offer – whether to achieve increased devolution, roll out the current 2012 settlement, or fashion a constitution post-independence. Will it be one that aims to create a space for women's voices, and offers possibilities for engagement, influence and change?

International experience suggests two key lessons: firstly, the importance of women mobilising to intervene at an early stage and the need to bring demands and concrete proposals to the table; and secondly, that without vigilance, active intervention and participation, visions that are expansive, inclusive and gender-sensitive can be quickly diluted or overlooked.

References

Curtice, A. (2012), 'Closing the Gap: Why Women's voices could be a deciding factor in the independence referendum', *Holyrood Magazine*, 5 November.

Ipsos MORI, (2013), *Scottish Public Opinion Monitor poll for The Times*, February.

Nairn, T. (2001), 'Gender Goes Top of the Agenda', *The Scotsman*, 28 December 1994, reprinted in Breitenbach E. and Mackay, F. (eds), *Women and Contemporary Scottish Politics*, Edinburgh: Polygon at Edinburgh.

Cultural Policy and the Constitutional Question

PHILIP SCHLESINGER

Introduction

CULTURAL POLICY IS made where culture, politics and the economy meet. It is an institutional system whereby government enters into a relationship with how culture is made, how it circulates, and how we use it.

Of key importance for the current debate about Scottish independence is the fact that cultural policy is characteristically focused on nations and questions of collective identity. Because this is the territory of symbolic representation, sentiments and emotion, it is inherently sensitive.

Cultural policy is invariably concerned with questions of value in more than one dimension. Whether we are cast in the role of viewers, listeners or readers – or increasingly, 'prosumers' and 'co-creators' – cultural artifacts and performances may move, excite, edify and otherwise engage us. If we are producers, the work of making is inextricably connected with making a living. In the world of cultural policy, therefore, the aesthetic dimension is connected with an economic one.

Public policy in the UK – of whatever ilk – is overwhelmingly focused on how culture generates revenues for the national economy in the context of global trade and how – through various forms of intervention – it might be made to generate even more. It is part of the wealth of nations question.

Most often, but not invariably, cultural policy comes under the purview of sovereign states, such as the United Kingdom. It therefore unavoidably and centrally involves public institutions. In the UK, the political focus of much explicit policy-making is the Secretary of State for Culture, Media and Sport together with his or her department, the DCMS. An increasingly prominent echo chamber for this policy world in the House of Commons is the Select Committee on Media, Culture and Sport. Beyond the Westminster-Whitehall axis, but highly dependent on its machinations, are various kinds of public agency that intervene in the cultural domain, such as Arts Council England and the British Film Institute. These are complemented by a veritable bevy of national bodies ranging from the British Museum, the Tate and the BBC to the London Philharmonic and the National Theatre, and many more besides. Such institutions constitute the highly visible official apparatus of British national culture.

However, in the context of the current debate about independence, we can hardly ignore the fact that sovereign statehood is by no means essential for at least certain kinds of cultural policy to be autonomously pursued. Scotland is a nation without a state. It is also a nation that until 1707 had a state, although it had shared a head of state with England since 1603. At the heart of the present campaign for independence is the idea of a nation that needs to restore its own state and that would otherwise be incomplete without taking this crucial step. In such a struggle, how could control over cultural policy not be of crucial importance?

The sheer density of Scotland's distinctive institutional world is at least in part a legacy of its original statehood and its long-standing, variable forms of autonomy within the United Kingdom. In common with many sovereign states, there is an extensive official Scottish cultural policy apparatus, comparable to that of the UK, but on a lesser scale. There is a Cabinet Secretary for Culture and External Affairs and a culture division in the Scottish Government as well as an education and culture committee in the Scottish Parliament. And just as in London, there is a complex of the classic national high-cultural institutions typical of a contemporary European nation state: the National Museums and Galleries of Scotland, the National Library of Scotland, the Scottish National Orchestra, Scottish Opera, the National Theatre of Scotland. The nominal repetitions not only flag the nation; they also muster resonant massed pipes and drums to sound the distinctiveness of the national dimension. A glance at the Scottish budget shows that expenditure on the national cultural apparatus includes the agency Creative Scotland, the Cultural Collections, and the National Performing Companies.

The Scope of Cultural Policy in Scotland

Under the present politically contested constitutional arrangements, cultural policy is a devolved power falling under the aegis of the Scottish Government and Scottish Parliament. This competence was set out in the Scotland Act 1998 in phase one of devolution. Devolution's phase two is embodied in the Scotland Act 2012, which – despite pressures from the SNP – did not expand the scope of cultural policy to include broadcasting.

Broadcasting policy – which deals with the major cultural forces of radio and television as well as the various and increasingly important kinds of online presence that range from websites to catch-up TV and podcasts – remains a reserved power, held by London rather than Edinburgh. Although the Scotland Act 2012 gave no significant ground on this matter, there have been pressures in Scotland over the past decade to treat broadcasting policy as part of cultural policy. Back in 2005, the first, tentative rethinking of the policy map on these lines came in the report of the Cultural Commission chaired by the former BBC executive, James Boyle. Jack McConnell, the last First Minister of the Labour-Liberal coalitions that ruled from 1999-2007, initiated this rethinking of cultural policy. The Cultural Commission asked Scottish ministers to introduce 'an element of devolution in broadcasting' and said that there was 'a strong case for the establishment of at least one [television] channel based in Scotland'. This was rapidly dismissed by the then Scottish Executive only to be picked up a couple of years later by the SNP minority government.

Despite devolution, broadcasting policy in the UK has retained its original centralist cast. It has always been marked by highly political considerations. This is evident in the long history of the BBC which, not without contradictions, has been – in the words of its first official historian, Asa Briggs – an 'organisation within the constitution' ever since the general strike of 1926 and subsequently through World War II, the Cold War, decolonisation, the Northern Ireland conflict, the Falklands campaign, the Iraq war, 7/7 and beyond. Moreover, ever since the advent of ITV as the first incarnation of commercial television in 1955, the development of the broadcast marketplace and its regulation have always involved the political management of economic interests and recourse to a succession of regulatory bodies deeply inscribed with Britishness, even as they offered various forms of territorial representation to the 'nations', namely, Scotland, Wales and Northern Ireland.

Broadcasting is so important to the independence debate because of its deep implication in the reproduction of Britishness – an obstacle if it is Scottishness that you wish to reproduce. In its very form, the national public service broadcaster is another of those cultural institutions of sovereign states enumerated above, although since the 1980s the classic role has increasingly been adapted to the challenge of commercial competition and technological change. The specific institutional framework of public service broadcasting (in the age of the internet increasingly termed public service media) developed in varied ways in Europe and elsewhere in the course of the 20th Century. Despite far-reaching media developments in the past three decades, a tenacious image of what is needed to complete the cultural sphere has continued to exercise a normative force in Scotland. In short, for the SNP to have a national state without a national public service broadcaster is simply inconceivable for the official cultural apparatus of a small European nation intent on finding its sovereign place in the European Union. Scandinavia and Ireland are often invoked by the SNP as providing models of what might be.

It is not surprising that one of First Minister Alex Salmond's first initiatives after forming his minority government in 2007 was to argue for the devolution of broadcasting powers to the Scottish Parliament 'to ensure the principle of editorial and creative control being exercised in Scotland on behalf of Scottish audiences'. Like his predecessor, Jack McConnell, he set up an inquiry – this time much more focused – in the form of the Scottish Broadcasting Commission, again led by a former BBC executive, Blair Jenkins. The SBC reported in 2008 and – not least due to dogged persistence and focus – together with regular formal updates to the Scottish Parliament on the state of play, the future of broadcasting has been on the political agenda ever since.

The forthcoming struggle over broadcasting has far-reaching implications for the future of the BBC in the event of independence post 2014, as well for commercial television. Legal powers in the field of broadcasting would be a key shift in the current scope of Scottish cultural policy and also highly relevant to any conception of the nation's creative economy, given the income and employment generated by radio and TV.

But before we venture any further into the thickets of the Scottish institutional landscape, we should discuss the invention of the 'creative industries', which by degrees have mutated into the 'creative economy'. The underlying ideas provide an ideological framework in Scotland, no less than in the UK as a whole.

Inventing the Creative Economy

The official ideas about managing culture in the interests of the national economy that dominate Scotland today were minted in London in 1997, by the New Labour government of Tony Blair. The Blairites were the first major popularisers of the creative industries thinking that has now circled the globe and captivated many policy-makers worldwide. But that mode of thought also hopped instantly over the Border. It was rapidly adopted by the Labour-Liberal Democrat coalition.

Since coming to power in May 2007, the SNP government's initiatives in broadcasting and cultural policy have likewise been deeply influenced by current thinking about the key role of the creative industries and the creative economy in conditions of global competition.

At the heart of all creative industries strategy is aggregation. One of the most quoted lists in the cultural policy field is that which identifies the 13 industries designated as creative by the DCMS in 1998: advertising, architecture, the art and antiques market, crafts, design, designer fashion, film, interactive leisure software, music, the performing arts, publishing, software and television and radio.

A passing inspection will assure the reader that this list is entirely arbitrary. Just consider what is missing. For instance, newspapers and magazines do not figure; nor do museums and galleries or sport. We have to understand the rhetorical and policy purposes of bringing together a number of quite distinct cultural practices in order to call these 'creative'. This denomination creates an object, originally the creative industries now called the creative economy, which remains an aggregation of different practices, and actually behaves that way too. Indeed, the continuing diversity and specificity of different sectors makes overall policy-making rather difficult.

For those adopting this strategy, having established a new focus or object for policy the task is to try and devise instruments to make it work better – in particular, to make more of a profitable business of culture. One of the consequences of this approach is to change the focus and functioning of public agencies operating in the public domain. This can involve renaming and reconstructing existing bodies or reorienting them profoundly by introducing new management styles. In Scotland, it was creative industries thinking that led directly to the establishment in 2010 of Creative Scotland, the national agency for Scotland's arts, film and creative industries.

Quite how the creative industries, and latterly, the creative economy, should be defined has spawned a massive literature among consultants, gurus and academics. Which industries are central, which peripheral? Has creativity become the new human resource? Can we distinguish between cultural and creative industries? To what extent are the statistics bandied about at national and international level concerning the value of the trade in creative products, employment levels and the returns to creators, actually reliable?

These questions have been debated extensively elsewhere. However, since the creative economy has become an increasingly taken-for-granted reality, we should take the ideas that led to them seriously and put them under the microscope of criticism.

We might start with the most obvious appeal of labelling something as creative. Who *doesn't* want to be called creative? It's so much better than being dull, mundane and boring, which is the implied alternative. But playing with romantic notions of cultural work – those extra-ordinary and god-like qualities of originality and inspiration – is only a small part of the story. The idea of creativity as such has huge appeal because it has a widespread ideological resonance: it accords with contemporary aspirations to seek fulfilment in work. Although often officially presented as inclusive and democratic, creative economy policy is ultimately focused on a small minority's cultural labour and its successful commodification through the exercise of intellectual property rights - because that goes with the grain of how cultural markets actually work, as is well attested in the academic research literature. Commercial success predominates.

At the heart of the official British vision of creativity has been the harnessing of culture to the growth of the national economy coupled with a grandiose post-imperial design to make the UK the 'world's creative hub'. This can take on an explicit polemical complexion as well as the more implicit one of generating sentiments of national solidarity. Thus, the successful Olympics of London 2012 were rapidly (and superficially) interpreted in some quarters as a notable rediscovery of Britishness, as the rebirth of Ukania (to use Tom Nairn's ironic term) through collective pride in Team GB's sporting endeavours. Dishing the nationalists in Scotland was one immediate, short-lived, follow-up unionist tactic after the Olympics. Such expedient manipulations of cultural events, however, are inherently open to a boomerang effect. With the 700th anniversary of Bannockburn, the Ryder Cup and the Glasgow 2014 Commonwealth Games all to come in the year of the independence referendum, no doubt we shall see the exactly same kind of instrumentalism used against the union.

Irrespective of the parties in power, the creative economy has moved increasingly to the centre of policy thinking in the UK. One fundamental logic remains in play – the tradability of intellectual property (IP) in cultural works and the contribution made by such trade to the national economy.

Creative economy thinking has also become globalised, if increasingly adapted to each country's particular needs. And this movement – while not yet universal – has continued apace. In East Asia, during the past decade, China, Japan and Korea have adopted creative economy strategies, and they are not alone in doing so. At a global level, it was in 2008 that the United Nations produced its *Creative Economy Report*, which advocated an IP-driven approach for all countries, at whatever stage of development.

Why has this happened? In the UK's case, part of the explanation at least, given the sway of post-industrial, 'new economy' thinking, with its strong bias towards knowledge production and non-material goods and services, has been the quest by nations for new sources of profitability and competitive economic advantage.

In similar vein, the present attraction for the Edinburgh government of a creative economy is obvious, not least after the precipitous loss of credibility by the major Scottish banks, concern about over-reliance on oil revenues, and the need to diversify Scottish sources of income generation. At the heart of the Scottish nationalist vision is the harnessing of culture to the growth of the national economy to contribute to the economic foundations of Scotland's independence.

There is, though, a deep continuity between the SNP's focus and present UK policy, just as there was with Scotland's own earlier coalition governments. Indeed, in its fundamentals, Scottish cultural policy is a scaled-down version of British cultural policy. This parallelism also extends to policy on communications infrastructure where the quest to build a digital Scotland with world-class capacity once again echoes another of the former Labour government's themes, first embodied in the 2009 report titled *Digital Britain*. The coalition government in London shares this aspiration.

Many different sources have come together from sociological and economic thinking to create a policy framework that so dominates everywhere. In the UK – and therefore Scotland – creative economy thinking came about at least in part through two mutations deep in the heartlands of social theory. It began in 1947 with a critique of the so-called culture industry by the leading Frankfurt School theorists, Theodor Adorno and Max Horkheimer. There was then a shift from critique into leftwing policy analysis notably in the 1980s through the work of French and British marxist political economists. And then the arguments were reworked in the late 1990s and early 2000s through the think-tank-erati of New Labour into more or less what we have now.

Making Cultural Policy in Scotland

If there has been common thinking about the creative economy between London and Edinburgh, since devolution there has also been continuity in broad institutional approaches from the Lib-Lab coalition to the Nationalists. One key decision, effected in April 2007 by the coalition in its dying days, was to move the national performing companies (Scottish Ballet, Scottish Opera, the Royal Scottish National Orchestra, the Scottish Chamber Orchestra and the National Theatre of Scotland) from being clients of the Scottish Arts Council to direct funding by the Scottish Government. That arrangement has remained undisturbed by the change of party in power.

The other main policy decision taken by the Nationalists was to continue on the path set by their predecessors and to set up Creative Scotland by amalgamating the Scottish Arts Council and Scottish Screen. The convoluted pre-history of the new cultural agency remains to be told in full. But in outline, phase one was a long gestation; phase two, the transition; and phase three, the launch of Creative Scotland as a non-departmental public body on 1 July 2010 with the passage of the Public Services Reform (Scotland) Act.

Creative Scotland's structure was intended to break with the previous model and was based in a critique of traditional arts council funding which was held to have created an unhelpful interdependency between arts officers and their clients. A novel relationship was conceived, mediated by a new-style officer, the portfolio manager, who would not 'own' a piece of cultural territory or work in a 'silo' and who could therefore evade capture by art-form interest groups.

Creative Scotland was conceived as a new prototype of the cultural agency: an investor rather than a funder, the leader of a number of partners sharing risks and finance. The blueprint for the organisation drew on the DCMS's ideas about the creative industries as well as those of the innovation think-tank, the National Endowment for Science, Technology and the Arts (NESTA). Prior to Creative Scotland's launch, the then culture minister, Mike Russell, recognised the tensions between entrepreneurial and cultural approaches but thought them to be reconcilable.

However, fundamental conflicts about cultural value cannot be wished away. In part, discrepant viewpoints fuelled the row that exploded in October 2012. A letter eventually signed by more than 400 artists, accused the agency of 'ill-conceived decision-making; unclear language; lack of empathy and regard for Scottish culture' and much else besides. It led to the resignation of Andrew Dixon, Creative Scotland's first CEO. Such arguments between artists and agencies are not unusual. On this occasion, however, the impact of creative economy thinking on Creative Scotland's organisational architecture may well have played a role in shaping the conflict. At this time of writing, the agency's future strategy is unclear.

The future of broadcasting is also quite an open question and depends on the outcome of the independence referendum. The stakes are high. Whereas Creative Scotland is a recent invention of the Scottish Parliament, the BBC was established under a Royal Charter in 1927. A fundamental institution of Britishness, it has a Scottish dimension in the shape of BBC Scotland.

Since 2007, the intensifying struggle between unionists and nationalists over the scope of broadcasting policy that has the initiative to date has lain with the nationalists, who have consistently argued for the creation of a separate public service broadcaster in Scotland, controlled by the Scottish Parliament. The argument has been deeply connected to the creative economy (more Scottish production), to national identity (more representations of Scottishness), and to politics (more focus on Scotland's public sphere).

The Scottish Broadcasting Commission's proposal in 2008 to create a publicly funded Scottish Digital Network within the devolved settlement – using part of the Television Licence Fee – won no favour with London politicians. The most dramatic turn in the story came at the Edinburgh International Television Festival in August 2012. There, Alex Salmond proposed the break-up of the BBC on independence, with the BBC's Scottish assets to be taken over by the new Scottish state. In that event, many complex issues would need to be addressed.

Conclusion

Aside from the creation of a national public service broadcaster, independence would not greatly change Scotland's existing cultural policy apparatus and institutions. There is no reason to suppose that debates familiar under devolution will cease. There will be arguments about the level of funding for culture, how this is apportioned, whether the arm's length principle is being observed by government and what models of support should be adopted. But whether it is statehood or stateless nationhood, the institutions are not likely to change.

However, if cultural policy were extended to include broadcasting, the game would change. At present it is all all-or-nothing one. The UK government will not entertain a more federal structure for the BBC or a change in its governance arrangements. There is no formal role for the Scottish Government and Parliament. Devolution means reserved powers over broadcasting and communications regulation; statehood means a Scottish Broadcasting Corporation and new regulatory powers.

But if a putative SBC were to fit the territory like a glove, come independence the commercial sector would be less tidy. Under current relicensing arrangements, the UK Culture Secretary has decided that Border TV's signal will remain part of the ITV network and straddle the Anglo-Scottish line. STV, the Channel 3 incumbent north of the Border, will not therefore extend its territorial footprint to satisfy the completist urge for a national commercial system. Arrangements to address the specific needs of Scottish viewers for their own news and current affairs will undoubtedly be brokered but perhaps not to everyone's satisfaction. In future, STV will be the backbone of ETV and GTV, the Edinburgh and Glasgow local television stations, set up in a DCMS-inspired initiative that directly contradicts the SNP government's desire to create a Scottish Digital Network.

The First Minister's proposal to take over the BBC's Scottish assets only opens up a lengthy chain of questions to be posed and resolved. How is the putative Scottish Broadcasting Corporation related to the Scottish Digital Network advocated by the Scottish Broadcasting Commission? What will be the governance arrangements for a new broadcaster under independence? What will be the relationship between the Scottish Broadcasting Corporation and the BBC (assuming quite reasonably, post Great Britain, that it will retain this global brand)? How will the new broadcaster be funded? The First Minister has intimated setting up a mixed model, with Ireland's RTE in mind, where advertising complements a license fee. How would this cash out for STV, ETV and GTV in the small Scottish advertising market?

Broadcasting is, of course, part of the converged regulatory system of communications run by Ofcom. The BBC Trust is the BBC's main regulator. But the Trust's own future status came into renewed question during the crisis of BBC management and governance that began in November 2012. Ofcom's Broadcasting Code also regulates the BBC, notably in respect of privacy and fairness. Ofcom regulates all commercial television as well as communications generally. Given the possibility of independence, what regulatory regime would Scotland develop for its media and communications landscape? Those who call for broadcasting regulation to be repatriated will find that in the converged world of communications, this would probably mean unwinding Ofcom's activities north of the border.

At this time of writing, there are certainly straws in the wind regarding the future regulatory regime. An expert panel chaired by the former high court judge and solicitor general, Lord McCluskey, has been charged by the First Minister with considering the possible creation of a distinct Scottish press regulator, in the wake of Lord Leveson's 2012 report into the culture, practice and ethics of the press. Furthermore, in February 2013, the Scottish Government also published a report on 'economic and competition regulation in an independent Scotland'. Communications – currently regulated by Ofcom – is one field identified for a new, National Regulatory Authority. The paper notes in respect of communications that 'elements could be contracted to RUK' and leaves it unclear as to what might be regulated in an independent Scotland apart from the economic dimensions of communications, although it is hinted that media content and spectrum might be either Scottish governmental or regulatory fields.

Scotland's public urgently needs to debate these questions, which so far have simply not received sustained attention and in some cases not even been posed. They are too important to be left to the closed world of the policy community because in the event of independence the choices made will deeply shape our common future.

Grasping the Fizzle: Culture, Identity and Independence

MARC LAMBERT

I hate it. All that purple stuff, vat's it called? Feather? Then all this green and orange and the blue sky. It makes me sick. It looks like a biscuit tin. And vat are those tings with spikes? Fizzles?
Alexander Korda on the set of *Bonnie Prince Charlie*, 1948

Culture Wars I

'Moderate your own fucking language...'

The reply was James Kelman's. The occasion: The Saltire Society's Book Awards 2012. The place: National Library of Scotland. The date: Friday 30th November – a certain Saint's Day.

Kelman was receiving his award for the best book of the year, *Mo Said She was Quirky*. £5,000 in a year where he had earned £15,000 in total, would you believe. His acceptance speech started slowly, but soon gathered power and pace like an avalanche, and with it came the percussive, rising notes of expletives, signifiers of his passion. Amongst the August gathering – which included many of Scotland's top academics and writers, the Minister for Culture, Chair of the Saltire Society Magnus Linklater, and its CEO Jim Tough (who had been, formerly, Acting CEO of the Scottish Arts Council before its dissolution) – was one who objected to Kelman's *style*. 'Moderate your language!' he roared, interrupting the avalanche. All things considered, it was a curious thing to say to Kelman. And it was far from the only irony on parade that evening.

The stushie was reported on the next day. But the real issue was not how much Kelman swore, that he had complained about his earnings, or that he 'fucking hates' the British Council, it was hidden in the hesitant, digressive beginnings of his speech.

Kelman began by speaking quietly about his Gaelic ancestors, the richness of their inner lives, the harshness of their material one, referencing the Clearances and his family's military service for Empire, tracing their line down to him. I was completely baffled by this opener, since it seemed to have no relation to the matter at hand. How wrong I was. In yet another layer of irony, it was a visiting English friend I had smuggled into the evening who deciphered Kelman's meaning for me. Living in Stockholm, an artist working across Europe for 30 years, he was electrified by the incident. Scottish culture was *live*. We were even *arguing about it*.

Kelman's impromptu genealogy, it transpires, was a response to the award made immediately previous to his. This was won by Sarah Fraser for her biography of the notorious 11th Lord Lovat, who rescued the Frasers from obscurity only to lose his head after Culloden. As a biographer Sarah Fraser had taken her duties seriously; she had married twice into the clan and produced an excellent study (Fraser, 2012). For his part, Kelman was asking, in so many words, 'Which Scotland are we talking about? Whose history? Whose family? Whose re-evaluation and representation?' During his speech, this broadened into a wider polemic on memory and truth, the deliberate suppression of history and language for political ends, the Scots' conflicted ignorance of their own culture, and much else besides. His opening remarks were consistent with an earlier reaction to Disney/Pixar's *Brave*, heralded as a game-changer for Scotland's international brand, derided by him as a cod-parable about 'loveable indigenous aristocrats'.

'Give Kelman the microphone at your peril', someone later remarked. It wasn't until the next day that I was able to think of a reply. Kelman had been speaking on this theme for years. Strange that we should celebrate his writing while remaining uncomfortable with his cultural politics. Especially weird, given those politics are so clearly indivisible from the substance and form of his art.

And yet, some weeks previously, in a room not far away across town...

Culture Wars II

... Creative Scotland, successor body to the Scottish Arts Council, established by Act of Scottish Parliament on 1 July 2010, was imploding. As it happens, I was in the room at the time. Part of a small delegation of representatives from the arts sector, we had been meeting with Creative Scotland management board, and civil servants from the Culture Division for months already, in an effort to Sort It All Out. 'It' being the policies, practices and values of Scotland's chief body for the Arts, increasingly under fire. This latest meeting, held at Victoria Quay on 8 October, coincided to the hour with the publication of a letter signed by 100 top artists and writers. It read in part:

> Routinely, we see ill-conceived decision-making; unclear language, *lack of empathy and regard for Scottish culture* [My emphasis]. We observe an organisation with a confused and intrusive management style married to a corporate ethos that seems designed to set artist against artist and company against company in the search for resources.

This letter is not about money. This letter is about management. The arts are one of Scotland's proudest assets and most successful exports. We believe existing resources are best managed in an atmosphere of trust between those who make art and those who fund it. At present, this trust is low and receding daily.

A sense of crisis had been gathering about Creative Scotland for months, even if those in charge seemed tone deaf to it. Here, however, was the *coup de grace*, as the horrified faces of senior management gathered around their CEO's Blackberry confirmed. So much for patiently grinding away in meeting after meeting. This was something else again – a devastating public statement of no confidence from those who really mattered.

At least some of us knew there was no way back. The penny took longer to drop for others. Creative Scotland's first reaction to this October revolution, combative, disastrously misjudged, only served to confirm the organisation as completely disassociated from its locus. On 3 December, the CEO resigned. On 20 December his second in command followed suit. Meanwhile the Board, belatedly waking to the challenge, met on 7 and 8 December in Pitlochry to consider two reports it had commissioned into the crisis. A flurry of contrite communiqués ensued, pledging a total reversal of Creative Scotland's *modus operandi* (Creative Scotland, 2012).

At a follow-up meeting with our group on 19 December, Sir Sandy Crombie, Chair of Creative Scotland and Senior Independent Director of the Royal Bank of Scotland Group plc, spoke of the commitment from the Board to change, not least because Board members felt the need to rescue their reputations. As if that was the point.

A Little History

A few years ago a friend sent me a paper by a respected Scottish academic which analysed arts policy in Scotland since 1999. The paper was accurate, solid, and well-researched. It was, I said, a fine piece of satire.

This was only half in jest. Since the Scottish Parliament was reconvened on 12 May 1999, an understanding of arts policy only seems bearable to those of a satirical cast of mind. In his 2003 St Andrew's Day speech, Scotland's then First Minister, Jack McConnell, announced his intention to make 'the development of our creative drive, our imagination, the next major enterprise for our society'. Shortly afterwards, Culture Minister Frank McAveety launched the Cultural Commission as part of 'a generational opportunity to look seriously and maturely at our culture and decide the framework for its support in the future.'

Pies brought McAveety down. A kilt did for McConnell. The Cultural Commission, led by the poacher-turned-gamekeeper James Boyle, former Chair of the Scottish Arts Council, fell foul of Labour politics. In 2005 it submitted a surreal report of more than five hundred pages, and couldn't even spell its own name right on the cover, despite having spent £487,000. Amongst the exhausting plenitude of recommendations, (there was no executive summary), two were taken up. The first was to place Scotland's national companies (Opera, Ballet etc) under direct control of the government's Culture Division, and the second, which had in effect already been decided, was to press ahead with the creation of a new body for the arts called Creative Scotland.

Given how this 'generational opportunity' was seized, the value-for-money realised, and that the new arts body then created operated with a 'lack of empathy and regard for Scottish culture' – what else but satire might do?

It would be tedious to recount blow-by-blow the slouching-to-wards-Bethlehem we have done in search of a policy for the arts in Scotland (and more widely in the UK), and the institutional convolutions this has entailed. But a few general elements need to be sketched because the historical fault-lines they describe are still unresolved.

The Arts Council of Great Britain was first set up on 9 August 1946. From the beginning there was an argument about purpose. Some saw it as promoting wide access and participation; others favoured a narrower strategy of funding 'the best'. Its first chairman, John Maynard Keynes, was in the latter camp and established the arms length principle. Under the chairmanship of Kenneth Clark (1955–1960) the Arts Council further developed its patrician style and its intrinsic 'art for art's sake' funding model. But Britain was changing. In 1967 the Arts Council was granted a new charter of incorporation, with the objectives of 'developing and improving the knowledge, understanding and practice of the arts; of increasing the accessibility of the arts to the public throughout Great Britain; and of advising and co-operating with departments of Government, local authorities and other bodies on any matters concerned.' That same year semi-autonomous committees (also designated 'Arts Councils') were set up in Scotland and Wales. The Scottish Arts Council received is funding from central government via the Arts Council of Great Britain but in practice most of its policy decisions were made without much interference from London, though also – in the absence of a parliament in Edinburgh – without much democratic oversight from within Scotland.

Various other regional permutations in England ensued as the Arts Council responded to charges of elitism and an excessively metropolitan focus during the eighties and nineties. (the 1984 report found that while the population of the capital comprised a fifth of the UK's total population, London was receiving at least half of the total funding available). In 1994 the Scottish Arts Council became entirely separate from the old Arts Council of Great Britain, receiving its funding directly from the Scottish budget. In its first years it was a fine champion of Scottish arts. Just over a decade later it was viewed by some as sclerotic – a hopeless example of dependency culture.

Meanwhile, the Thatcher government (1979–1990) came and went, leaving an indelible mark on Scottish psyche and society. In the arts, a neo-liberal, instrumental paradigm came to hold sway, one that had already been hinted at in the 1967 charter: the arts were responsible for 'co-operating with departments of Government, local authorities and other bodies on any matters concerned.' The final collapse of the arts into a branch of education, the economy and international branding came during the Blair years (1997–2007), with a focus on monumental projects (Dome, Angel of the North, etc), the creative industries, the knowledge economy, and the 'Cool Britannia' brand. Art's purpose was to serve these national and economic priorities.

At the same time, policies of fiscal deregulation begun under the Tories and adopted by New Labour gave rise to newer, more strident voices, those for whom public sector reform had never properly been fulfilled. Art and the structures put in place to deliver it came under the lens for being part of a nationally damaging culture of dependency. Arts leaders were feckless and irresponsible; the organisations they ran were inefficient and ineffective; subsidy ensured there was no pressure on them to be entrepreneurial; and a narrow cabal of bureaucrats funded the same old time and time again.

Those pursuing these arguments did so despite the new precariousness of their own positions. Following the crash of 2007, the UK's financial sector, having engaged in criminal practices including rate fixing, mis-selling financial products and money laundering on an unprecedented scale, remains the biggest single dependant on the British people and State. We are back in the space of satire. What we need is a latter-day Juvenal. What we got was Creative Scotland.

Creative Scotland was meant to be a neo-liberal dream. Combining Scottish Screen with the Scottish Arts Council in a leaner body would enable it to finally make good on the potential of the creative industries, while rationalising and re-purposing the existing framework of arts delivery in a much needed shake-up which would bring it into line with national objectives. Chief among those was developing Scotland's international brand. The aim: to deliver for Scotland – whichever 'Scotland' that is (see Kelman).

It didn't get going with much élan. From the start there were questions – still unresolved – about its value-system, its independence from government, and its operating remit, particularly in relation to the creative industries (at one point *Antiques* was mentioned). This fuzziness, alongside the presentation to Parliament of financial memoranda described by the chair of the scrutinising committee as the worse he had ever seen, ensured that the first Bill fell on 18 June 2008. Prior to this, hilariously, the transition director, tasked with shepherding Creative Scotland into being, had gathered arts leaders to come short on detail but long on claim: Creative Scotland was to be a 'Big Brain' organisation.

Brains were not much in evidence. Having publicly expressed dismay at the failed legislative process, I was summoned for a meeting. Nothing much transpired, but I did notice that the transition director Anne Bonnar served tea out of very nice porcelain cups. Her absurdly lucrative term was soon up. A team of bankers, led by Ewan Brown, the then vice chairman of the Edinburgh International Festival and former chairman of

Lloyds TSB Scotland, was drafted in. During the first two-and-a-half years of its existence Creative Scotland perfectly expressed the cultural understanding of its makers.

The annual salary for the CEO was £120,000.

Culture Wars III

One of the principal fantasies of neo-liberal policy making is that Everything Can be Managed. Everything, that is, except money, speculation and the processes and institutions relevant to these operations globally. At the same time as these particular freedoms are claimed, surveillance of the populace is increased while civil liberties are eroded (Grayling, 2010). The rise of managerialism and regulation across all aspects of British life has been pursued without irony, even as aggressive and exceptionalist arguments against regulation have been successfully made by the financial sector. (It's farcical that the charities regulator OSCR has more teeth than the FSA, for instance). All the same, radical free market ideology, constantly presented as the *sine qua non* of 'doing business successfully in the 'modern' world', did not prevent banks running to the state once their free markets had failed. So much for Darwin, then. That survival of the fittest only works when you are winning is axiomatic.

This intellectual dishonesty, accompanied by a great deal of 'we'll show you' arrogance, is both reprehensible and sadly comic when transferred to the sphere of culture. Comic, because it rests on the hopeless idea that culture, and cultural production, can actually be precisely managed towards certain pre-arranged ends. Kelman, again: 'For the political authorities 'the role of literature' is primary. For writers it is beyond that, way, way beyond. Literature has no 'role'. Literature is art and art is life' (Kelman, 2012). Nevertheless, chasing the chimera of pre-determined outcomes in culture was Creative Scotland's task, one which clearly demonstrated that those in charge had not the slightest idea of what art is. It is against this insulting ideological and intellectual background that one understands the common charge that Creative Scotland expressed a lack of respect for and understanding of Scottish artists and culture. At the most basic level, artists were appalled to find their achievements subsumed in a corporate marketing operation which interfered in the free expression of their meaning.

But the leeching of neo-liberal discourse into Creative Scotland went much further than this. It is clear, from the language of investment it adopted, the policies it pursued, and the professional composition of its governance structure, that what Creative Scotland really wanted to be like was *a bank*. This understood, all else falls into place – the early declaration that it was not interested in being a funding body, but would be free to pick and choose, by opaque private processes, its investments; the disconcerting (but often self-confessed) habit of the CEO to offer money to artists and projects he happened to like, acting like a private sector investor; the butchering of its client base in the name of entrepreneurial efficiency; the strict vertical nature of its internal hierarchy; the short-termism of its strategic horizons; the treatment of art as product it owned; its almost compulsive focus on marketing and control; and its attitude to artists as just another set of dependants supplicating at the high table of the Masters of the Universe.

This crude attempt to map business onto art, in order to marshal culture into conformity with a set of ideological precepts, economic priorities and marketing imperatives was desperately dim. Art doesn't easily simplify, and an art which doesn't pose more questions than it answers is not art but propaganda. 'Awkward questions are a sign of independent and well-tended minds' writes Janice Galloway (Hames, ed., 2012), adding elsewhere that 'artists are the awkward squad'. Despite the mock-heroic rhetoric, ('Creative Scotland's priority is to invest in talent ... We think Scotland's arts, screen and creative industries are worth shouting about. We'll lead the shouting.), Creative Scotland never understood this basic cultural truth. And its collapse as Scotland's chief cultural body has left us with the open question of how best to represent Scotland, and support Scottish culture, in a post-1999, pre-2014/post-2014 scenario. There are battles going on here too.

Grasping the Fizzle: Culture and Identity

Ah dinna ken whit like your Scotland is. Here's mines.
National flower: the thistle.
National pastime: nostalgia ...

Liz Lochhead (Lochhead, 1987)

The cultural achievements of 80s and 90s Scotland are commonly related to the infamous 1979 referendum on devolution. These various works of art and literature had a triple burden to bear. Not only did they have to be aesthetically successful in their own right, standing equal with, or at least comparable to, the best of art produced elsewhere in the world; they also had to preserve the idea of a nation denied politically by representing its continued existence in art. As Alasdair Gray put the dilemma (and the fear): 'People who care nothing for their country's stories and songs ... are like people without a past – without a memory – they are half people' (Gray, 1992). Similar ideas can be found in Lanark, which despite being 30 years in the making is treated as the Ur-text of the period (Gray, 1981). Finally, in a burden placed retrospectively, these works of art also needed to be selectable and sortable within a pre-determined narrative frame, or schema – one where 1979 meets 1999 meets 2014. Once so arranged, by academics and cultural activists, they proved the thesis. The dangers of this methodological circularity have been cogently pointed out by Alex Thomson: 'something akin to a re-nationalisation of literary history seems to be taking place...' (Thomson, 2007).

This approach flattens the essential heterogeneity of works of art, which are co-opted to a single significant meaning through the violence of a pre-determined theory. Further, the theory rests on an conflation of culture and politics: the representation provided by each is completely different in kind and not easily mappable. That much of Scotland's cultural production, not just in this period, but over centuries, has been 'about' Scotland, is of course true; that it has preserved/created an idea of identity/nation true also. Scotland's art arises naturally and obviously from its historical, linguistic and cultural milieu (but is not contained by it). James Robertson's short essay on this subject for the Scottish Parliament is probably the best and most balanced overview we have:

> Perhaps what characterises the category 'Scottish writing' more than anything these days is a refusal to be easily categorised... Is it possible that ... in a twenty-first century, democratic and multi-voiced Scotland the best thing about our national identity is that it cannot be readily pigeon-holed? We need our history, to be aware of it and to understand it, because it is the story of who we have been and where we come from, but we also need not to be restrained by it. (Robertson, 2005)

Scotland is not alone in Europe in having to deal with the relation of art to politics and national identity. Milan Kundera called the gravitational pull of nationalist discourse in relation to art a 'small-scale terrorism' (albeit in a more fraught political context). 'The Czech nation', he writes, 'was born (several different times born) not because of its military conquests but because of its literature. And I don't mean literature as a political weapon. I mean literature as literature.' The same is true of Scotland. But in the same volume Kundera notes the attitude of another Czech exile, Vera Linhartova: 'The writer is above all a free person, and the obligation to preserve his independence against all constraints comes before any other consideration. And I mean not only the insane constraints imposed by an abusive political power, but the restrictions – all the harder to evade because they are well-intentioned – that cite a sense of duty to one's country' (Kundera, 2010). Norman MacCaig – as alive as any to Scotland – wittily summarised the same idea in his poem Patriot:

> My only country
> is six feet high
> and whether I love it or not
> I'll die
> for its independence.

As the contributions to the volume already cited (Hames, 2012) amply demonstrate, most Scottish writers and thinkers continue to take a nuanced, intelligent attitude to all of these questions. Just occasionally is a bum note struck, as with Alasdair Gray's essay *'Settlers and Colonists.'*

Many angry words have been exchanged over this essay, which has been characterised as licensing anti-English sentiments. A careful reading of the text does not support the charge. Instead, more serious issues are at stake here. These are to do with legitimacy, identity, history and truth. A discussion of them is directly relevant to how Scotland might be represented in the 21st Century, and symptomatic of the difficult passage between culture and nationalism.

The first issue is that of identity and definition: who defines? In his attempt to categorise not just difference, but the terms of *acceptable* difference, Gray assumes *a priori* that there is a historically stable, continuous, coherent and homogenous entity to work against. Incomers to Scotland are placed by him, in relation to this homogeneity, either as exploiters of it, or in a sub-set of that homogeneity. These latter ('settlers') appear to have won their place through a mysterious process of legitimisation that remains opaque and which is not administered by them. This is a worrying taxonomy that rests on an order of preference which Gray has no particular right to define – or at least that we have every right to reject. And, if the criterion of value here is a respect for, commitment to, and knowledge of, Scottish culture, many Scots would themselves not qualify. Are we to call these Judases 'internal exiles'?

The attempt to place a single overarching value on the shifting variousness of identity is a chimera, and demonstrates one of the intellectual traps of monolithic nationalist thinking. Identity is a thrawn dialogue – a babble, not a monologue. There is no gold standard. At which level of description are we to define *sufficient* Scottishness? Parentage? Birthplace? Accent? Education? Class? Cultural knowledge? Length of time spent in Scotland? DNA? Even if we were able to agree on a particular level of description, the idea that this is what defines us *in toto*, and happens to be the most important thing about us, is to take part in a radically simplified national mythology which is both intellectually, existentially and historically dishonest. Nor does Gray, in setting up the discussion in these terms, leave any room for those who regard national identity as a trap or others who, because of their backgrounds (or politics), are unable and unwilling to ascribe themselves unequivocally to any one nation, or to nationalism tout court. Like Kelman, I might reject nationalism altogether. Or I might talk of my father's ancestors, Jews from the German-Polish border, or my Mother's, Italians from Trieste, that liminal Austo-Hungarian, Slovenes, Piedmont and Italian city. And yet, when I open my mouth, what you'll hear is English public school...

In reply to Gray, one might say that there are more interesting facets of identity and identification than those he seems to allow for, Osip Mandelstam, the great Jewish-Russian (or Russian-Polish-Jewish) poet once wrote: 'A *raznochinets* [rootless cosmopolitan] needs no memory, it is enough for him to tell of all the books he has read, and his biography is done' (Mandelstam, 1988). Unpacking that sentence would require an essay in itself, but Gray presumably agrees with a biographical premise which places at least as much stress on individual cultural sophistication – on intellect and knowledge in the republic of letters – as it does on national identity. Why else would he publish his monumental 'Book of Prefaces'? (Gray, 2002). Indeed it's evident that most Scottish writers and artists, starting from a natural appreciation of their own culture, also display, as Mandelstam did, a 'longing for world culture' – as in Tom Leonard's postulate (Hames, *ibid*):

> The local is the international.
> The national is the parochial.

The second issue raised by Gray's essay is the spectre of bad history. In this respect using the terms settlers and colonists to categorise incomers to Scotland is highly loaded. Granted, he acknowledges that Scots have themselves been colonisers, but then truncates the complexity he introduces, serving only to shift the argument onto a false ground where everything evil Scots have done takes place *elsewhere* (and at the behest of others), and where, therefore, the only *visible* evil worth crying out about is that done to Scots on their own territory.

If Scotland is really to construct a healthy 21st Century identity, honest history is required. Where, in the general public discourse of and in Scotland, is the acknowledgement that Scots have spilt far more blood in internecine conflict than with the English? That Scot also fought against Scot at Culloden? That Scot cleared Scot from the land? That Glasgow merchants of the industrial revolution and Empire regarded the workers (often Gaels) who peopled their factories as less than human, as *beasts*? That the dictates of class have played a far greater role in Scottish sorrow than invaders? Who knows that handsome black-boys 'to be disposed of' could be bought for domestic service in late 18th Century Edinburgh, or that the *Glasgow Courier* opposed any rights for slaves well into the 1820s? Why do we think that adjacent to St Kitts, an infamous slave entrepot, and the site of a stomach-churning museum of slavery which details torments as revolting as Treblinka, is an island called *Nevis*? Only one major novel has dealt with these subjects in recent years (Robertson, 2003).

Even if some Scottish historians have begun to address the complexities of history, (Cameron, 2011; Devine, 2012; Finlay, 2004; Macdonald, 2009) popular attention is still more devoted to a victimology that buttresses the inflated claims of nationalist mythology. Did Scots really invent the modern world? (Herman, 2002). One might say, half in jest, that if they did, they didn't make a very good job of it ... Nor are the claims of innate national character in today's Scotland any the less equivocal. That Scots are naturally community minded and politically inclined to a moderate socialism, is an old saw. This in a country which has in some regions male life expectancy rates lower than most other countries in Europe, and where the link between deprivation and educational attainment is more acute than most other countries in Europe (Scottish Government, 2011). Overall, Scottish (and UK) society remains one of the most economically and socially unequal amongst developed nations (Wilkinson and Pickett, 2009). There are clear disjunctions here between facts and ideas, rendering these ideas mythological.

'It looks like a biscuit tin' said Alexander Korda of Scotland, while filming yet another myth – the noble, virtuous and bonnie prince. The task of those who make cultural policy, of those who make culture, and of those who are responsible for representing that culture to others, is to deny the shorthand of the biscuit tin, and to present Scotland in all its heterogeneous complexity. There are no easy answers, because culture is not a finished object. This requires the kind of fearless, independently minded artists we are fortunate to have ('moderate your own fucking language...'), and artistic producers and policy makers who know how to represent the nation to itself and others with real integrity: people, in short, who are prepared to 'grasp the fizzle', with all the pain and pride that involves. It is, after all, a spiky thing.

References

Cameron, E.A. (2011), *Impaled upon a Thistle: Scotland since 1880*, Edinburgh: Edinburgh University Press.

Creative Scotland (2012), http://www.creativescotland.com/about/our-people/our-board

Devine, T. (2012), *Scotland's Empire: The Origins of the Global Diaspora*, London: Penguin.

Finlay, R. (2004), *Modern Scotland 1914–2000*, London: Profile Books.

Fraser, S. (2012), *The Last Highlander*, London: Harper Collins.

Gray, A. (1981), *Lanark*, Edinburgh: Canongate.

Gray, A. (1992), *Poor Things*, London: Bloomsbury.

Gray, A. (2002), *The Book of Prefaces*, London: Bloomsbury.

Grayling, A.C. (2010), *Liberty in the Age of Terror: A Defence of Civil Liberties and Englightenment Values,*, London: Bloomsbury.

Hames, S. (ed.), *Unstated: Writers on Scottish Independence*, Edinburgh: Word Power Books.

Herman, A. (2002), *How The Scots Invented the Modern World*, London: Fourth Estate.

Kelman, J. (2012), 'The British Council and the Edinburgh Writers Conference', Word Power Books, 13 August, http://www.word-power.co.uk/viewPlatform.php?id=601

Kundera, M. (2010), *Encounter*, London: Harper Perennial.

Lochhead, L. (1987), Mary Queen of Scots Got Her Head Chopped Off, first performed by the Communicado Theatre Company.

Macdonald, C.M.M. (2009), *Whaur Extremes Meet: Scotland's Twentieth Century*, Edinburgh: John Donald.

Mandelstam, O. (1988), *The Noise of Time*, London: Quartet Books.

Robertson, J. (2003), *Joseph Knight*, London: Fourth Estate.

Robertson, J. (2005), *Voyage of Intent*, Edinburgh: Luath/Scottish Book Trust.

Scottish Government (2011), *Literacy Action Plan*, Scottish Government.

Thomson, A. (2007), '"You can't get there from here": Devolution and Scottish literary history', *International Journal of Scottish Literature*, 3.

Wilkinson, R. and Pickett, K. (2009), *The Spirit Level: Why Equality is Better for Everyone*, London: Allen Lane.

Who Speaks for Scotland? Entitlement, Exclusion, the Power of Voice and Social Change

GERRY HASSAN

Introduction

THE SCOTTISH PARLIAMENT and 'devolution project' did not come from nowhere; it was born of certain political expectations, interests and ideas. This chapter sets out to investigate some of the key unexplored assumptions about the Scottish Parliament: the idea and practice of 'devolution', the rhetoric of 'the new politics', 'civic Scotland' and promise of 'consensus politics'.

It will offer an analysis of Scottish politics post-devolution, in terms of who has been included and gained voice and influence, and who has been marginalised and excluded. From this overview, it will attempt to make some observations about political and social change in contemporary Scotland which are relevant to the context, the run up to and beyond the independence referendum.

The analysis will also anchor an understanding of the Scottish dimension in the work of Albert O. Hirschman and his seminal text, '*Exit, Voice and Loyalty*' (1970). In this he posits that traditionally the right have championed the power of 'exit' in the form of individual power and choice, and the left the notion of 'loyalty' in collective solidarity, but what both have tended to ignore and downplay is the power of 'voice'; of people gathering, mobilising and bringing about change. For all the Scottish narrative of difference, this chapter will argue that the Scottish debate(s) have been shaped by this context.

The Limits of 'the New Politics' Thesis

The establishment of the Scottish Parliament saw the articulation of a host of hopes and expectations about what it would achieve and represent. Some of this was grounded and to be expected: the creation of a democratic voice whereas previously there had been none, and the righting of the wrong of the increasingly problematic 'democratic deficit' of how Scotland was governed.

However, a number of other deeper and more problematic claims and assumptions were made. One was that the Parliament would introduce an era of 'new politics' whereby Scottish politics, democracy and society would be rejuvenated in a culture of engagement, participation and better policy. There was in this a critique of the limitations of Westminster politics and its adversarial culture and practice, and a belief that north of the border with a new institution elected by proportional representation, things could be very different.

There was pre-devolution in the campaign for a Scottish Parliament in the 1980s and 1990s, and post-1997, in the work of the Consultative Steering Group set up under the auspices of Henry McLeish, a eulogising of consensual ways of working and of reaching agreement which bordered on naivety, and ignored the dynamics of party competition and political disagreement (Consultative Steering Group, 1998).

The 'new politics' school of thought had little understanding of the realities of contemporary party politics, and the propensity towards adversarial, combative conflict and disputation. Instead, it talked a warm, inviting language of participative democracy, consultative processes and inclusivity, without addressing how this was to come about in an environment of party politics and ideological disagreement. Within these assumptions were two core ideas that I will explore in turn, first, the idea of 'devolution', and second, of 'civic Scotland'.

The concept of 'devolution' entered the modern political lexicon of Scotland and the UK with the rise of the SNP in the late 1960s. The response of the then Labour Government was to set up a Royal Commission on the Constitution as a way of being seen to do something, and part of the political conversation looked at ways Scots autonomy that could be enhanced within the union via a devolved directly elected Assembly. In the 1970s as Labour shifted back to being pro-home rule and explored how to combine this with maintaining the territorial integrity and settlement of the UK and a unitary idea of politics, its limited concept of 'devolution' came into focus.

In the 1980s and the Thatcher administration, Labour's commitment to a Scottish Assembly slowly morphed into that of a Scottish Parliament, and the rhetoric of 'the new politics' was for some swept up in the hopes and expectations of wider constitutional reform and Charter 88. However, the political motivation of 'devolution' increasingly across the entire spectrum of anti-Tory Scotland became about mitigating the effects of the Thatcher administration and maintaining the more institutionally corporatist and managed set of networks which defined government and public agencies. In the Labour version of this, it was motivated by defending the internal Scottish status quo and Labour state. 'Devolution' became about narrow political change, institutionally focused on achieving a Parliament, and placing it in a polity and civil society, which only needed this change to renew and revive itself. And simultaneously, it allowed the political elites to take charge of a vision of change in which their position was central, maintained and remained unchallenged.

'Devolution' can thus be seen as an idea and ideology, bringing together the appearance of political change and democracy, with the point of restricting and restraining it, and maintaining the complex set of arrangements which governed Scotland pre-Thatcher.

The Nature of 'Civic Scotland'

The story of who established and feels that they have a sense of 'ownership' and 'claim' over the Scottish Parliament as an idea, a sort of social 'Claim of Right' is about power and legitimacy. There are competing claims in this. For one, there is the Labour version which can be seen in the accounts explored above, which state, 'Labour delivered the Scottish Parliament'; then there is the Nationalist account which emphasis that without the pressure and electoral threat of the SNP, Labour would have done nothing.

Beyond these party beliefs there is a more powerful, persuasive explanation which lays claim to the idea of the Scottish Parliament, and that is the story of 'civic Scotland'. It states that throughout the 1980s, a host of initiatives, including most prominently the Scottish Constitutional Convention, gave voice to the consensus for a Parliament, which became known in John Smith's revealing words as 'the settled will of the Scottish people' (*The Scotsman*, 12 March 1994). The Convention was a gathering of a significant part of the Scottish political class and institutional elites (local government, churches) who had been locked out of large aspects of power by the Thatcher administration, and felt compelled to do something about it; the body via '*A Claim of Right for Scotland*' document and declaration in 1988-89 invoked a language of popular sovereignty, legitimacy and politics. Crucially, it did not do anything to advance these ideas beyond its existence and issuing reports; no clarion calls to radical or direct action were made, nor were experimental forms of democracy embraced.

'Civic Scotland' came to the fore as a term in this period as an explanation for the non-state gathering of centre-left opinions which felt it was excluded by Thatcher, and as a statement of intent about difference and autonomy. It was nearly always used as a positive declaration of the diverse, pluralist, rich nature of Scottish public life, and almost never in the negative or even in a self-critical, reflective way. In the 1980s and 1990s, writers such as Iain Macwhirter, Joyce McMillan and Ruth Wishart, used this term continually to define the Scotland of the centre-left, in the space beyond the political class and before the state.

This became one of the defining periods of the anti-Thatcher era: the mobilisation not of a people but a myth, folklore and story which has shaped how we think of change, power and the past. It has entailed a romanticising of the near-past, and in particular the 1980s, which is still a constant in the writing of some of the key public figures of the time. For commentators such as Macwhirter and McMillan, the passing of time has only reinforced their sepia-like nostalgia for the 'golden era' of the 1980s, when everything was more straightforward.

There are a number of critical factors missing from the use of the term, 'civic Scotland'. Any sense of definition and differentiation between the concepts, 'civil society', 'civic society' and 'civic Scotland' is conspicuously absent. These terms are all used and invoked interchangeably, yet they are not the same; 'civil society' is a recognised term in political theory given modern meaning by the Scots philosopher Adam Ferguson; the term 'civic society' is a subset of the former, and 'civic Scotland' is an organised, orchestrated and narrower version of the second.

The barriers and boundaries of 'civic Scotland', what are the criteria, entrances and exit points of membership, are never examined in the numerous evocations of the term. Jean Barr in her challenging book, '*The*

Stranger Within', is one of the very few writers to explore and challenge the dominant perspective, observing:

> Clearly, people on the street are not civil society, only the organised are; nor is civil society completely separate from the state or necessarily any less politically partisan. Civil society does not even necessarily promote democracy, such that the more civil society there is the more democracy there is. Civil society (and civil societies) pursue political and often partisan objectives and can promote socially exclusive behaviour. (2008: 100)

The New Class of Devolved Scotland

The professional classes and institutional Scotland have shaped a large part of the public life of Scotland. This goes back at least to the nature of the Acts of Union agreed between a pre-democratic Scotland and England and which defined and protected an autonomous Scots civil society. This centred Scots identity in the union around the 'holy trinity' of education, law and the Kirk, putting centre-stage these professional and specialist groups.

As the role and reach of the state expanded from late Victorian times onward, a Scottish embryonic state emerged in what was a stateless nation without democratic scrutiny and accountability. This contributed to the rarefication of professionalism, experts and authority, which could be found at a British level, but was even more extensive in Scotland, as a managed society arose within the closed order of high Scotland.

The expansion of the state across post-war times saw increased public expectations and the creation of a distinct Scots public sphere, with increasing pressures for more autonomy, often from elite opinion. With the election of the Thatcher administration in 1979, this began to coalesce into the demand that it be a more Scottish state held accountable to the people. This set of factors led to the establishment of the Scottish Parliament in 1999, which by then had come to be seen as a normalising action.

'Devolution' can be seen in this context as the moment of triumph and re-legitimation of professional class Scotland, which paradoxically, open it up to challenge and scrutiny. What it did was two-fold: it incorporated the relatively weak forces of radical Scotland and elements of the new left in the constitutional project, while also acting as a blockade to new right thinking and critique.

It is not surprising that out of institutional Scotland a new devolution class has arisen who have gained position, influence and status out of the new arrangements. This has had an association in the early days of devolution with the extended Labour state and its patronage and preferment, but the same practices, often with the same individuals, has continued under the SNP minority and majority administrations. Part of this is the collective intelligence of civil service Scotland and its search in its 'usual suspects' drawer for people who are a 'safe pair of hands' who will perform the tasks asked of them. Public life is littered with commissions, expert groups and panels made up of such personnel who know nothing of a particular subject but are happy to be used as window dressing to give some kind of legitimacy to an initiative.

Yet, devolution has proven to be as well as the greatest opportunity also a threat to the existence and maintenance of the new class because it has amplified public expectations and provided a platform which did not exist before. It has also been an experience which has revealed to a significant extent a large part of the professional classes attitude of disdain and disappointment at the people, who did not respond in the neat, tidy, rationalist way they are meant to by the system.

The devolution class have, in the last decade, shown a fundamental inability to engage in self-reflection or self-criticism; instead their exhaustion and retreat has been evident in a host of pronouncements. One has been the search for a form of language, philosophy and practice which continues to give them legitimacy for their centre-stage, while offering some explanation for the state of Scotland. Thus, we have the Chief Medical Officer Sir Harry Burns adoption of an 'asset-based approach' as the silver bullet to address health inequalities (Friedli, 2012); elsewhere there have been mantras about 'confidence' and 'well-being', both of which are now less in fashion, along with focuses on 'resilience'.

What all of these have in common is articulating change as being the responsibility of the individual, with a pathologising and blaming of people for wider structural, economic and social change. This has resulted in the Scottish Government seeing one of the main problems as 'a culture of dependency' which illustrates the accommodation of the new class to the ideas of the new right, with concepts such as 'underclass' and 'dependency culture' used all the time in public deliberations. One senior health professional told me that 'there was no interest in Scotland in structural change' and that the best prospect of wider change was a retreat into

some inner psychic change defined by new age values; this can surely only
be seen as an outlook of complacent retreat and passivity.

The Missing Scotland

The Scottish Parliament has arrived at a time of deep disconnection in
politics generally, and what is seen as a crisis of trust, age of cynicism and
anti-politician mood. While voters continue to show identification with the
idea and institution of the Parliament, and rate it higher than Westminster,
politics north of the border have been affected by this wider crisis.

If we look at the most recent Scottish Parliament and Westminster
elections and assess the turnout in comparison to the 1992 UK election
levels in Scotland, we find in the 2011 Scottish elections, 989,540 voters
missing and in 2010 UK election in Scotland, 446,954 voters missing.

The parliamentary constituency which had the lowest turnout in 2011
was Glasgow Provan in which only 34.5 per cent of voters went to the
polls. This produces a seat with 16,809 missing voters, 30 per cent of all
of the prospective electorate. And in the 2012 council elections, the
Glasgow leader, Gordon Matheson, was elected for the ward of City/
Anderson with a 23.6 per cent turnout, the lowest in the city.

Glasgow was not always like this. In the 1951 UK general election the
city had a turnout of 81 per cent which, by the Scottish Parliament elections of 2011, had fallen to 41 per cent (Hassan and Shaw, 2012: 207,
209). The city's 15 constituencies then split eight Labour, seven Conservatives and were in most places competitive, showing little variance from
the average turnout; 60 years later, the city's constituencies, all of which
were Labour from 1987–2011, showed a much wider variance from the
average. As the socio-economic and health inequalities in the city have
widened, it is not an accident that inequalities of political engagement
have widened as well; but while we have a burgeoning industry on 'the
Glasgow effect' on health inequalities, we have next to no research on the
cross-generational trends of political disengagement.

Glasgow Provan's turnout (as Camlachie) was 82.4 per cent in 1951,
and this was a seat competitive enough for the Tories to win it briefly in
a 1948 by-election (admittedly with a split Labour-ILP vote). When the
seat became Provan in 1955, Labour held it against the Tories by a mere
180 votes, and there is a strong correlation between competitiveness, the
Tory vote (49.7 per cent in 1955) and turnout (74.7 per cent in the same

year). In the 1999 Scottish elections, turnout was 47.8 per cent and it has fallen in every subsequent election: 39.4 per cent 2003, 38.9 per cent 2007, 34.5 per cent 2011.

Why this has happened is important for understanding the fragility of Scottish democracy, the failure of 'the new politics', and the effect of devolution. Many of these changes predate the Parliament, and are rooted in the powerful economic and social forces which acted like a tsunami over large parts of Scotland in the 1970s and 1980s; as well as the long retreat of the mainstream parties and civic bodies from places such as Provan. In the 1950s, areas like Provan had active, representative political parties (although Labour has historically had a problem in the East End of Glasgow at least from the 1950s), trade unions and civic organisations which filled the lives, streets and communities of the areas; no longer can this be said. This leaves the critical question, of how do people in an area like Provan feel that politics is something other than remote from them and a set of alien processes?

Provan's streets and neighbourhoods, Dennistoun, Alexandria Park, Riddrie, Blackhill, Robroyston and Easterhouse, were once filled with political discussions, hope and activism; but that is sadly no longer the case. Its streets and areas have proven beyond the reach of 'the new politics' or the appeal of 'civic Scotland'. This has produced a politics distorted by a truncated electorate and democratic practice, which is increasingly focused on a narrow section of voters, those who are more affluent, professional and older, with the over 65s in particular, turning out to vote; while those who do not vote are younger, poorer, have less assets, and are more likely to live in social housing. This can be seen as a Scottish expression of a Western phenomenon known as 'the truncated electorate', but the divide is particularly acute in parts of missing Scotland, and flies in the face of the comforting story of an inclusive, compassionate country.

Social Democracy of a Narrow Bandwidth

Despite all of the above, the disconnection, marginalisation and exclusion of a whole swathe of Scotland, the prevailing account of politics emphasises Scotland's centre-left and social democratic credentials. Indeed, in the first years of the Parliament, one account emphasised that Scotland was 'too social democratic', with a political culture leaning too far to the left, based on uncritical producer capture and an over-extended state.

This account spread from *The Scotsman* under Andrew Neil's tutelage, to New Labour's critique of Scotland.

Scotland's social democratic sentiment has become associated with a number of totemic policies: free care for the elderly, no tuition fees for higher education, free prescription charges, and bus passes for the elderly. These have become the narrative of difference of the social democratic settlement, marking out our supposed progressive values, and our divergence from the fragmentation of English welfare and policy choices.

This could be seen in the debate around Johann Lamont's 'something for nothing' speech, in which the Scottish Labour leader called for a reassessment of the above headline policies and a debate about priorities and choices in public spending (Lamont, 2012). Lamont's speech, which invoked the populism of the new right in part of its language, was met with an avalanche of criticism from political opponents and the media. This was revealing, with the ghostly influence of Thatcher and Blair cited to close down a debate; and illustrated what many saw as the boundaries of permissible debate in politics and public policy (Hassan, 2012). Here was a supposed social democratic culture which could not bring itself to debate how best to distribute resources, tackle exclusion and aid those most in need. Instead, the cumulative *status quo* and inherited choices of politics had to in some strange Burkean conservative sense, not be examined and changed.

The Lamont episode was but one episode which illustrated the limits of what William Mackenzie called 'the community of communicators', made up of those in public life and positions of influence (1978:165). This is for all its social democratic references, a political culture which is shaped by included, entitlement Scotland and the insider groups who are embedded in and know how to influence the system. Then are those who don't have a voice or status, who do not sit within the confines of this entitlement culture and are outsiders, who paradoxically are the people who would most gain financially from a genuine social democratic Scotland.

The narrowness of Scotland's political landscape, shaped as it as by the conservatism and inertia of its political and professional classes, affects numerous debates. First, there is an over-concentration on politics and institutions as the main way of bringing about change. An apposite example of this is how the SNP talk about independence, as being about the Parliament attaining full powers, which is a very restrictive idea of independence. One government minister told me that independence could be achieved 'by gradually extending the Scotland Act [1998] over each aspect of domestic life': a sort of Whig-like gradualist progress towards independence.

Second, the realm of where political ideas can be drawn from is incredibly narrow. Scotland's devolution environment has not produced an ecology of think tanks, research centres and political campaigning organisations; most MSPs are not actually in the real sense political actors or activists, making influential speeches and public interventions. Third, the exit and entrance points to public life in Scotland, how policy, administration and consultation are undertaken, show a deep sense of caution, control and risk averseness. This is a public culture which privileges not letting go, not making mistakes and rewarding people who are a 'safe pair of hands': the competence of the devolution new class who won't ask difficult questions.

All of this reinforces a public culture which espouses social democracy, but is far removed from it; instead it has become defined by two dynamics: the self-preservation of elites and insider groups who have talked progressive values, but have been more than happy to engage in their corrosion at the hands of market fundamentalism and managerialism; and the struggle for the soul of anti-Tory Scotland which is at the heart of the Labour-SNP contest, and what a large part of the independence debate has so far been reduced to.

Values, Voice and Vessels: Self-Government and Self-Determination

There is an assumption across large swathes of Scotland that we as a society know how to do social change: that we collectively have not voted for the Tories, did not like Thatcher, and rejected the values and ideas of Thatcherism.

This assertion does not stand up to greater scrutiny. Change does not come from institutional Scotland or enlightened authority; nor does it come from the myth and ideology of 'civic Scotland'; and nor does it come from ideas being floated or postulated on their own. Instead, social change comes from a combination of three crucial factors: *values, vessels and voices*.

Values matter and inform what we do in public life. There is a prevailing assumption that the values of Scottish society and institutions are good values: that we have progressive, compassionate, inclusive values which inform policy and practice, and that we have collectively taken a positive decision to turn our back on the free market vandals gathered at the border. In this conjecture, significant parts of public life and agencies find it comfortable to have a near complete absence of self-examination, self-criticism and reflection on the limits of current practice and approaches. There is overall a collective belief in the efficacy of Scotland's progressive credentials and that these work and animate the public life of the nation.

Voice is critical in understanding who has it, who hasn't and why. There does seem to be across public life a complete absence of interest in what I would call 'relational space', which means an understanding of who is involved in a conversation or relationship, what the dynamics of power are, and who is missing and why (Hassan, 2013). Andrew Marr, the broadcaster said recently that 'all Edinburgh was involved in the discussions of the Scottish Enlightenment', a comment which belies a complete historical ignorance of the age he was invoking, of class, gender and profession; that was a complete failure to grasp the importance of 'relational space' and instead be drawn towards the powerful totem of the Scots egalitarian myth (see Hassan, 2014).

Then there is the subject of *vessels*. This is about a sense of collective agency which people feel they created and own, and can express themselves and find their genuine voice in, rather than having to speak through the codes of the system. Once people felt this about political parties, trade unions and church bodies, but for most, if not all people, this is no longer the case. Membership of political parties in the UK and Scotland (despite the SNP's recent surge) is a distinct minority pastime which is north of the border not even the equivalent of a good Saturday gathering at Celtic Park or Ibrox; and then there is the issue of what such parties do and allow their existing memberships to engage in.

What is missing in Scottish debates is an understanding of how to advance, nurture and create social change, build alliances and movements, and create new forms of voice. These would build into and amount to an ecology of self-government, which show people self-organising, mobilising and resourcing their own lives and priorities, leading to a culture and practice of self-determination. Such a politics would be very different from the paternalism, statism and control managerialism, which has been the diet on offer from all our mainstream political parties.

Fortunately there are increasing signs that the nature of this benign authority driven, managed and cossetted society will not remain unchallenged in perpetuity. First, Scotland is not immune from wider Western political trends, and is thus as influenced by the crisis of authority, decline in deference and loss of faith in professionals, as elsewhere; this may take longer in Scotland, or find voice in a very different form from other Anglo-American democracies, but it will undoubtedly find form and influence here. Second, the lost decade of the UK economically whether in the union or independent, will focus a debate on distributional consequences which Scottish politics has consciously and conspicuously avoided; and while this could have a reactionary, populist edge, it can only ultimately be seen as a positive development.

Then there are the creation of a range of fuzzy, messy spaces which have increasingly challenged 'the official story': initiatives such as the Radical Independence Conference (RIC), Poverty Alliance's Poverty Assemblies, and the potential of groups such as the Citizen's Assembly. Each of these has created powerful spaces and places which have sat outside institutional Scotland, not been about access to power and insider status, and brought people together in a genuine, uncontrolled way. It is also not an accident that two of the three examples use the good Scots word, 'assembly', with its connotation of cultivating, gathering and soft power. In a previous project addressing how people imagine and create their own future, examining the missing issue of agency, we came up with the idea of 'assemblies of hope', initiatives which were not owned by the system, but engaged with it, and that is what these three examples are (Hassan, Mean and Tims, 2007).

Part of this has to involve a different kind of politics: one in which there is an artistic and cultural intelligence to how politics is undertaken, and a political understanding to how cultural activism is done. This is about a broader, rich tapestry of how the radical imagination is conceived, and activism, protest and engagement created, which breaks with some of the dour, prescriptive, holier-than-thou attitudes which have passed for left traditions across Scotland. Some may think that this culture is anachronistic in today's world, but it has been able to exist in places, despite the left's retreat over the last 30 years. And the undoubted anger and indignation that is felt about a variety of Conservative-Lib Dem coalition polices from public spending to welfare, has to entail a wider palate of opposition styles and methods than the usual left menu of marching, sit-ins, demos and petitions; fun, humour and creative imagination are crucial in this.

Devolution has not produced a social democratic polity or dividend. What it has achieved is that the mantra of social democratic rhetoric over a politics of restricted practice and vested interests has proven good enough for part of Scotland's supposedly centre-left, radical political community.

Scotland has not yet become a fully-fledged political democracy. The UK – starting from the analyses of Tom Nairn (1977), Will Hutton (1995) and Patrick Wright's 'On Living in an Old Country' (1985) – is not only not a democracy, it is not even a modern country, increasingly shaped by living in a permanent conversation with the past and its dead generations. Witness the seemingly constant celebration of various British imperial military adventures, from in the last decade, the Battle of Trafalgar to the Battle of Britain, and forthcoming, the onset of the First World War.

Scotland has its own ghosts and shadows as well but it has the collective potential to become a modern nation, European, inclusive, hopeful and humble, one which notes and cares for the welfare and well-being of all its citizens. But for that to happen, the current debate has to notice some rather unpleasant truths about the current state of supposedly progressive Scotland, who gains from it and who has been permanently excluded. The potential of the independence debate is that it could be one of the catalysts which aid this and which contribute to the slow democratisation of Scottish society. And for that to happen, there has to be the emergence of a culture of values, voices and vessels which aid a pluralist culture of self-determination, and which refuses to leave politics to the world of 'the official story' and 'civic Scotland'.

References

Barr, J. (2008), *The Stranger Within: On the Idea of an Educated Public*, Rotterdam: Sense Publishers.

Consultative Steering Group (1998), *Shaping Scotland's Parliament: Report of the Consultative Steering Group on the Scottish Parliament*, Edinburgh: Scottish Office.

Friedli, L. (2012), "What we've tried, hasn't worked': the politics of asset based public health', *Critical Public Health*, http://www.centreforwelfarereform. org/uploads/attachment/353/the-politics-of-assets-based-public-health.pdf

Hassan, G. (2012), 'Searching for the 'New Tartan Tories' of Scottish Public Life', *Scottish Review*, 11 October, http://www.gerryhassan.com/blog/searching-for-the-new-tartan-tories-of-scottish-public-life/

Hassan, G. (2013), *State of Independence: The Scottish Political Commentariat, Public Spaces and the Making of Modern Scotland*, University of the West of Scotland PhD thesis.

Hassan, G. (2014), *Caledonian Dreaming: The Quest for a Different Scotland*, Edinburgh: Luath.

Hassan, G., Mean, M. and Tims, C. (2007), *The Dreaming City: Glasgow 2020 and the Power of Mass Imagination*, London: Demos.

Hassan, G. and Shaw, E. (2012), *The Strange Death of Labour Scotland*, Edinburgh: Edinburgh University Press.

Hirschman, A.O. (1970), *Exit, Voice and Loyalty: Responses to Decline in Firms, Organizations and States*, London: Harvard University Press.

Hutton, W. (1995), *The State We're In*, London: Jonathan Cape.

Lamont, J. (2012), 'Speech: Scottish Labour Leader', Scottish Labour Party, Edinburgh, 25 September, http://www.scottishlabour.org.uk/scottish-labour-leader-johann-lamonts-speech-in-edinburgh

Mackenzie, W.J.M. (1978), *Political Identity*, Harmondsworth: Penguin.

Nairn, T. (1977), *The Break-up of Britain: Crisis and Neo-nationalism*, London: New Left Books.

Wright, P. (1985), *On Living in an Old Country: The National Past in Contemporary Britain*, London: Verso Books.